Business International's Guide to International Licensing

Also published by McGraw-Hill

Shirley Dreifus, Editor
BUSINESS INTERNATIONAL'S GLOBAL MANAGEMENT DESK REFERENCE

Business International's Guide to International Licensing

Building a Licensing Strategy for 14 Key Markets Around the World

Thomas J. Ehrbar
Business International Corporation

McGraw-Hill, Inc.
New York St. Louis San Francisco Auckland Bogotá
Caracas Lisbon London Madrid Mexico Milan
Montreal New Delhi Paris San Juan São Paulo
Singapore Sydney Tokyo Toronto

Library of Congress Cataloging-in-Publication Data

Business International's guide to international licensing / by the Business International Corporation.
p. cm.
ISBN 0-07-009332-6
1. Foreign licensing agreements. I. Business International Corporation. II. Title: Guide to international licensing.
K1530.B87 1992
341.7'53—dc20 92-10847
CIP

1 2 3 4 5 6 7 8 9 0 DOC/DOC 9 8 7 6 5 4 3 2

ISBN 0-07-009332-6

The sponsoring editor for this book was David Conti, the editing supervisor was Kimberly A. Goff, and the production supervisor was Donald F. Schmidt. This book was set in Palatino. It was composed by McGraw-Hill's Professional Book Group composition unit.

Printed and bound by R. R. Donnelley & Sons Company.

Contents

Preface xi

Introduction xvi

Why License? xvii
Some Benefits of Licensing xvii
Limitations of Licensing xviii
International Issues xx
IPR: Variations on a Theme xxii
Into the 1990s xxiv

1. Argentina 1

Legal Context 2
Trademarks 2
Patents 5
Industrial Models and Designs 6
Copyright 7
Technology Transfer 8
Licensing Experience in Argentina 9
Approval Criteria 11
Practical Advice 12
Taxation 14

2. Brazil 15

International Treaties 15
Federal Legislation 16
Patents 17
Unpatentable Products 18

Remittance Restrictions 19
Trademarks 19
Remittance Restrictions 20
Copyrights 21
Software 22
Licensing and Technology Transfer 24
Remittance Restrictions 25
Practical Matters 26
Requirements of Licensing and Technology-Transfer Agreements 27
Licensing Experience in Brazil 28
Tax Consequences 31
Tax Rates on Royalty Remittances 32
Tax Incentives 32

3. Mexico **34**

Why Mexico? 34
The Regulatory Framework 37
The New Intellectual Property Law 40
Tax and Financial Considerations 40
Practical Matters 40
Intellectual Property in Mexico 41

4. Venezuela **45**

Foreign-Investment Regulations 46
Technology Imports 48
Legal Context 48
The Industrial Property Law 49
Decree Law 727 51
Copyright Law 53
Registration Expenses 54
Royalties and Fees 54
Proposed Bill on Monopolies and Cartels 55
International Legislation 55
Practical Matters 56
Patent and Trademark Protection 57
Payment Instruments 58
Other Problems 58
Tax Consequences 58
Patents and Trademarks in Venezuela 59
Royalty Remittances 60
Corporate Income Tax Rates 61
Licensing Experience in Venezuela 62
Tax Treaties 65

5. Japan **66**

Transfer of Technology 68
The Legislative Framework 68
Royalty Payments 72

Tax Consequences 72
Practical Matters 73
The Pharmaceuticals Case 74
International Disputes 75
Patents and Trademarks in Japan 76

6. South Korea **79**

Attracting Foreign Technology 80
Foreign-Investment Preferences 82
Patents and Trademarks 84
Patents and Trademarks in South Korea 85
The Corporate Response 86
Legislation 89
Tax Consequences 91
The Road Ahead 92

7. Taiwan **93**

Technical-Cooperation Agreements 95
Intellectual Property Laws 96
Patents and Trademarks 97
Pressure for Change 101
Copyrights 102
Enforcement of Intellectual Property Rights 103
Intellectual Property Laws 104
Legal Matters 107
International Conventions 107
Licensing Outside the System 107
Practical Matters 108
Tax Consequences 109

8. Thailand **111**

The Legal Context 114
Patents 115
Copyrights 117
Trademarks 118
Registration of Licensing Agreements 119
Practical Matters 119
Government Attitude Toward Business 120
The Legal Tradition 120
Patents and Trademarks in Thailand 121
Payment Instruments 122
Tax Consequences 123
Political and Cultural Considerations 124
Licensing Experience in Thailand 126

9. China **127**

Finding a Partner 128
Legal Context 129

Technology Transfer 129
Negotiating and Approval Requirements 131
Practical Matters 133
Lack of Funding 133
Countertrade Clauses 134
Secrecy 135
Payment Terms 135
Progressive-Payments Clauses 136
Other Practical Matters 138
Patents, Trademarks and Copyrights 139
Fluke and the PRC: The History of a Relationship 140
Patents 143
Trademarks 146
Patents and Trademarks in the PRC 148
Copyrights 151
Tax Consequences 152

10. India **153**

Industrial Policy 155
Technology Transfers 156
Foreign-Investment Requirements 158
Investment Classifications 158
Incentives 159
Intellectual Property Laws 160
Patents 160
Copyrights and Industrial Designs 161
Trademarks and Trade Names 161
Payment Practices 162
Restrictions on Royalties and Fees 162
Patents and Trademarks in India 163
Tax Consequences 166

11. Czechoslovakia **167**

Problems 168
Reforms 169
Special Funds and Priority Areas 169
Guide for Western Negotiators 170
Basic Licensing Procedures 172
Contact Organizations and Responsibilities 172
The Decision-Making Process 174
Unplanned Imports 175
Taxes on Royalties and Fees 175
Patents 176
Legislative Basis 176
Author's Certificates 177
Protection of Industrial Designs 177
The Office for Inventions and Discoveries 178
Compulsory Licenses 179
Infringement 179

Validity and Revocations 180
Licensing Experience in Czechoslovakia 181
Patents of Czechoslovaks Abroad 182
Trademarks 182
Registration 182
Duration of Protection 183
"Use" Provisions 183

12. Hungary **185**

Approval Requirements 186
The Licensing Agencies 187
License Payments and Taxes 188
Licensing Experience in Hungary 189
Patents 190
Patent Agents 191
The Patent Information Center 192
Patent Regulation in Hungary 193
Trademarks 194

13. Poland **196**

Policy Background 197
Licensing Procedures 198
The Central Fund for License Purchases 198
Selling Licenses to Poland 199
The Role of Polservice 200
Taxes on Royalties and Fees 201
Double-Taxation Treaties 201
Patents 202
Types of Patents 203
Industrial Designs and Models 204
Co-Ownership 205
Application Procedures 205
Infringement and Legal Recourse 207
Compulsory Licensing and Annulment Proceedings 208
Trademarks 208
Licensing Experience in Poland 209
Application Procedures 210
Infringement and Legal Recourse 210
Trademark Infringement in Poland 212

14. Russia **213**

A Market in Transition 213
The 1991 USSR Code 215
Protecting JV Inventions 216
Five-Year Tax Exemption 217
Not an Invention 217
Licensing Opportunities in the Former USSR 218

Appendix A. What to Include in a Foreign Licensing Agreement 220

Appendix B. Typical Licensing Agreements 223

I. Trademark and Know-How License Agreement for Argentina 223
License Agreement 223
II. Modifying the Trademark and Know-How License Agreement for Brazil 234

Appendix C. Questions to Ask When Fixing a Price on Patents Abroad 239

Index 242

Preface

This book examines the licensing environment in 14 developing markets in Latin America, Asia and Eastern Europe. As a group, these countries constitute a sizeable share of the world market; in fact, they account for over 80% of the world's production outside North America or Western Europe. The potential for licensing is enormous, but strategies vary widely from country to country. As much as they afford certain opportunities, all of the countries analyzed here pose particular difficulties for foreign firms. In countries where routes such as direct distribution and joint ventures are difficult, a well-conceived licensing approach can prove to be a better initial step in market entry. Although international standards for intellectual property protection certainly exist, many countries fall severely short of them. Increasingly, corporations have the need for tactics to combat serious infringements of their patents, trademarks and copyrights in unfamiliar environments. The individual chapters examine the current developments and future prospects in the licensing situation of each country; in addition to these in-depth overviews, the book offers practical details that corporations can utilize in building their own licensing strategies.

Argentina's intellectual property legislation, which was greatly reformed in the early 1980s, is among the most favorable in the Third World. Licensing procedures are relatively smooth and the legal system affords protection against infringement. Still, certain sectors remain without patent protection, most notably pharmaceuticals, due to strenuous objections by local industry. Menem's economic plan has reined in hyperinflation and reactivated production by increasing consumer demand. The government has embarked upon a program of privatization and is further reducing the state role in the economy through deregulation. As its economy improves and its bureaucracy is trimmed, Argentina will provide increasingly advantageous opportunities for licensing.

In the 1970s and 1980s, severe lack of adequate protection led many multinationals to slow the transfer of technology to **Brazil**. Now the Collor administration is trying to make up for years of technological isolation by improving the intellectual property code. The law will expand patent protection to pharmaceutical and biotechnology and augment enforcement. Trademark infringement has been rampant in Brazil, but new guidelines promise to improve protection. Despite reforms, the government control still maintains too much control over the licensing environment: registration requirements remain strict and exchange controls can slow payments. Despite continuing economic difficulties, Brazil remains the third largest market in the Western hemisphere. In certain sectors—such as software, in which piracy was endemic—foreign companies have responded to the improved licensing regulations by quickly establishing local operations.

Since 1972, **Mexico's** licensing environment had been marked by heavy government regulation and lax protection measures. A new intellectual property law—enacted in June 1991—has improved conditions significantly. The legislation extends patent protection and strengthens trade-secret protection. Deregulation has meant that licensing is automatic in most cases, a sharp contrast to previous cumbersome approval procedures. Even so, licensing is still interpreted to be the sale rather than rental of a technology. There are few legal instruments to fight patent and trademark infringement. Some consumer-goods companies have used licensing primarily as a direct means to circumvent counterfeits, some of which are exported to the US. The fortuitous change in IP regulations under Salinas will attract many licensors who were discouraged by previous conditions.

In the past decade, there have been a number of proposals to reform **Venezuela's** severely inadequate Industrial Property Law, but none has been implemented. The economic crisis has led to greater concern for foreign trade issues; the promulgation of a new foreign investment law and increased pressure from the US might eventually even lead to improvements in intellectual property legislation. For the near term, however, protection remains a serious problem for foreign firms, many of which not only refuse to license, but also to export new technologies to Venezuela. Registration procedures and legal recourse are time-consuming and cumbersome, so some firms have decided to combat potential pirates by being first on the market with their products.

In **Japan**, where impediments to direct means of market entry are legendary, licensing is a particularly strong alternative. Many firms have used licenses to establish alliances with Japan's powerful distribution system. The import of foreign technology through licensing has played an essential role in the post-war development of Japan's economy. Although Japan continues to be a net importer of technology, the gap has been closing rapidly as Japanese licensing in Asia escalates. Industrial and intellectual property legislation is well-codified, but many problems exist due to differing conceptions of the nature of patent and copyright protection, such as giving "first-to-file" instead of "first-to-invent" priority to competing inventions. American high-tech firms have fought with Japanese firms over charges of copyright infringement in both Tokyo and Washington. These long and expensive battles ultimately serve to underscore the importance and problematic potential of the Japanese market.

Firms have used licensing in **South Korea** both as a means of reaching the growing domestic market and taking advantage of lower production costs for export. The Korean government's favored foreign-investment vehicle continues to be the joint-venture. However, since a number of foreign firms have experienced complications in the management and financing of these JVs, many prefer to license. With trademark protection difficult to obtain and enforcement grossly insufficient, South Korea has become the world's largest producer and exporter of counterfeit goods. Bowing to US pressure, the government has offered some accommodation, including protection of trade secrets and retroactive patent protection of certain chemicals and pharmaceuticals. While the domestic market has undergone rapid expansion, IP protection has increased relatively slowly.

Although **Taiwan** has introduced broader intellectual-property legislation, including the extension of copyright protection to foreign works and a pending extension of the patent term, enforcement remains an intractable problem. It is a major issue in the regularly scheduled trade talks with the US, since American industries have lobbied for greater protection in Taiwan. Foreign firms choose licensing over litigation as a means of controlling infringement. Tax benefits for licensors and licensees also act as an impetus. In addition to a government-sanctioned licensing program, a considerable amount of licensing is done by firms operating outside the state's formal parameters. The gradual build-up of an indigenous technology base has ameliorated the IP situation, but since Taiwan continues to operate largely as an offshore manufacturing site, the need for imported technology persists.

Due to its rapidly industrializing economy, **Thailand** is a market hungry for technology. The government actively promotes majority Thai equity in joint ventures and, in many cases, the foreign interest licenses technology to the Thai-registered JV. The tax code also offers incentives for licensing, by offering advantages to firms when they pay royalty fees instead of remitting profits. Because of the absolute lack of patent protection for computer software and pharmaceuticals, Washington has threatened Thailand with trade sanctions. Equally problematic is the calculated lack of enforcement in legally protected items such as apparel trademarks and audiovisual copyrights. Trademark owners must instigate investigations themselves. While trademark piracy is rampant, consumers are increasingly demanding the genuine articles, which greatly increases licensing opportunities for foreign licensors and, because of low costs, export possibilities for their Thai licensees.

In the 1980s, the People's Republic of **China** turned to technology imports as an alternative to costly turnkey projects. With foreign exchange extremely scarce, however, the environment for licensing has become much more formidable. Technology transfers now require built-in mechanisms that reduce or compensate for their hard currency outlays, such as export-oriented production. Since China does not have a market economy, market-entry strategies such as direct sales face insurmountable barriers. In China, technology is considered a commodity that is purchased, and can be used freely. Confidentiality agreements are essential in licensing agreements in the PRC, as is shrewd bargaining with regard to compensation. Only a decade ago, China possessed virtually no legislation on intellectual property rights. Despite its substantial body of laws, the code has myriad shortcomings, the most notable of which is its failure to provide copyright protection for US works (an action that costs the US $400 million a year in trade losses).

India continues to have one of the world's most autarkic national economies, one in which foreign trade and multinationals play a conspicuously small role. Due to the drastic restrictions on foreign involvement mandated in India's pervasive industrial policy, foreign firms have generally found it easier and quicker to establish a licensing agreement (dubbed "technical collaboration") with a licensee than to arrange a joint venture with an Indian firm. Even so, approvals are often strictly contingent on a project's ability to generate exports. Patent protection is sufficient (except for foods and pharmaceuticals), but copyright infringement remains prevalent, especially in the publishing industry. Payment for the use of foreign brand names is strictly prohibited for nationalistic reasons, yet such names have no legal protection when they are appropriated by Indian firms. India's enormous emerging middle class has great potential for licensors of consumer goods, but liberalization of the state's economic regulations is progressing only very fitfully. The debate over IP protection in India focuses much more on national sovereignty than international standards.

In **Czechoslovakia**, the lack of hard currency continues to curb the import of technology. Licenses have also acquired the reputation of not being cost-effective, due to the expense of buying project-related equipment and raw materials. There is often a long time span between the opening of license negotiations and the start-up of licensed production. In some cases, bureaucratic delays have made a technology obsolete even before it is implemented, depriving the country of up-to-date technology.

Traditionally, intellectual property protection has been strong. Foreign firms have experienced very few incidents of patent infringement.

A major component in the current restructuring of **Hungary's** economy has been the acquisition and implementation of new technology. The bureaucratic procedures governing licensing have been eased significantly. Enterprises authorized to conduct foreign trade are now permitted freely to purchase licenses. Three foreign trade organizations, however, have traditionally specialized in license purchase and technology transfer. Because of foreign exchange shortages, there is an emphasis on licenses which will produce exports. The IPL code of Hungary is considered to be up-to-date.

Poland has had a host of bad experiences with license imports, which often entailed enormous expenditure on inputs. Licensing has also diminished because of acute cash shortages. All license imports must be able to pay for fees, equipment and raw materials through an "export multiplier effect." The Polish market for consumer products is overrun with goods labeled with pirated brand names. Ironically, Polish customers usually prefer authentic goods, so some of the pirated goods are exported to other Eastern European countries. A recent case established a precedent by which to pursue trademark violators and take effective action against piracy. Even so, foreign firms rarely take actions; because Poland is a small market, their commercial interests are generally not threatened.

With the formal fragmentation of the USSR in 1992, the former Soviet laws applying to technology and licensing agreements are in an indeterminate state. By the second quarter of the year, the only individual republic that had passed its own intellectual property laws was Lithuania—though this legislation is very short and pertains essentially only to company names and trademarks. The **Russian republic**, on the other hand, has made the most headway in putting forward numerous draft proposals that are on their way to superseding the older Soviet legislation. In addition, all Russian enterprises now have the right to conclude licensing agreements directly with foreign companies, and the limitations on import of foreign technology have been lifted. For these reasons, Russia is most likely to make the transformation in its treatment of intellectual property most quickly and, possibly, most fundamentally. While MNCs looking to initiate licensing agreements in any of the Commonwealth of Independent States are strongly advised to follow the evolution of the legal system, many elements of the old structure are likely to remain influential for some time. Until the new legal structure is firmly in place then, there is still much to be learned from the experience of Western firms in the USSR.

Introduction

The transfer of technology from its owner to another party—*licensing*—has traditionally been a major option for doing business internationally. It may be an alternative to exports, joint ventures and wholly owned subsidiaries, and is often a component of these strategies as well. It can involve know-how as well as patents; sale, leasing, operation and maintenance of machinery and equipment as well as blueprints; training and engineering assistance; supply of special components and/or raw materials; marketing and promotion programs; and various forms of management assistance, including ongoing management contracts.

And the licensee can be more than a simple supplier of payments. Besides improving the technology, the licensee can also offer related technology, new marketing experience (tailored to a specific environment and possibly applicable elsewhere), and general experience and contacts that result from doing business in the licensee's home market.

Licensing today takes place in an extremely complex arena for technology management. To begin with, technology takes an increasing number of different forms, including process technology, product technology, management technology and quality control. All these elements must be managed in an international environment dominated by an accelerating pace of innovation, the globalization of the economy and technology, and increased world competition. An indication of the sheer growth of cross-border transfers is given in the table on p. xxv, which shows the "trade balance" in technology for the Group of Seven countries. Some of the most important factors shaping this environment include:

- advances in communication technology, which have led to the globalization of the marketplace;
- an escalation in the costs of research and development, product commercialization and production facilities; and
- an acceleration in technological development and a general shortening of product life cycles.

Why License?

The importance of technology transfer is widely recognized by small and large companies alike. Many small firms realize that licensing is the best way to reap substantial earnings from markets they could not penetrate on their own. Even large multinationals with extensive equity investments include licensing as an option in their overall growth strategy. For companies of all sizes, licensing can be a first step toward expansion through acquisition or joint-venture arrangements.

Companies also use the licensing process to lower risks and costs associated with direct investment, or simply as an alternative when direct market penetration is unfeasible. Depending on the political and economic environment in certain markets, the prevailing corporate attitude toward direct investment and other factors, licensing may be the best and most cost-effective way to expand overseas and maximize earnings from proprietary technology. Export sales in some situations face mounting tariffs and other barriers, for example, and direct investment is often costly, legally restricted, unacceptably risky or a combination of these.

Some benefits of licensing

Licensing offers numerous advantages, the most important of which are summarized below.

Freedom of action. A company can pursue business programs and execute specific strategies through licensing, which permits access to new markets as well as to the licensee's marketing strengths and other assets.

Revenue generation. Such diverse sources as royalties; up-front fees; lump-sum payments; counterpurchase; the sale of raw materials, components and certain special models of licensed products; and other services provided to licensees can provide substantial income.

Entry to and competition in a market. Often at low risk and without the investment of sizable amounts of money or time, licensing can prove useful to a firm in gauging a market's possibilities or testing a product or process by letting the licensee run the risks of start-up and implementation. Participation in the market can later be expanded to manufacture or joint-venture operations.

Gateway to the worldwide market. A company can open up global markets to its products and services through licensing, especially in countries where direct export sales or investment are unfeasible or undesirable.

Cost and resource effectiveness. For some companies, a shortage of capital or human resources precludes acquisition or new investment. Licensing lowers both the cost and risk of overseas expansion, and reduces management time involved in starting up a new operation.

From an investment perspective, the costs of a licensing agreement are modest. No capital outlay is usually required of the licensor, nor is there substantial drain on its management and technical resources. Licensing may also be less vulnerable to the effects of recession and other economic or political problems than are many other strategies. If the licensee is unsuccessful, or if political or social trouble of any real substance and duration develops, the licensor may emerge relatively unscathed.

Suitability to a particular market. A market may be too small to offer a sufficient return on direct investment or exports. Environmental conditions—such as restrictive policies on foreign firms, economic uncertainties, high duties or transportation costs—may also discourage or prohibit more intense involvement. Furthermore, a market may be dominated by competitors that are firmly entrenched, and the potential licensor may possess inadequate knowledge of the marketplace to operate effectively there.

Protecting patents and trademarks. For some companies, the protection of technology is more important than the earnings to be derived from a licensing arrangement. Companies grant licenses as a safeguard against patent or trademark infringement, particularly in regions where infringement is common, such as parts of Latin America and Asia.

Limitations of Licensing

Although licensing offers many benefits to a company, it does have drawbacks as well, including the following points.

Limited income potential relative to other business alternatives. While licensing involves lower capital investment and therefore lower risks, income is also usually a much smaller percentage of gross sales than the profit that could be derived from direct manufacture and sale to the market.

The possibility that a licensee might become a competitor of the licensor when the agreement expires. Some companies license competitors to forestall the development of similar technology that could then be used to compete against their own (and earn royalties in the process). But other firms, particularly smaller ones, eschew licensing for this very reason: They do not want to give competitors access to their core technology, especially if this would boost sales of the competitors' related products.

Concern that the licensee would aggressively seek to market outside its territory, or even outside its geographic region, through direct sales or sublicenses, thus perhaps competing with the licensor or its other licensees. Some agreements contain provisions restricting the licensee's market, but in many cases such clauses are illegal.

The licensee's inability to meet acceptable business standards. The quality of the product may, for instance, be substandard because of management or manufacturing problems; the company may develop a poor reputation because of misleading or inappropriate sales strategies; the lag time between receipt of the technology and effective exploitation of the market may exceed that originally forecast; or the company may simply not live up to its potential and fail.

Misunderstandings and disputes that may require prolonged discussion or even arbitration or litigation. The difference between each party's national laws and business practices can be a serious operational stumbling block.

The tendency of licensees to renew only on conditions more favorable to them. Royalty fees are often negotiated at lower rates in renewed agreements.

The limitations set by some countries on outward payments for licenses. Strict exchange controls, restrictions on royalty percentages and prohibition of local tax deductibility for these payments are some of the limitations that can crimp technology transfer. Parties should also be familiar with double-taxation treaties that afford some relief from local withholding tax requirements.

Exchange rate uncertainties. Exchange rate volatility can have a serious effect on the royalty stream. This situation can be mitigated by specifying in the contract the currency to be used for payment and providing a mechanism whereby the royalty rate is indexed to compensate for currency fluctuations. However, this route may be impossible in countries with strict controls on royalty rates. Other, more informal methods can also be used, including sale of materials to the licensee and barter or countertrade.

The appendices at the back of this book include a summary of items that should be included in a foreign licensing contract, as well as suggestions on how to price patents in foreign countries.

International Issues

Greater efforts are also being made to confront international infringement problems. Intellectual-property concerns are now increasingly linked to international trade issues. The US Trade and Tariff Act of 1984, for example, added intellectual-property considerations to trade laws. The first trade law amended was Section 301 of the Trade Act of 1974. Under Section 301, the government may take action to enforce US rights under trade agreements or to eliminate policies—including intellectual-property-rights infringement—that restrict US commerce. The 1984 act enhanced the trade representative's authority to initiate motions against a trading partner and redefined the acts and policies that constitute such infringement abroad. The second US trade law amended was the Generalized System of Preferences (GSP), which authorizes the president to waive tariffs on many imported products from developing-country beneficiaries. The 1984 act also extended the GSP program to 1993 and added adequate intellectual-property-rights protection as one criterion for eligibility.

Multilateral efforts to foster greater recognition of intellectual-property rights are also under way through the General Agreement on Trade and Tariffs (GATT) negotiations. As a result of such bilateral and multilateral attention, a number of countries notorious for not respecting intellectual-property rights, such as some Asian nations, have begun to change their attitudes by recognizing the value of enforcing these rights. Despite the pressures of GATT, the US Trade Representative placed four countries—Brazil, China, India and Thailand—on the "priority watch list" in 1990 as a result of their IPR-related trade barriers.

While many developing countries appear to have declined in importance in licensing activities, this trend is largely being reversed in Asia, which has seen its market for technology suppliers grow. Technology licensing in Latin America, on the other hand, is receiving less emphasis—due largely to unstable economies, foreign exchange shortages and poor protection of intellectual-property rights.

The legal aspects of international licensing have also become increasingly more complicated. Despite developments strengthening patent protection in many countries, legal problems in the patent area may grow trickier as applications—and disputes—grow more complex, particularly for emerging technologies in the pharmaceuticals and biotechnology areas.

Complicating overseas licensing are the requirements in many countries that licensors prepare proposals for and deal with government and quasi-government agencies, departments and banks in addition to the licensee. Also, government interference has sometimes manifested itself in the establishment of preconditions for approval of licensing agreements. Governments in technology-importing countries, for example, often try to limit technology payments in a variety of ways. Many regulatory regimes either prohibit or severely limit intra-firm technology payments, which they fear may lead to abusive transfer-pricing practices. General payments regulations focus on limiting royalty rates and controlling payment terms that are considered abusive. A ceiling of 5% of sales is often used. Higher payments may be allowed when the technology to be supplied is considered exceptionally valuable, and lower ceilings can be applied to particular industries and categories of payments (e.g., pure trademark agreements unaccompanied by any other technological input).

Government legislation restricting the export of sensitive technology has also complicated the licensing process and other international ventures. These export controls must be thoroughly assessed when planning any international venture that involves transmission of technology to a foreign country.

Under the US Export Administrations of 1979 and the Export Administration Amendments Act of 1985, for example, the president of the US is empowered to control the export and reexport of certain commodities and technical data to prohibited (generally communist) countries. Export controls related to national security are administered in conjunction with the Consultative Group Coordinating Committee (COCOM), a committee composed of members of the NATO alliance. This group controls the export of products and technology to the Eastern bloc and has agreed that no member country can export products and technology on a special list to Eastern bloc countries without securing the prior approval of COCOM. The US has been pressured by its allies in COCOM to loosen up the 42-year-old embargo as hostilities of the cold war era fade. In October 1991, the US Department of Commerce published a shorter and more specific list of products and technologies that require special government licenses before they can be exported. The new list eases many restrictions on exports to the USSR and its former Eastern bloc satellites. It does, however, retain curbs on technologies that might be put to military uses, as well as advanced telephone systems, including many fiber-optic and microwave systems.

(US concerns were primarily responsible for the continued tight controls on fiber-optic technology, a decision that has hampered US West's plans to modernize the Soviet Union's telephone system.) On the legislative front, meanwhile, Congress is moving toward codifying the Cocom liberalization, though it is also considering a bill to restructure the US's export control regime; President George Bush vetoed a similar bill in 1990.

IPR: Variations on a Theme

Protection of intellectual-property rights vary greatly from country to country. ***Eastern bloc*** countries such as Czechoslovakia and Hungary have been virtually free of piracy until recently. As business conditions in Eastern Europe become less regulated, however, the risk of piracy will certainly increase. Poland, on the other hand, has long been notorious for Western trademark piracy. In 1985 a new trademark law was passed, prompting a multitude of Western companies to register their trademarks to enjoy increased protection. The Soviet Union uses unusual categories of patents, such as "inventor's certificates," which are issued instead of patents for chemicals, pharmaceuticals and biotechnology. The protection provided by this system of certification is often inadequate and is due to be phased out.

Latin America has a long history of intellectual-property abuses, which are slow to change. Although Brazil still offers lax protection for chemicals and pharmaceuticals, computer hardware and software were granted increased protection by the Collor government at the same time they were removed from the list of prohibited imports. Mexico has only recently improved protection. In Venezuela, patents and trademarks are well protected by the letter of the law, but because enforcement is meager, trademark piracy remains a severe problem.

In many countries in ***Asia***, Western firms license to local companies to offset piracy. Although enforcement is a problem in Taiwan, for example, licensing is a good means of offsetting competition. In Korea, Western firms must go a step further and become registered resident foreign companies if they are to enjoy trademark protection under amended copyright laws. Thailand—perhaps the worst offender in the region—is especially rampant with enforcement problems; piracy of books, records and movies is common, and representatives of Western companies and industrial associations trying to secure IPR protection in the country report that they have even met or been threatened with violence.

Differences in registration also exist. Companies in Korea still use close imitations of Western brand names, while a nationalistic Indian law virtually forbids the domestic use of foreign trade names. Japan offers strong protection, but its legislation has loopholes—such as allowing different companies trademark rights in different sectors—that mandate a degree of caution. Much of the patent and trademark legislation in China was ratified only in the past decade, and the degree to which it will protect foreign intellectual property has yet to be proven in actual suits.

Government control

One of the most striking but consistent ways in which the non-Western governments differ from those in North America and Western Europe has been in their strong commitment to industrial policy. Any company that has been primarily used to working in a laissez-faire environment must be prepared to face a good deal of red tape in licensing products in these nations.

Because of its need for Western technology, for example, Hungary has greatly liberalized its regulations and increased its imports of technology. No government approval is needed for a technology transfer that will produce items on the liberalized-import list, which comprises about 40% of imports. Even so, the Foreign Trade Organizations charged with licensing are still involved in the coordination of a high percentage of licensing deals. In the former USSR, control for technology transfers were decentralized. Transfers of technology to Czechoslovakia still require government approval, but there as elsewhere in Eastern Europe the legislative framework has been changing rapidly.

In Venezuela, foreign contracts no longer require government approval, merely registration. Argentine law requires government review only for transfers of technology from foreign companies to their foreign subsidiaries; transfers between independent firms need only be registered. The Salinas administration in Mexico adopted liberalized regulations for technology transfer. Despite liberalization under Collor, however, Brazilian ministries continue to exercise a great deal of control over details of licensing contracts.

Under Taiwanese law, companies can choose to do a licensing deal either through government channels or privately, whichever is more advantageous. In both Japan and Korea, government ministries exert a great deal of control over industrial policy. As a result, technology-transfer contracts in Korea go through long processes of government review. The situation in China varies. While technology transfers to enterprises in Beijing or Shanghai, for example, still require centralized review, those to enterprises zones such as Shenzhen are more flexible.

The Indian government, which stipulates that all foreign collaboration must involve technology transfers, has liberalized some of its industrial legislation, but transfers often require several years of red tape before approval.

Payments and foreign exchange

The convertibility of local currencies has a strong impact on national licensing conditions. Even though some Eastern European countries have instituted convertibility, the sheer lack of hard currency makes it difficult to finance licensing deals. Poland is virtually unable to do licensing deals without tying them to export projects that repay the hard-currency outlay. In Hungary, however, the government is looking toward new financial mechanisms to enable enterprises to import the technology they need.

In many countries, bureaucrats set ceilings on royalties and other remittances. The National Institute of Industrial Property in Brazil determines what it calls "fair market value" on licensing contracts and prefers lump-sum payments to royalties. Under new Venezuelan legislation, though, the government limits regulation of royalties to those between foreign firms and their subsidiaries. Because inflation in Latin America can reach astronomical levels, the stability of a currency, along with the difference between parallel and official rates, becomes a major factor for foreign firms.

The international trade ministries in both Japan and Korea stay on the alert for potential foreign technology to transfer, and likewise watch over royalty rates. Foreign exchange problems make licensing in the People's Republic of China and India particularly difficult; the authorities often ask for some sort of export provisions. In addition, it is difficult to negotiate for royalties based on output in China.

Into the 1990s

An economic climate characterized by slower growth and intensifying competition—and the 1990s may well be a decade of contraction in the world economy—places a premium on the ability of companies to reduce costs and increase efficiency. Technological considerations, therefore—including especially the ability to transfer technological knowledge across borders—are certain to gain in importance. The purpose of this report is to outline the regulatory regime for the transfer of technology in 14 countries where licensing makes good sense as a business strategy—either because it is preferable to direct investment or it is the preferred means of entering a protected or limited market. The organi-

Technology Transfers, 1970-87
($ millions)

		1970	1975	1980	1983	1985	1987
US	Exports	2,134	4,008	6,617	7,531	16,669	22,281[1]
	Imports	225	473	762	230	6,215	8,877[1]
Japan	Exports	—	233	644	1,124	982	1,490
	Imports	—	592	966	1,303	1,229	1,958
Germany	Exports	153	264	430	636	614	1,081
	Imports	413	679	1,025	1,269	1,206	2,443
France	Exports	173	394	688	969	894	1,348
	Imports	282	472	823	1,074	1,064	1,732
UK	Exports	407	589	779	1,131	848	980[2]
	Imports	378	578	672	887	692	908[2]
Italy	Exports	—	90	233	208	144	301
	Imports	—	480	662	842	546	788
Canada	Exports	—	53	—	211	393	425[2]
	Imports	—	190	—	449	534	541[2]

(1)Revised wider coverage, 1985-. (2)1986.
Source: OECD.

zation is broadly regional, starting with Latin America, moving to the Asian NICs and Japan, then westward into Thailand, China and India before finishing with Eastern Europe. The successful companies profiled in each of these very different environments prove that cross-border licensing continues to play a leading role for companies wishing to expand their operations internationally.

Acknowledgments

Business International would like to thank all the people whose cooperation made this book possible. Thanks go especially to the law firms of Kuhn & Mueller, and Sena & Berton Moreno, for their help in preparing the Argentina chapter; to Alexander Hoagland and Gabriel Navarrete of Hoagland Jauregui Abogados in Mexico City for assistance with the new Mexican licensing regulations; and to Paul, Weiss, Rifkind, Wharton & Garrison for their contributions to the China chapter. The editors of BI's *Doing Business with Eastern Europe* service were also kind enough to make their expertise available.

This book was edited in New York, from reports in the field, by Tom Ehrbar, with extensive support and assitance from Lance Lattig.

Business International's Guide to International Licensing

1

Argentina

The administration of Carlos Menem has introduced sweeping reforms and liberalization measures in order to stabilize Argentina's often erratic economy. Since 1989, when the Peronists came to power, Argentina has had to cope with waves of hyperinflation, with consumer prices often increasing by 100% a month. In April 1991 the government instigated an economic plan that curbed devaluation of the austral, reactivating production through heightened consumer demand. Simultaneously, the Central Bank slashed interest rates to counter inflationary pressures. By August 1991, inflation had been reduced to 1.3% per month. Declining interest rates and new financial instruments have given Argentine firms new access to capital markets, at home and abroad.

Menem's market-oriented economic strategy focuses on reducing the state's traditional participation in the economy through deregulation and privatization. Privatization of the petroleum, telecommunications and transportation sectors have bolstered domestic and foreign investment after several years of serious decline.These policies have garnered strong support abroad—from both the Bush administration and the IMF. The government is hoping to use a fiscal surplus to service its monumental foreign debt without resorting to inflationary monetary tactics. By September 1991, arrears on interest payments to commercial banks totaled $8 billion.

Various influential groups within Argentine society—the opposition parties as well as factions within the ruling Peronist Party (Partida Justicialista); business and industrial sectors whose privileges have been affected by privatizations and other anti-oligopolistic policies; and the powerful labor unions—have vigorously opposed Menem's policies. In the September 1991 midterm election, however, the Peronists were rewarded for the recent period of economic stability and social peace.

In 1991 the goverment enacted legislation reducing import and export duties; mounting imports and plummeting exports are reducing the trade surplus (which was $8 billion in 1990). While laws governing foreign trade are being reformed, other problems remain for foreign firms doing business in Argentina. In one of several scandals that involved Menem's administration in 1991, the US Embassy accused Argentine government officials of soliciting bribes from MNCs.

Legal Context

Argentina recognizes five basic types of intellectual property: trademarks (*marcas registradas*), trade names (*nombres commercials*), patents (*patentes*), industrial designs and models (*diseños y modelos industrials*), and copyrights (*derechos de autor*). The country does not attempt to focus on any one kind of technology by giving preferential tax or other treatment to certain kinds of imports.

Trademarks

The Trademarks and Trade Names Act, No. 22,362 of December 1980, and Decree 558/81, which adopted an international classification system, controls trademark registration in Argentina. Rather than defining the nature of a trademark in general, these laws confine themselves to defining what can and cannot be registered as a trademark. According to this legislation, the following qualify for registration as trademarks:

- one or more words without meaning;
- drawings, emblems, monograms, engravings, prints, seals, images, bands, distinctive combinations of colors applied in a specific place to goods or to their containers;
- wrappings and containers;
- combinations of letters and numbers, and letters and numbers with a special design;
- advertising phrases; and
- distinctive reliefs or any other distinctive sign.

The following items cannot be registered as trademarks:

- a name, word or sign that is the generic or habitual term for the goods or services to be protected, or that is descriptive of their nature, function, quality or other characteristics;

- names, words, signs and advertising phrases that were in general use before the application for trademark was filed;
- the natural or intrinsic color of goods, or a tint applied to them;
- trademarks identical to others that have already been registered or applied for, to distinguish or protect the same goods or services;
- names of origin, whether national or foreign—for example, the name of a country, region, place or geographical area used to distinguish a product coming from the area and whose characteristics are exclusive to that place;
- trademarks likely to be misleading with respect to the nature, properties, merit, quality, manufacturing techniques, purpose, origin, price or other qualities of the goods or services to be protected;
- words, drawings or other elements contrary to morals and good customs;
- letters, words, signs or symbols used (or to be used) by the national, provincial or municipal government, or religious and health organizations;
- letters, words, signs or symbols used in foreign countries and international organizations recognized by the Argentine government;
- the name, pseudonym or portrait of a person (or his existing heirs up to the fourth degree) used without that person's consent;
- the names of activities used to distinguish products; and
- advertising phrases lacking originality.

Registration with the National Institute of Industrial Technology (INTI) secures trademark rights. Sec. 4 of the Trademark Act states that "the property of a trademark and exclusiveness of use are obtained by registration thereof." The *use* of a trademark is considered a necessary condition for the renewal of the registration (see below).

The term of a registered trademark is 10 years, and renewals may be made indefinitely for a similar period provided that the mark has been used in the commercialization of the product, in the rendering of a service or as part of the name of a business within the five years prior to each expiration date.

Trademarks are considered immaterial property under the Argentine judicial system, and are therefore assignable among living parties or by last will of the deceased. Also, the assignment or sale of the goodwill of a business includes the assignment or sale of its trademarks, unless otherwise stipulated.

While trademark rights are granted on a priority basis according to the time of filing (following the Paris Convention, Lisbon Act of 1958, and ratified by Argentina in Act 17,011), a trademark can also be jointly registered by more than one individual, in which case they must act jointly to license, assign or renew it. Any of the owners may defend the trademark and use it, unless an express provision to the contrary is granted.

Trademarks may lapse through waiver of the owner; expiration of term (when no renewal is sought); or a judicial finding of nullity.

A trademark may be canceled under the third option if it has been registered against the provisions of the law; if it was registered for commercial purposes by someone whose habitual business is the registration of trademarks merely to keep them in use; or if it was registered by someone who knew, or should have known, when applying, that the trademark belonged to a third party. These provisions for cancelation, together with Sec. 6 of the Paris Convention, have greatly simplified the persecution of trademark piracy and the cancelation of infringing trademarks in Argentina.

The Trademarks and Trade Names Act also contains formal provisions that detail the procedures for registering a trademark and criminal penalties for the violation of its statutes. Criminal action may be taken against any person who counterfeits or fraudulently imitates a registered trademark; uses a fraudulently imitated trademark belonging to a third party without his authorization; or sells, offers for sale, or markets products or services bearing counterfeited trademarks or a fraudulently imitated trademark.

The penalties range from three months to two years imprisonment, in addition to monetary fines. The damaged person may request the liquidation of the merchandise and other elements that bear the infringing trademark, along with the destruction of the infringing trademarks and names of all those elements bearing such a trademark if they cannot be separated from these elements. These must all be carried out at the expense of the violator, who must also pay for the publication of his sentence.

A trademark that has not been used may also be canceled by judicial action on the part of a third party. Any third party with a "legitimate" interest may request from the court the cancelation of a trademark that has not been used in the country within the five years prior to the filing of the judicial action. There are two restrictions on this method of cancelation. An unused trademark cannot be canceled if it has not been used for reasons of force majeure (under Sec. 16 of the act)—e.g. a trademark that will be used (but has not yet been used) to distinguish a medicine that has not yet been approved; or if it is a part of the name of its owner (under Sec. 26 of the act)—e.g. Philip Morris Inc.

Trade names

Act 22,362 also regulates trade names, stating that "the name or sign used to designate an activity, whether for profit or otherwise, is considered a property by law." Hence, a trade name is a generic concept that includes the name of a profit or nonprofit organization, the name of a commercial establishment, or a mercantile sign or design.

Any person with a legitimate interest may oppose the use of a trade name, and a corresponding action must be instituted within a year from the date when the third party began to use it "in a public and manifest way," or within a year of the plaintiff's first knowledge of its use. Criminal provisions applicable to the infringement of trademark rights also apply to trade-name violations.

Patents

Patents of invention are regulated in Argentina by Act 111, dating from 1864 and based mainly on the French patent law of 1844. Sec. 4 of the act explicitly prohibits pharmaceuticals, financial plans, discoveries and inventions of a purely theoretical nature with no industrial applications, as well as those contrary to morals or the laws of the country.

Secs. 1 and 3 of the act define patentable inventions in the following ways.

New discoveries concerning inventions in all fields of industry confer upon the authors the right to its exploitation for the period of time and under the conditions defined by law. Certificates of registration, known as patent letters, are issued by the state. For a patent of invention or discovery, absolute novelty within and outside the country is required.

Each patent must address a single invention, i.e. all elements must be combined in such a way that the invention cannot be used without making use of all of them. If more than one invention is involved—if the parts are not combined but juxtaposed—an individual application must be filed for each one.

Patent rights cannot be issued for a product or service that merely substitutes a technical equivalent of a known means for the same purpose and application.

Patented inventions must constitute a positive technological contribution—i.e. they cannot be the mere application of known technical processes for a generic or equivalent purpose. In addition, the invention should not be considered obvious or foreseeable to a person skilled in the art.

The law theoretically provides for terms of five, 10 and 15 years, which are supposedly determined by the merit of the invention and the will of the applicant. In practice, however, patents are always granted for a term of 15 years. It should be noted that patents cannot be renewed. Foreign patents, though, may be revalidated in Argentina for a maximum of 10 years. If the foreign patent expires in the country of origin in six years, for example, a revalidation patent may be granted for six years.

As with trademarks and trade names, patents can be canceled if they are not used for a period of time. In this case, the law states that validly issued patents expire after two years of issuance if the protected invention has not been exploited, or when exploitation is discontinued for the same period of time, except in cases of force majeure. Patents canceled in this way for lack of use immediately fall into the public domain.

Law 111 also provides for "additional" or "precautionary" patents. Additional patents allow anyone who has improved a patented discovery or invention to request a certificate of addition, which cannot be granted for a period of time longer than the time left for the original patent to expire.

Precautionary patents relate to the development of an unfinished invention. The duration of these patents is one year, and within this term no other patent related to the object involved may be issued without a previous notification to the holder of the precautionary patent, who must file an opposition within three months of notification to block a related patent.

Act 111 also establishes penalties for counterfeiting patented articles. In addition to monetary fines and compensation for damages, violators of patent rights may be imprisoned for one month to six years.

The pharmaceuticals debate

Several amendments have been introduced to bring pharmaceuticals under the patent umbrella, but none has ever succeeded. Local drug manufacturers, however, fearing such a move would result in monopoly control of the industry by foreign companies, have objected strenuously to such protection. In fact, even though the Constitution protects intellectual-property rights, the legislation as it is written specifically excludes pharmaceuticals patents. After the US began to impose retaliatory measures against countries that do not recognize pharmaceuticals rights, however, the Argentine Congress tabled a draft bill that would change the provisions of Law 111 within the next two years. As a result, the US has currently suspended actions against Argentina.

Industrial models and designs

Industrial models and designs are governed by Decree Law 6,673 of 1963, ratified by Act 14,478, which is based on Art. 17 of the Argentine Constitution. (Art. 17 recognizes exclusive ownership by authors and inventors of their work, inventions or discoveries.)

Secs. 1 and 2 of the act state that the author of an industrial model or design and his legitimate heirs have a property right, which includes the exclusive right to exploit, transfer and register it for the time and under the conditions stated by law. The same rights are granted to authors of industrial models and designs created abroad (and their legitimate heirs) provided the respective country grants a reciprocal right to Argentine authors residing in Argentina. An industrial model or design is defined by law as the "form or aspect given to an industrial product, which gives it an ornamental character."

In order to enjoy these property rights, the author must register the model or design with the Registry of Industrial Models and Designs, a department of the National Board of Industrial Property. As with patents, a sine qua non qualification stipulates absolute originality as a condition for valid registration. Models or designs whose elements are a part of the function of the product, as well as those in which the only change from previous models or designs is insignificant (e.g. color changes) cannot be registered, nor can anything that is considered to be "contrary to morals or good customs."

Registered industrial models and designs are protected for a period of five years, and may be renewed at the request of the owner for two consecutive periods of five years each. Renewal applications must be filed six months before the expiration date.

Industrial models and designs are not subject to any type of review process by the Patent Office with regard to the intrinsic value of the product submitted for registration (as patents are, as described above). Applications are rejected only when the formal procedure has not been followed. Consequently, the validity of an industrial model or design may only be challenged by a formal lawsuit and the registration may only be canceled by a court of law at the request of a third party.

Copyright

Copyright is governed in Argentina by Act 11,723 of 1933. This law defines the intellectual property that may be copyrighted as follows:

- scientific, literary and artistic works, including writings of any kind;
- dramatic, musical, cinematographic and pantomime works;
- drawings, pictures, sculptures, architecture models, works of art or science applied to commerce or industry, fine arts, photographs, engravings and records; and
- other literary, scientific, artistic or didactic works, whatever the reproduction process.

The property right of a literary, scientific or artistic work comprises the author's right to use, publish, play, represent and publicly exhibit it, as well as to sell, translate and adapt it or to authorize its translation and reproduction in any way.

With regard to anonymous works or those signed with pseudonyms, a publisher can acquire the author's rights and duties by filing evidence that he is the publisher. Authors who sign their works with pseudonyms may also register them, however, thus acquiring them as property.

Copyright coverage extends over the author's lifetime, and continues for 50 more years for his heirs. If there is more than one author, the heirs' copyright commences at the death of the last coauthor. The copyright of anonymous works belonging to institutions, corporations or juridical persons lasts 30 years from the first publication.

Intellectual property that may be copyrighted must meet the following requirements:

- it must be a complete intellectual work (a mere idea is not enough); and
- it must be original and novel.

Scientific, artistic and literary works published in foreign countries are also protected by Argentine law as long as they comply with the requirements established for copyright protection in their home country. The protection granted by Argentine law to foreign authors is never longer than the term recognized by the laws of the country where the work has been published.

Political or literary speeches and lectures on intellectual matters cannot be published by a third party if not expressly authorized by the author. Parliamentary speeches cannot be published for profit without the author's authorization.

Act 11,723 also created the National Registry of Intellectual Property, which serves as the repository of information for all copyrighted materials in Argentina. All materials must bear an imprint detailing the date and place of publication and the name of the publisher.

As for punishment for copyright infringement, violators can be fined, and imprisoned from six months to eight years.

Technology Transfer

Transactions involving the transfer, assignment or licensing of technology or trademarks by a foreigner in Argentina are subject to Act 22,426 of 1981. Approval must be granted for contracts between foreign firms

Licensing Experience in Argentina

McDonald's

McDonald's Corp has a subsidiary in Argentina that operates under the name of McDonald's Restaurants de Argentina SA. This company holds 49% of Arcos Dorados and Golden Pampa, which operate in Argentina under the license of McDonald's Corp.

Arcos Dorados pays royalties to McDonald's for the use of trademarks and designs, most notably the "golden arches" from which the firm's Spanish name derives. Under Argentine law, it is an independent company, since the Argentine affiliate of McDonald's holds 49% of its shares—the legal limit on independent status. "Trademarks and patents are owned by the corporation," explained Arcos Dorados Chairman Woods Station. "They were registered in Argentina before we started using them. When we began our operation in 1988, we found that several patents registered by the corporation were being used. A cookie factory was using Ronald McDonald in its logo, and a retail store was using the golden arches.

"But the law is very clear and strong in this area. It was easy to cover the patents. All we had to do was talk with their lawyers. In both cases, they stopped using our designs," Station added. "We've never had difficulties with the remittance of royalties, not even when the government imposed exchange controls or restrictions on the transfer of funds."

Station also noted that registration before INTI presents no major difficulties. Comparing Argentina to other countries, specifically Third World nations, he asserted, "It's much easier to establish here. If the economy were more stable, it would be a perfect place."

Siemens

In Argentina, the Siemens group operates mainly in the telecommunications field. Through its subsidiary KWU, it is a partner of the state in electricity generation via nuclear plants.

Discussing Siemens' recent experiences in Argentina, Public Relations Manager Miguel Ritter stated, "The current legislation is quite liberal in comparison with the previous law. Over the past nine years, it has proven to be a useful and easy framework for licensing."

Ritter said that if a contract signed with an independent company

(Continued)

is not registered with INTI, the process is "extremely easy and fast, taking three to five days." As for contracts between subsidiaries and their parent companies, he noted that "INTI must first approve the transaction, which generally takes several months."

Siemens' experience shows that all contracts are subject to close scrutiny when they are first presented. Although some 10-20% are rejected, the rest are approved if the requested corrections in the original contract are made.

The company also noted that in certain cases INTI tries to reduce the rate of royalties for technology transfers by valuing them under the legal limitation of 5% of net sales.

INTI also objects to contract clauses regarding the liability of the parties. The supplier may want to limit its responsibility to the purchasing company or third parties when the quality of the products produced under license are defective or when third-party patents are violated, for example. Sometimes INTI will demand the elimination of such clauses, but other times it accepts, for instance, a figure equivalent to one year of royalties as the supplier's limit of responsibility.

and their subsidiaries; those between independent firms need only be registered with INTI. Transfers involving the armed forces or other defense organizations are also exempt from approval if they are related to national security. The most common cases of this involve nuclear-energy contracts, which are signed under confidentiality provisions.

In the case of agreements executed between a local company with foreign capital and a company located abroad that directly or indirectly controls it, the payment of royalties for trademark licensing is not permitted. In practice, two contracts must be signed by such companies: one relating to the transfer of technology, which takes account of know-how transferred to the local company, and another that covers the

Transfer-of-Technology Contracts
(number presented before INTI)

	1982	1983	1984	1985	1986	1987	1988	1989*
Independent companies	331	377	351	326	307	332	315	130
Parent-subsidiaries	64	68	95	84	41	58	39	28
Total	395	445	446	410	348	390	354	158

*First half of 1989.
SOURCE: INTI.

licensing of the trademark for products produced with that know-how. Remittances for both must be made as profits.

INTI sets a 90-day limit on application responses; if the office does not reply before this deadline, its silence is interpreted as a sign of approval. Rejections may be appealed up to 30 days after the notice is served.

Apart from the restrictions set out in Argentina's antitrust law, there are no restrictive clauses that are not allowed to be included in technology-transfer agreements, whether between dependent or independent parties. In this regard, the Argentine Defense of Competition Act stipulates that business transactions that "limit, restrict or eliminate competition, or constitute an abuse in the market by a dominant party, [and] work to the detriment of the general economic interest" are forbidden and punishable. Decree 580 of 1981 also addresses the issue of technology transfer in Argentina. According to its provisions, the subject matter of a license agreement may include

- patents of invention;
- industrial models and designs; and
- any technical knowledge required for the manufacture of a product or the rendering of a service.

Once an application is accepted (or merely recorded, if approval is not necessary), INTI grants a certificate, which must be filed with the central bank. The certificate includes information about the contracting parties, such as the names and domiciles of the supplier and receiver of the technology, the place of payment, the duration of the contract and the dates when payments must be made, plus a clause detailing the type of exchange and currency in which the debt is to be paid.

Art. 3 of Decree 580 stipulates that payment may not exceed 5% of the net value of the sales of products manufactured or services provided through the technology transferred. Net value is defined as producer price minus discounts and the deduction of domestic, value-added or other taxes.

Approval Criteria

For contracts that require approval (e.g. those between parent companies and their subsidiaries), the conditions imposed by the supplier must agree with those of the local market, and royalty payment should be set according to market rates. In the case of parent-subsidiary operations, though, the law bans the payment of royalties as such; as noted above, remittances must be made as profits.

Practical Advice

Transfer-of-technology contracts are usually negotiated with the assistance of local specialized law firms. Fees average $100/hour, with an estimated 70 hours needed for the approval of a contract. One partner with a leading local firm in this field advises companies to take the following steps:

- Make an in-depth study of the legal and tax consequences of all contracts, especially the tax advantages of registering contracts before INTI.
- Sign separate contracts when dealing with the transfer of different items, such as technical-assistance fees and know-how. Because these two items have different tax rates, if they were both included in the same contract, the higher tax rate would apply.
- Remember that while most contracts are signed for a four-year period, they are generally and easily extended to five years.
- Delineate clearly the responsibilities of each of the parties involved, particularly when considering possible difficulties that may be brought up by a third party. When problems such as forgery of a licensed trademark arise, the local company is usually subject to legal action.

INTI charges a fee to issue certificates of registration: 1.5% on a contract for independent/foreign companies transactions, and 2.5% for contracts between foreign parents and their subsidiary companies.

According to INTI estimates, about one sixth of the roughly 300 applications submitted every year are rejected. Most rejections are based on formalities, such as out-of-date applications or the attempt to register a transaction that does not actually deal with technology transfer. According to the institution's figures, an average of nine applications are rejected every year for other reasons, usually because the technology to be transferred is available in the local market.

There is an ongoing debate on the issue of software—i.e. whether it can be regarded as the transfer of technology or not. Presently, INTI does not approve software-licensing contracts, claiming it is not a transfer of technology.

Technology Transfers, 1977–88

(Percentages of technology-transfer contracts based on approved or estimated values)

Contracts by Industry

Sector	1977–83	1984–88
Automobiles	7.1	13.0
Clothing (except shoes)	1.8	6.8
Construction	3.7	6.5
Oil refining	4.4	5.3
Power and electricity	8.6	5.1
Pharmaceuticals	4.9	4.9
Electrical machinery	3.5	4.6
Cosmetics	1.7	4.4
Basic chemical substances	8.0	4.2
Plastics, synthetic resin	3.3	3.5

1977–83 total, $2.09 billion; 1984–88 total, $1.05 billion.

Origin by Country

Country	1977–83	1984–88
US	38.6	35.4
West Germany	9.6	20.0
Switzerland	12.9	9.2
France	8.3	10.1
Italy	4.2	4.9
UK	5.1	1.3
Netherlands	2.5	4.3
Spain	4.0	1.0
Canada	3.5	0.7
Japan	2.8	1.8

Private vs Public Companies

Type of company	1977–83	1984–88
Private	72.5	88.2
Public	27.5	11.8

SOURCE: INTI.

Taxation

Under the present income tax law, foreign companies transferring technology to Argentina must pay a 36% tax, which is the result of a 45% tax on 80% of the remittances. This 36% tax is reduced to 27% in the following cases: when the contract involves technical assistance, engineering or consultant works exclusively; when it is registered with INTI (registration for independent and parent/subsidiary operations is not mandatory, but it allows this deduction); or when the services to be transferred cannot be found in the country, as determined by INTI.

If a technology-transfer contract does not fall into any of the abovementioned categories, the foreign company must pay a 45% tax on total remittances. The local company, by the same token, cannot deduct the purchase from its annual fiscal balance. In addition, there is a legal sealing tax of 1% on the amount of the contract.

Argentina has signed bilateral agreements to avoid double taxation with Bolivia, Brazil, Chile, Austria, France, Germany, Italy and Sweden.

2
Brazil

Brazil recognizes intellectual property in the categories of patents, trademarks, copyrights and know-how.

The following types of patents can be granted for novel products: patents of invention; utility and industrial models; and industrial designs. If the registration guidelines for a patent cannot be met, protection is often available as intellectual know-how.

Trademarks can be words, logos or composite elements; both manufacturing and service marks are recognized.

Copyrights can be issued for the protection of an idea's expression, but not the idea or concept itself. Included are books and other published text, maps, music (with and without lyrics), sheet music, films, photographs and works of art.

Know-how in the form of manufacturing processes and procedures, commercial techniques, trade secrets and other types of industrial property are recognized and protected, but they cannot be registered.

International Treaties

Brazil is a signatory member of the Stockholm Convention, which instituted the World Intellectual Property Organization (WIPO). WIPO administers the Paris Convention, The Berne Convention, the Nice Union, the Lisbon Union, the Budapest Union and others. Brazil is also a signatory member of the Strasbourg Agreement on the International Classification of Patents, and of the Patent Cooperation Treaty. Although Brazil signed the Madrid Treaty, the government has announced that it would not abide by the treaty's guidelines for copyrights and trademarks.

Brazil has often been criticized as being a violator of international treaties because of its reservation of markets in the following industries:

hardware, software, chemicals and pharmaceuticals. While some of these barriers (especially in the computer and informatics field) are falling because of President Fernando Collor's plan to open the economy, Brazil has always made the argument that emerging industries, according to GATT, can be protected at the national level. Certain federal restrictions still result in frequent abuses of foreign property rights in these sectors.

Following his election as president, Fernando Collor de Mello assembled a commission to propose changes to IP legislation in 1990. The commission's report became the foundation of a revised IP code awaiting Congressional approval. In response, the US government lifted the trade sanctions it had imposed.

Federal Legislation

In February 1991, the government announced an overhaul of the rules restricting the terms of technology transfer and other licensing contracts. Contracts will no longer be controlled as to royalty levels, duration, forms of payment or control of technology after licensing contracts expire. Ambiguity remains in the fact that the National Institute of Industrial Property (INPI) must still approve contracts in order for the central bank to provide hard currency for royalty remittances, but officials say that approval will be virtually automatic for legitimate contracts. The major obstacle—not only to normal technology relationships, but to normal trade, credit and investment patterns—is the existing system of exchange controls that force officials to be vigilant in all areas involving the transfer of hard currency overseas. The government has hinted at lifting these controls, but no action has been taken since the floating of the commercial exchange rate in March 1990.

Of the four intellectual-property categories, only copyrights are currently classified as intellectual property, which is covered by civil law. Patents, trademarks and know-how are classified as *industrial* property and are covered by commercial law. The present regulations regarding licensing, the registration of trademarks and patents, and the transfer of technology are contained in the Industrial Property Code of 1971. While these regulations were intended to protect domestic firms from multinational domination, they have ultimately limited the transfer of technology into Brazil. Strict registration requirements, severe limits on royalty payments, and lax protection of technology can make licensing in Brazil an operation of limited profitability.

The primary agency responsible for the administration and control of industrial property is the National Institute of Industrial Property (INPI, originally controlled by the Ministry of Industry and Commerce, but now headed by the Ministry of Justice). The INPI regulates the registration of patents, trademarks, software copyright, licensing contracts and other agreements relating to the transfer of technology. A distinction should be made between the registration of patents and trademarks, and licensing contracts regarding their use. In evaluating international licensing agreements and treaties, the role of the INPI is to establish a "fair market value" and determine the duration of contracts.

Patents

The liberalized intellectual property legislation proposed in 1991 includes expanded patent protection and tougher enforcement. This motion follows other changes that cut red tape for cross-border licensing contracts. Once ratified by Congress, these new rules will resolve many of the conflicts Brazil has had with MNCs and foreign governments over intellectual, though critics assert that officials still have too much power over the private flow of technology.

Key points of the proposal are as follows: Patents on inventions (now 15 years maximum) would be renewable for an additional five years. Patents on utility models (now 10 years maximum) would be renewable for an additional three years. Penalties for violation of patent and trademark rights would be stiffened. Imprisonment of three months or more would be mandatory for counterfeiting and other crimes.

Patents on pharmaceuticals, certain other medical items, foods and biotechnology products (now unpatentable) would be allowed. Only plant and animal species are excluded. A phase-in period proposed by the government, although not specified in the code, would make processes in these areas patentable in 1993, and products in 1994. Removal of the ban on pharmaceutical, biotechnology and food patents is the most important element in the proposal. In the past, Brazil defended the lack of such patents with arguments ranging from balance-of-payments concerns to the need to protect nascent industries. Now, the administration is focusing on the damage caused by technological isolation.

Under the present code, patents must meet certain novelty requirements; they cannot be a mere modification of an existing design. They must not have previously been patented, divulged or utilized within Brazil or abroad. To safeguard rights, and to qualify for royalty payments in licensing contracts, patents should be filed in Brazil within one year of being granting abroad, except for those patents protected by priority rights under international conventions. A foreign patent is not protected if an application has not been published or approved by the INPI.

Patents are classified as patents of invention, utility models, industrial models and industrial designs. Patents of invention are valid for 15 years, and the other three are valid for 10 years. (The duration is calculated from the time of initial application.)

The patent application including the intended use or objective, along with supporting specifications and descriptions, must be submitted to the INPI. If in existence, proof of foreign patents must accompany the application or be presented within 180 days of filing. Both the application and the proof of foreign patent must be filed in Portuguese.

During a preliminary examination period, there are no communications between the INPI and the applicant. The next step is a publication of claims, which is made at least 18 months after the application, unless an earlier date is requested by the applicant and approved by the INPI. A request for formal technical examination must be made, either by the applicant or by a third party, within two years of the publication; otherwise no further action will be taken. Opposition to the application must be made within 90 days of the request for examination.

In practice, it has been very difficult to contest a patent, as virtually no details are released in the publication. Little more than a title is provided as a description of the patent. An opposing party must prove that the patent under consideration is already in the public domain, or it must own or have applied for a similar patent. If opposition is made, the INPI may request additional information from the applicant, who has 90 days to respond. The INPI will reach a conclusion, which the applicant has 90 days to appeal. The final step is approval or issuance of the patent certificate. In the past, some patents took eight years for approval, but the length of time has been greatly reduced in recent years.

Patent rights are forfeited in the following situations: if annual fees are not paid; if the patent is not worked in Brazil within four years of issuance; if the patent is the subject of a licensing agreement and the licensee has not worked the patent within five years of issuance; or if the patent remains unexploited for two consecutive years thereafter.

In certain instances where demand is not currently being met, if the patent is not exploited within three years of issuance or remains unexploited for one year thereafter, the patent may be released for compulsory licensing to interested parties.

Unpatentable Products

Currently, unpatentable items include pharmaceuticals, food and medical products. Not patentable also is the process for obtaining them. Most other chemical products, or products made through a chemical process, are not patentable, while the process of obtaining them is. The field of biotechnology in general has suffered from lack of protection, which caused many multinational pharmaceutical companies to reduce or abandon their operations in Brazil. Under a bill introduced in Congress in 1991, pharmaceutical patents will be valid, but only if the product is manufactured in Brazil.

Note that products not qualifying for patent protection can be protected as trade secrets, as is the case in the pharmaceuticals and chemicals industries. If the proper safeguards are not taken in protecting trade secrets, protection may be forfeited.

Remittance Restrictions

To be eligible for royalty remittances, a foreign patent must be filed in Brazil within a year of its registration in the home country. For approval of a licensing contract, the patent must be published in Brazil. According to commercial law, the licensing agreement is limited to the duration of the patent: 15 years from the filing date in the case of patents of invention, 10 years for other patents. But a patent cannot be the subject of a licensing agreement during the preliminary examination period (normally 18 months from initial application), and no royalties can be paid on a license contract until the patent certificate has been issued. This makes the effective term of a patent license less than the 15-year maximum.

Under an agency restructuring, the INPI has established a permanent technical group to increase the processing efficiency of patent-licensing contracts for MNCs. The group works closely with institutions such as the Central Bank and other government agencies.

According to attorneys familiar with the procedures, licenses for issued patents are frequently approved with few restrictions, as the patents themselves have already been researched and approved. Royalties are permitted in the 1-5% range, depending on the industry, with heavy industries receiving the higher rates. Other industries, such as luxury goods, fall in at the lower end of the spectrum.

Trademarks

A trademark can be a word (word mark), symbol or emblem (logo), or a combination including a stylized word (composite). It can represent specific products, groups of products, firms, etc. Not available for registration are generic terms when not accompanied by specific symbols or official names, and marks giving false impression of origin or quality.

Trademarks must be registered to be protected, as prior use is not grounds for protection. Applications must be submitted to the INPI, followed by a preliminary formal examination, then published.

Oppositions must be made to the INPI within 60 days. Cancellation of trademarks based on Industrial Property Code violations, however, can occur at any time within five years of registration. If trademarks are not used within two years of registration or if not used for two consecutive years thereafter, protection will cease. Foreign marks are also protected under international legislation to which Brazil is signatory (WIPO, the Paris Convention), but Brazil has renounced the international trademark guidelines outlined in the Madrid Agreement.

Trademark infringement has been commonplace in Brazil, partly because of favoritism toward smaller national firms. Under Brazilian law, the first company to register a trademark becomes the rightful owner as long as the mark is not used on the same *category* of products for which it is already registered outside of the country. Brazilians have used this strategy to appropriate foreign trademarks owned elsewhere by Nike, Ellesse, Sergio Valente, Calvin Klein, All Star and Apple. The president of INPI announced in 1991 that Brazil will no longer grant registration of well-known trademarks to anyone other than the internationally recognized users of the name.

In order to protect trademarks in Brazil, the following actions should be taken:

Company trademarks should be registered in all categories of goods in which the firm is interested, even if the mark is not yet in use in the home country. The applicant should claim priority based on the Paris Convention.

Once registered, the mark should be used in Brazil within two years. Products can be imported, produced locally, or licensed for production in Brazil. The French firm Lancôme successfully defended its trademark Magie Noire by selling the product in a duty-free store in one of Brazil's international airports.

If possible, a certificate of notoriety should be obtained. The certificate designates that the trademark is well known and associated with a specific product by the Brazilian public. It is difficult to obtain, but the process can be facilitated by a market survey performed in Brazil demonstrating that the trademark is associated with a particular product.

Remittance Restrictions

It is extremely difficult to remit royalties to foreign firms for the use of trademarks. To be eligible for remuneration, the trademark must be registered in the home country for no more than six months before being registered in Brazil (assuming no conflicts with previously registered trademarks). The trademark is then considered a "foreign trademark" and eligible for royalty remittances not to exceed 1% of net sales for a period of 10 years. Subsidiaries, however, cannot pay trademark royalties to a foreign parent.

A trademark that has been registered in the home country for over six months can be registered in Brazil as a "national trademark of foreign title," but no royalty remittances are allowed.

Both kinds of trademark registrations are valid for 10 years, and are easily renewable.

Companies used to circumvent these strict trademark royalty-remittance rules in the following way: Toward the end of the 10-year term, the firm would register a new trademark, similar to the existing trademark, in its home country, then reapply in Brazil within six months. Royalties could be collected for another 10 years this way. The INPI, responding to this scheme, issued a normative act in 1982 stating that new trademarks that were determined to be similar to previously registered trademarks in Brazil would not be eligible for royalty generation.

Copyrights

As mentioned above, copyright—an author's exclusive right to the expression of an idea—is protected in Brazil by civil law (No. 5.988, 1973). Criminal law (Penal Code, Art. 184) covers unfair competition, including that which results from infringement of patent or trademark rights. Only the expression of an idea is protected, not the concept itself.

Copyright registrations are controlled by the National Copyright Council (CNDA) under the Ministry of Culture. The registration of a copyright is not required for protection, but it is helpful in case of litigation. Proof of ownership is not required for copyright registration; lack of ownership must be proven by a third party if it chooses to make an opposition on this basis.

While illegally reproduced video and audio cassettes have been widely available for years in Brazil, the situation seems to have improved recently. International film companies have successfully invoked Brazil's copyright laws to protect their movies. Walt Disney Productions and Universal Studios filed suit several years ago against the Associaçao Brasileira de Distribuidores de Videocassettes and Video Cassette Rent Club Ltda for unauthorized rentals. The courts ruled that the rental of films without the express authorization of the holders of the authors' rights is illegal. While raids on videocassette rental outlets are commonplace, copyright infringement remains a problem.

Software

The administration of Collor de Mello announced that restrictions on foreign participation in the computer industry will end in October 1992. In April 1991 the government's National Council on Informatics and Automation (Conin) voted to remove all remaining restrictions on foreign software. These include regulations that have barred foreign software houses from setting up their own distribution companies in Brazil, ordered federal registration of all imported programs, and prohibited imports of programs that compete with similar Brazilian-developed programs. Under earlier legislation, sales were reserved for domestically controlled distributors and final corporate users were prohibited from directly importing software.

Responding quickly to the liberalization policy, many foreign software companies began local operations, terminating the under-the-counter software piracy that marked the retail sector during the 1980s. Officials, who have anticipated the end of the "informatics reserve," began to allow many transfers of technology through licensing agreements that would earlier have been blocked.

Until law is formally amended, current copyright law provides one form of protection for computer software, as covered under the Software Law, Law No. 7646 of 1987. This law, put into effect in May 1988, grants protection for 25 years to foreign applicants, providing that their home country allows equivalent protection for software developed in Brazil. Penalties for the violation of software copyright are six months to two years in prison, plus fines.

While copyright registration of software is not a legal requirement in Brazil, it is very helpful as a means of proof in cases that go to litigation. When software is registered, proof of authorship is not required; rather, authorship must be disproved by a third party. In practice, however, all the copyright laws provide for is protection against direct copying of the finished product.

The software's underlying logic (such as a linear program, heuristic technique, algorithm, simulation, or sequence of commands) is not protected by copyright law; however, the logic is eligible for patent and trade-secret protection. An exception—under Art. 7 of the Software Law—is made if the underlying logic is deemed "necessary" in order to arrive at a desired objective; then the logic is not patentable. While direct copying and distribution of copyrighted software is prohibited, once the software is released very similar national versions can be (and usually are) released shortly thereafter. This can be done legally when the logic is not patented but protected as a trade secret, and then obtained through reverse engineering. The end result of this lack of protection is that inexpensive copies of most PC software packages are readily obtainable in Brazil.

Software registrations are controlled by the INPI, but the National Copyright Council (CNDA) under the Ministry of Culture is ultimately responsible. Direct responsibility was delegated to the INPI in October 1988, as policy-makers felt that software was more appropriately controlled by the organization in charge of inventions and the industrial applications of technology. This move was also made in an effort to step up protection rights, due at least in part to pressure from the US and WIPO. In case of doubt or conflict, however, the CNDA still retains the final say. If doubts arise about software packages—of which the INPI receives roughly 1,500 per month—the INPI cannot register the software until approval is received from the CNDA, which may in turn consult with the Special Informatics Office (SEI). The SEI, formerly associated with the military, feels that items relating to software and information processing are matters of national security. If a request for copyright protection is denied, the author has 15 days to contest the decision with the CNDA, which then consults the SEI before rendering a final decision. With this many players involved, the level of frustration can be very high.

The National Informatics and Automation Council (CONIN) is a political body made up of government and industry representatives, to which the SEI is subordinate. CONIN, guided by the Brazilian Informatics Policy (PNI), is concerned with developing the capabilities of the Brazilian informatics industry, determining and coordinating appropriate strategies, preventing monopolies, and taking other steps to encourage and regulate economic development.

The commercial aspects of software and other information technology—its import, manufacture and distribution—are under the control of the SEI, although registration with the INPI is required if the contract is for the transfer of software technology. The INPI and the SEI jointly analyze all contracts relating to informatics technology transfers before approving or disapproving contracts. Among other things, it considers whether a Brazilian version of the software exists and if the technology is capable of being absorbed.

Severe restrictions apply to the marketing of software in Brazil as well. It can only be marketed by domestic firms, except in the limited situations where the software is to be applied to hardware marketed in Brazil by foreign firms. Though the law is undergoing significant change at the moment, for many years software could neither be imported nor marketed in Brazil if a national equivalent were already in existence. The SEI, responsible for administration of the Software Law, has a great deal of discretionary power in ruling on such matters, since equivalency and other determinations are not always clear cut. Some industry experts have expressed concern over a federal bureaucrat's technical competence to analyze algorithms, heuristic techniques, and the various other types of processes which underlie software logic—especially when his decisions have a direct impact on the nation's industrial development.

Licensing and Technology Transfer

Licensing and technology-transfer agreements must be registered with and approved by the INPI. Rules issued in February 1991 streamlined procedures, reduced INPI interference in contract terms and permitted licensors to maintain control of technology after a contract expires. Efficiency of the INPI has improved, but while approval time has been reduced, it can still take over a year to reach a decision. The INPI classifies licensing and the transfer of technology according to five categories:

(1) licensing of trademarks;

(2) licensing of patents;

(3) industrial-technology agreements (related to the production of consumption goods);

(4) technical industrial-cooperation agreements (related to capital goods); and

(5) specialized technical-service agreements (planning, implementation, installation, inspection and operational support, such as specialized engineering services).

The US is the largest source of licensing and technology-transfer agreements, followed by Germany, the UK, France and Japan.

Under Normative Act 32 (1978), the INPI requires a prior consultation before contracts are finalized. A draft of the proposed contract must be presented to the INPI, which analyzes it, researches any patents or trademarks involved, consults with other agencies regarding technical aspects, and offers preliminary approval or rejection. The applicant can then amend and finalize the agreement before resubmitting it for final approval.

Under Normative Act 60 (1982), however, a prior consultation is not required for specialized technical-service agreements of less than $35,000. Nor is this procedure required for "urgent technical services," such as those needed to start up production again in a plant that had been shut down due to technical difficulties. All requests are reviewed on a case-by-case basis, and a great deal of discretion is used in the interpretation of urgency.

Licensing agreements will not be approved if the contract places any restrictions on exports. Exceptions may be granted as provided for under international treaties with Brazil, or when the home country has explicit restrictions on exports to specific countries, such as Communist countries.

Remittance Restrictions

The INPI exercises great discretionary power in evaluating the merit of intellectual know-how to determine if the technology is useful to Brazil. Under Normative Act 15, passed in 1975, the agency also rules on whether the technology to be transferred is capable of being absorbed. Its chief concern is that local firms might not fully realize that they are acquiring technology that later proves to be inoperable. By avoiding the unnecessary import of technology, the act was intended to accelerate the transfer of useful technology to Brazil.

Royalty payments for technical-assistance contracts between a Brazilian subsidiary and the foreign parent have the most severe restrictions. Payments at the higher end of the scale (5%) require lengthy negotiations with the INPI and the Central Bank and are difficult to obtain. Industries that use sophisticated technology and invest large sums of foreign capital in Brazilian operations (such as petrochemicals) receive more lenient terms. The Brazilian automobile industry, considered essential to economic development, is highly protected. The government protects the Brazilian operations of foreign auto manufacturers by prohibiting imports; as part of the bargain, however, the auto manufacturers cannot collect royalty payments for specialized technical services or technology-transfer contracts. An exception to this rule, as outlined in Normative Act 30 (1978), may be made for specialized technology relating to engines and advanced components not available in Brazil. Royalty payments are not tax deductible for subsidiaries.

Additionally, the INPI may place restrictions on Brazilian firms receiving technology, such as specific expenditures for R&D, and may make the receipt of technology conditional upon implementation of these expenditures.

The INPI does not allow payments for the transfer of technology (for nonpatented items) to be calculated exclusively as a percentage of sales. It prefers simple lump-sum payments, or lump sums plus a percentage of sales; lump sums based on sales performance; and percentages of sales subject to a specific ceiling.

The duration of technology-transfer agreements has traditionally been limited to five years, though recently this has been extended. In agreements for specialized technical services, there are no specific regulations regarding time limits. Agreements over five years are difficult to obtain, although extensions may be allowed when additional time is needed to complete the technology-transfer project.

Once the term of the technology-transfer contract has expired, the Brazilian firm is free to use the technology as it pleases. It may sell the technology at home or abroad, increasing competition with the original licensor. For this reason, *technology licensed to a Brazilian company may be considered as effectively being sold rather than licensed to the national firm.*

The result has been a tendency for foreign firms to license less-than-leading-edge technology in Brazil. Ironically, federal legislation that was intended to foster the country's industrial and economic development by accelerating technology transfers has had precisely the opposite effect by discouraging transfer of the most advanced technology.

While patent and trademark royalties may not be paid by subsidiaries, technical-assistance fees may be remitted up to the 5% limit. Detailed negotiations are required with both the Central Bank and the INPI, however, and the results are often less than satisfactory. In practice, the actual percentage allowed depends on the types of production and activities. Remittances of up to 5% are generally only allowed in the case of certain heavy industries, for projects requiring large capital investments and sophisticated ongoing technological input—the petrochemical industry is a good example. Where the assistance provided is considered less essential in furthering national interests, little or no fees can be paid to the parent. Fees in excess of the limits are treated as a transfer of profits.

Practical Matters

According to one industry expert, Brazilian law is "grossly inadequate" for the protection of technology and the policy-makers are among the most uncompromising of any Latin American country. Still in existence is an archaic mindset that Brazil should not pay royalties on technology relating (but not limited) to consumer and durable goods.

But things are loosening up somewhat. When the SEI barred the import of the computer operating system MS-DOS because of the existence of a national equivalent, the decision was quickly overturned. Most foreign software is now being freely imported and receives greater protection. Since 1987, the approval of licensing and technology-transfer agreements has been eased, with more flexibility in the acceptance of terms and a marked increase in the actual processing of contracts. Previously, rulings were rendered in closed sessions; now they are held in an "open courtroom" style. While corporate representatives do not directly influence proceedings, they can at least amend their agreements more easily to conform to regulations. As a result, there has been a dramatic increase in the approval rate for patent and trademark licenses and technology-transfer agreements, from 70% in 1985 to 96% in 1989.

The standard five-year "rule" limiting technology-transfer agreements is not actually stated in the Normative Acts, but rather is an interpretation of the law by the INPI. This was upheld in a 1985 court ruling, which determined that the INPI had the right to alter the duration of technology-transfer contracts in a case against Resana SA Industrias Quimicas. There are recent indications, however, that the INPI is allowing more

Requirements of Licensing and Technology-Transfer Agreements

All licensing and technology-transfer agreements—of domestic or foreign origin—must be registered with and approved by the INPI. The agency requires the following information:

- technical data and specifications (in the case of patent licenses, the application must include information about processes, designs, formulas, models and any other technical data critical to the use of the patent);
- the value of the technology being transferred (essential for determining the depreciation or amortization rates);
- plans for employee training at the licensed firm;
- R&D plans;
- how long the transfer process will take; and
- agreements regarding the ownership of the techniques and new technologies developed out of the technology being transferred.

After INPI approval, licensing and technology-transfer agreements are published—not the actual contracts, but a summary of the contracts, which are then available for public inspection. Included is a title or brief description, the parties involved, time limits and payment amounts.

Licensing Experience in Brazil

Because of the extensive outlays on R&D required for product development (among other factors), multinational companies tend to dominate the agricultural chemical market worldwide. The average agricultural firm spends about $70 million a year on R&D, with some spending more than $200 million. With a minimum R&D commitment of around $40 million, Brazilian companies are basically "me too" firms. New products often take eight to 10 years to reach the market, with a best-case scenario of around six years. This is due to extensive laboratory and field testing, data generation and information collection, publication of applications, and so on. Because of these extremely high development costs, the dominant firms must look to global markets for the distribution of their products.

Despite any desire to feed the local population, many products that have been proven and are in current use in other countries are held up in the pipeline or not allowed into Brazil. With over 30 companies importing, producing and distributing pesticides in Brazil, those importing agricultural chemicals are subject to duties of 30% if the product is not produced nationally. If it is produced nationally, then duties are listed at 60%. In practice, however, import licenses have been virtually unobtainable under these conditions.

Brazilian economic regulations intended to foster national industrial development and encourage local technology efforts have had, as in the case in most industries, a major impact on the agricultural chemical industry in Brazil. The result has been to foster the development of inefficient (lacking economies of scale), high-cost producers of off-patent products, with Brazilian firms unable to compete effectively in the global marketplace. These high costs are of course passed on to the farmer. Likewise, farm equipment is very expensive in Brazil as a result of protective measures. The impact on Brazilian agriculture—by far the nation's largest employer—is high costs and lower crop productivity.

Piracy problems

"Company A" is the Brazilian subsidiary of a large, highly diversified MNC. Its agricultural chemicals division is a major competitor in the Brazilian pesticides market and currently employs all the following strategies: extensive R&D for new product development; in-house production; importation; technology transfer; and licensing arrangements.

Due to the technical nature of the business, the firm has registered numerous patents in Brazil for chemical processes (not products), formulas and specialized equipment.

In the case of insecticide patents, applications must be made to the INPI, and registrations for the use of these products must be made with the Ministry of Agriculture, the Ministry of Health, and the Environment Secretary (a post created last year). When Company A was involved in developing an insecticide, it was careful to abide by the regulations in order to gain patent protection. Its experience is relevant for many MNCs operating in Brazil.

The first firm to register a new pesticide is required to develop and publish a comprehensive toxicology, use and environmental-effects report. The publication, available for public inspection, must contain extensive proprietary data. The cost of developing this information averages $5-10 million for a single product, and has cost Company A as much as $40 million in the past.

Brazilian firms, however, can and do take advantage of this very costly published technical information, without sharing in any of the expenses. One local firm "developed" a product using different raw materials and a different synthesis process, but ended up with an impure version having the same basic active ingredient as an insecticide registered by Company A. It was able to register the pirated product by citing the toxicology, use and environmental-data report already developed and published by Company A. Despite the unknown level of impurities the product contained, the regulatory agencies read the report and believed it to be as safe as the similar product registered by Company A.

Trade-secret theft

Licensing is used by Company A when demand exceeds capacity constraints. While not a major part of the business, it is an effective means of capitalizing on otherwise foregone revenue. Additionally, the company licenses technology from its foreign parent and makes no royalty payments, because it is forbidden by law. Fortunately, it has had no problems with licensing contracts being delayed by the INPI or other agencies due at least in part to its familiarity with procedures, requirements and format.

(Continued)

Company trademarks are used on all items produced in-house. In some instances, an approved product is also sold with a company trademark to another MNC who markets the product. In these cases there are no concerns with contract registration, since the product was already approved and no royalties are paid for the use of the trademark. An insecticide using the same production process can also be directly marketed by another MNC under the original trademark and directly by the original manufacturer under a different trademark.

Conditional approval has been received for the production and use of some of the firm's insecticides, which can only be applied using specialized machinery manufactured by Company A. The process involves the application of insecticide to seed, and the use of the company's equipment is meant to increase safety levels in the use of toxic compounds. In this case a complete package including the provision of specialized technical services, specialized equipment, and the insecticide itself is offered to the customer.

Some modification of the specialized equipment was necessary for its use in Brazil, however, so the local subsidiary imported technology from the parent that was used in a version produced elsewhere. Changes were made to further increase safety levels, generalize some applications and develop a portable version. Once the designs were completed, the equipment was put into production. While there was a patent involved, most of the project was protected as trade secrets—in the form of technological know-how.

One of the men involved in developing the equipment left the company and established his own machine-making business. As it turned out, a national competitor was interested in marketing a similar toxic insecticide that, in order to be approved, also had to be provided in conjunction with specialized equipment. Despite the fact that he had signed a contract with Company A that prevented him from taking propriety information with him, the ex-employee went into business with the competitor to produce the required machinery.

A court battle ensued, and an injunction was granted. Company A had two rulings in its favor, but in a third, binding judgement the case was decided in favor of the national firm.

Despite these setbacks, the company continues to expand operations in Brazil.

exceptions to the standard rules. One example is the approval of "rolling five-year periods" where five years of protection are allowed from the time the technology is disclosed, effectively pushing the length of the agreement to nearly 10 years. Recently the INPI approved a 15-year technology-transfer contract involving a major US chemical company.

While President Collor has not announced all the details of his plans to modernize Brazilian industry, he has made some changes that affect the accountabilities of the various regulatory agencies. The INPI, formerly controlled by the Ministry of Industry and Commerce, is now part of the Ministry of Justice. (However, in the charter for the Ministry of Justice, there is no mention of the regulation of the transfer of technology.) Additionally, there is a newly created Department of Industry and Commerce reporting to the Ministry of Economics, and the power to regulate the transfer of technology may shift from the INPI to the new department, where contract terms may be interpreted more liberally. Some industry experts speculate that this indicates a dawning realization that low royalty remissions combined with limited terms of protection have resulted in the acquisition of second-rate technology in Brazil.

Tax Consequences

Licensing of technology is not generally used by foreign firms as a strategy for the generation of tax benefits, but the proper configuration of technology-transfer agreements can reduce tax liabilities. There are some implications under the US Tax Reform Act of 1986, for example, that should be considered when structuring technology-transfer agreements.

If a US firm is in the position of having excess foreign tax credits (FTCs), the firm should attempt to classify royalties as "foreign-sourced" so that tax credits can be applied. Selling technology that is deemed to be not "contingent on the usefulness of the intangible to the buyer" or transferring technology as a contribution to capital will generate revenue that is usually classified as domestically sourced.

If the US firm is in a position of needing capital gains to offset capital losses, it might consider the sale or transfer of technology as a contribution to capital, as both will normally generate capital gains, while, for tax purposes, licensing usually generates ordinary income.

For firms analyzing various options for penetrating the Brazilian market, it is important to consider the regulations that apply to Brazilian branches or subsidiaries (50% or more owned, directly or indirectly, by a single group or investor). Generally, the distribution of profits or dividends abroad are subject to a 25% withholding tax. Exceptions are made when the home country has an approved tax treaty with Brazil where the withholding tax can be reduced for profit remittances, interest payments, capital gains and royalties (see below). Additionally, profits transfers of over 12% of registered foreign capital (on a three-year average) are subject to supplemental income taxes of 40-60%.

Payments for technical assistance are not deductible by the subsidiary, nor are payments of patent or trademark royalties allowed. Any remittances for these purposes would be treated as profit transfers, normally taxed at 25% and subject to supplemental taxes.

For Brazilian firms, the deductibility of royalties and fees is determined by the Ministry of Finance. The deductibility limits set forth on the payment of royalties, while established for tax purposes, have long been used as guidelines by the INPI in establishing technology payment limits—the 5%, five-year limit (Law 4131) is the best example of this. The INPI, however, has been authorizing more lenient terms on such payments—which may exceed tax-deductibility limits. While it is possible to petition and receive increased deductibility limits, many experts feel that the tax laws should simply be updated to reflect new realities.

Tax Rates on Royalty Remittances

Generally, payments remitted abroad are taxed at 25% by the Brazilian government, except for those countries having tax treaties with Brazil. Tax-treaty countries are assessed at the rates shown at the following rates.

- Trademarks—25%: Argentina, Austria, Belgium, Denmark, Finland, Italy, Japan, Luxembourg, Norway, Sweden and West Germany.
- Copyrights for scientific, literary, artistic works—10%: Austria, Belgium, Finland, France, Portugal and Spain.
- Copyrights for films, and recordings for TV and radio—25%: Norway, Luxembourg and Japan. Japan pays 12.5% on all other royalty remittances.

Other royalties by countries listed above are taxed at 15%.

Tax Incentives

A number of financial/tax incentives are given to Brazilian firms that meet certain criteria in the area of informatics, including R&D activities;

human-resource development and technical training; production of informatics goods and services; exports of computer hardware, software and services; and software development. The informatics law also permits deductions of double the expense of obtaining software if the firm is the first user of the software and the software is determined to be of national interest.

While the tax benefits of national firms may not have a direct impact on foreign firms, they may increase the bargaining power of foreign firms if specific contracts and arrangements aid in the acquisition of such benefits. Tax and financial incentives are offered for firms establishing operations in geographic regions the government considers economically disadvantaged, and for firms offering employee incentives such as professional training and food programs. In the duty-free zone of Manaus, import and export incentives are offered. Incentives under the Industrial Development Council (CDI) include accelerated depreciation, reductions on equipment-import taxes, and preferred loans.

In some cases involving Brazilian exports, taxes paid by foreign firms on receipts from national firms may be reduced via export incentives.

3
Mexico

Mexican President Carlos Salinas de Gortari is breathing new life into licensing as an attractive business strategy for MNCs in Mexico. A new intellectual property law—enacted in June 1991—represents one of the most important changes to Mexico's legal system since Salinas took office in December 1988. The Salinas administration's attitudes and philosophy toward technology transfers represent a significant departure from the harsh controls and heavy government intervention that have discouraged licensing since 1972. As a pragmatist, Salinas recognizes that private investment and technology, whether foreign or domestic, are critical forces in the plan to propel Mexico into the twenty-first century.

Like other reform measures introduced by the Salinas government, the revised IP law should greatly improve the operating environment for foreign companies. Because it is in the form of a law rather than an administrative decree, the new code improves upon earlier reform measures—such as the 1990 *reglamento* liberalizing technology transfers. Practically speaking, however, executives and legal experts say that only time and experience will determine the actual degree of freedom and facility firms will enjoy under the new regulations.

Why Mexico?

The pros and cons of licensing in Mexico depend considerably on the specific characteristics of the individual company—the firm's objectives, needs, resources, industry, products and type of technology, for example—as well as the investment commitment management wants to make and the strategic importance of the Mexican market vis-à-vis the markets of other countries. In addition to these internal factors, executives point to several environmental issues that firms may want to factor in to their licensing decisions. MNCs list the following benefits and pitfalls of licensing vis-à-vis other options, such as exporting or direct investment.

The benefits are significant...

Taps strong market growth potential. With a population of 80 million and growing, Mexico is a large and potentially lucrative market for many companies, particularly those in the consumer-goods area. After six years of zero or little expansion because of the debt crisis, the Mexican economy is now enjoying stronger growth.

Foreign MNCs may also gain an edge from the dramatic opening of the Mexican economy over the last few years. After years in which Mexican consumers had no choice but to buy overpriced, poor-quality domestic products, their appetite for foreign products is strong. Mexico represents a lucrative virgin market for many internationally recognized brands and products.

Keeps up-front investment costs low. For firms with limited resources, licensing provides a foothold in the Mexican market at lower costs than establishing a subsidiary or joint venture. With licensing, firms can gauge the market and test for product possibilities with minimal up-front cash outlays.

Maintains close tabs on the market. Some executives say they can better monitor the market and third-party counterfeiters with a licensee than a distributor because a licensor typically has little influence or say over what a distributor does. In fact, they say that the substantial risk that a third party will pirate brands and products in Mexico is a good reason to secure the more direct involvement of licensing. This is particularly true for MNCs in industries such as clothing, luxury items, leather products and sporting goods, which have the highest incidence of piracy.

Benefits from an insider's position. With a licensee, a company has an opportunity to gain first-hand knowledge of the local distribution channels, regulatory framework, bureaucracy, labor relations and customs. Licensing is often used as a "toe-in-the-water" approach, serving as a first step toward either a closer relationship with the licensee (via a joint venture) or a go-it-alone strategy (by establishing a subsidiary).

Capitalizes on the deregulatory spirit. Several bold initiatives, including an overhaul of intellectual property and foreign-investment regulations, signal the Salinas administration's commitment to provide a fertile, noninterventionist environment for business in Mexico. By eliminating many of the rigid restrictions on what licensing partners may do, the new regulations make it considerably more attractive for multinational firms to rely on licensing to build market share in

Mexico. Furthermore, the government's program of privatization and deregulation is opening up new business opportunities in key sectors—such as telecommunications, petrochemicals, energy and transport—for MNCs interested in licensing their technology.

Exploits franchise opportunities. The new regulations pave the way for franchise operations in Mexico. The government's attitude toward franchises is a sharp turn away from the previous view of them as a corrupting influence on Mexican culture and society. Officials now openly recognize the potential benefits of the arrangement, such as new investment, creation of new jobs and skills and the development of local suppliers. Many analysts expect strong growth in the franchise business, given the Mexican market and its appetite for foreign brands, products and services.

...But hazards remain

Be aware that enforcement of intellectual-property laws has been insufficient. In the past, major shortcomings in intellectual-property protection have been a serious deterrent to licensing in Mexico. Inadequate resources to enforce the laws have made counterfeiting a problem. Even when a company does uncover an unlawful infringement of its patents or trademarks, Mexico has few legal instruments, such as injunctions, to bar the illicitly sold or transferred intellectual property in the marketplace.

Watch out for your trade secrets. Protection of trade secrets—the valuable know-how and proprietary technical information and experience that often make up over 50% of a technology transfer—is another concern, and it applies whether firms license to unrelated third parties or to affiliates. The new IP code has modified the law to limit the very broad definition of trade secrets as originally provided in the draft version.

Consider Mexico's proximity to the US. One US textile firm says Mexico's proximity to the US makes licensing troublesome. Suppose the licensing relationship sours, for instance, and the contract ends. The licensee may have no hesitation about continuing to use the technology and export the products to the large US market, where they compete head on with the output of the former licensor. In fact, when the textile firm was downsizing its Mexican subsidiary several years ago, it considered switching to a licensing arrangement. Management abandoned the idea, however, because the temptations for a Mexican licensee to encroach on the US MNC's home market posed a genuine risk.

Take advantage of import liberalization and deregulation. As a result of the opening up of Mexico's economy over the last few years, tariff rates have fallen from over 100% to a current average of 9.5%. The government also deregulated the trucking industry in mid-1989, thus lowering transportation costs for companies generally.

Both factors may make it more efficient—in terms of time, money and resources—for firms to rely on an export strategy. One company suggests establishing a marketing affiliate in Mexico with a few key executives to manage and oversee a warehouse for incoming exports rather than using an unrelated distributor or licensee. That way, the business is in immediate touch with what happens in the market and can confront problems directly. At the same time, its overhead costs and investment are minimal. If economic conditions or policies worsen, management can easily shrink the operation and wait for better times to expand.

Factor inflation and price controls into licensing decisions. While not an exclusive concern of MNCs interested in licensing, inflation cannot be ignored. Wage and price pacts among business, government and labor to control prices have put pressure on profits of multinationals in Mexico. Any company interested in licensing in the country should consider the possible impact of price controls on profitability.

Mesh with global strategy. MNCs with a global strategy under which products may be sourced from one location—such as Mexico—for worldwide or regional distribution say they must operate through a subsidiary or a joint venture. The companies say that having only licensees does not give them the necessary infrastructure and resources to oversee suppliers and manage operations for continuous production of top-quality goods in a demanding global market. Licensing for these companies is viewed as a second-tier strategy. For instance, management may achieve some cost savings by having a Mexican subsidiary sublicense other firms for components.

The Regulatory Framework

The Law for the Promotion and Protection of Industrial Property of 1991 extends patent protection (from 14 to 20 years), broadens patent definition to cover numerous categories which previously had little or no protection, and limits compulsory licenses.

Contracts must be approved and registered with the National Registry for Technology Transfers, which is an arm of Secofi. Otherwise, the agreements have no legal validity. Firms may also face stiff fines and be denied tax deductions for royalties. Trademarks, commercial and trade names, and patents must be registered with the patent and trademark office at Secofi.

Transfers of Technology

In January 1990, Mexico published new technology-transfer regulations applying to the licensing law enacted in 1982. These rules, which took effect immediately, should radically improve the licensing landscape in Mexico, at least on the legislative front.

On the positive side, the new regulations create a better environment for the transfer of technology in Mexico.

Firms are exempt from the onerous restrictions of the original law. Perhaps the most important provision of the technology-transfer regulation is Art. 53. Companies that can provide one of the following nine benefits to Mexico may be exempt from the restrictions and prohibitions on licensing outlined in the 1982 law and its implementing regulations: (1) create permanent jobs, (2) improve the technical skills of employees, (3) provide access to new export markets, (4) manufacture new products in Mexico, particularly goods that replace imports, (5) improve the balance of payments, (6) lower unit production costs, (7) develop local suppliers, (8) employ nonpolluting technologies, or (9) establish or expand local R&D activities.

As long as a licensing agreement results in one of the above nine benefits, registration is virtually automatic. This eliminates a cumbersome procedure in which firms had to undergo an arduous approval process for the contract before it could be registered. The only requirement is that the licensee must provide proof of one of these nine benefits within three years.

According to one Mexico investment expert, "If a company is unable to provide one of the nine benefits, then the firm probably should not be in business." This provision, he notes, creates an exception to the 1982 law that is about as large as the 1982 law itself. With Art. 53, many of the reasons for denying registration under the 1982 law no longer apply. Under the old rules, registration could be refused for a variety of reasons—for instance, if the agreement contained clauses that required the purchase of raw materials from the licensor, granted management power to the licensor, included grant-back privileges, set production or export limits, or outlined restrictions on a licensee's R&D activities. Technology partners now have a much freer rein to determine the design, scope, structure and length of the contract.

Confidentiality provisions are strengthened. The regulations now permit licensors to extend the confidentiality period beyond a contract's normal expiration date, thus enabling firms to better protect their technology. In the past, confidentiality was restricted to the maximum 10-year period allowed for contracts. There is, however, at least one important caveat: The licensor must make some improvement to the technology in order to extend confidentiality.

Suppose a US licensor, for instance, extends its manufacturing technology for widgets to a Mexican firm under a 10-year licensing agreement. In the seventh year, the US licensor enhances its widget technology. If the licensor provides this new production know-how to the Mexican licensee, the partners can agree to extend the confidentiality period for another 10 years. Consequently, even though the contract ceases in three years, the licensee must keep the technology confidential for seven years beyond the expiration date.

Royalty payments are liberalized. Licensors are no longer confined to a restrictive 1-6% range. Instead, firms have free rein to determine and set royalties.

Registration for computer programs is easier. It is no longer necessary to register the mere sale of software programs to end-users.

The discretionary powers of the authorities is minimized. Under the old rules, the government frequently acted as an "uninvited third party," imposing rigid and often unrelated conditions on the technology partners. For example, the government might approve a licensing agreement only if the firms also engaged in an R&D program. Mexican businessmen have long resented having the government "baby-sit" them, while foreign executives often rejected licensing deals because of unprofitable and burdensome conditions.

The new regulation prevents the authorities from using discretionary powers to intervene and mandate additional conditions for registration. In the spirit of deregulation, the new code specifies the role and functions for the National Registry as a "promoter" rather than a "regulator" of technology.

Simple franchise guidelines are established. The new regulation for the first time legally defines and outlines procedures for setting up franchises. Similar to licensing contracts, franchises may also be exempt from the restrictions of the 1982 law if the franchisee proves, within the first three years, that the operation leads to one of the nine benefits. Procedures under the new regulations simply require the franchisor to register a "model" agreement that can then be used for all franchisees and subfranchisees: Every six months, the franchisor simply files the newly signed agreements. It is not necessary to register each one separately. Previous conditions, such as requiring franchise operations to generate export earnings, have also been lifted.

But bear in mind, the technology is still transferred... permanently. The new regulations continue to view licensing as a sale rather than a rental of technology. Consequently, when the contract expires, the licensee is freely permitted to use the technology to compete head-on with the licensor or sell the know-how to third parties.

The New Intellectual Property Law

Chief among the new provisions (see the box on p. 41) of the 1991 Promotion and Protection of Industrial Property Law are the extension of the patent term and the widening of the scope of product-patent coverage. The legislation also allows product patents in areas such as chemicals, pharmaceuticals, biotechnology, metal alloys, agrochemicals and food processing.

In addition, the new law strengthens trade-secret protection and restricts compulsory licensing. Registration procedures are also being streamlined to expedite the application process.

Tax and Financial Considerations

Mexico has no exchange controls on royalty remittances. Some firms use a forward contract, known as a *cobertura cambiaria,* to cover exchange rate risks. The maximum term for a *cobertura cambiaria,* which can entail a rather high premium, is 90 days.

Over the past few years, Mexico has implemented several tax reforms that place the country on a competitive footing with many other nations in terms of the tax treatment of royalty payments. For instance, the withholding tax on dividends has fallen from a high of 55% to zero for income that previously had been taxed at the corporate level. The most recent tax changes, which went into effect in January 1991, altered the withholding rate on royalty payments. Under the new structure, the rate on income from trademarks (with or without technical assistance) is 15%; from patents, 35% (but 15% with technical assistance); from copyrights, 15% plus a 15% VAT, which is credited against any income tax paid by the company.

Practical Matters

MNCs interested in licensing technology in Mexico may want to consider some of the following pointers when seeking to identify a partner, negotiate a deal, or manage the relationship. Some tactics may also help existing licensing partners take better advantage of the new technology-transfer regulation.

Consider renegotiating old contracts. One prominent partner in a Mexico City law firm suggests that MNCs may want to renegotiate agreements to take advantage of provisions such as the liberalization of royalties under the new law. In fact, several firms with

Intellectual Property in Mexico

Application fees. The registration of all intellectual property—patents, trademarks, inventor's certificates, and industrial designs and models—carries application fees. However, the charges, particularly in dollar terms, are nominal.

Patents. Patents of invention or improvement now last 20 years from the date of issuance, instead of 14. Terms are now counted from the time an application is submitted, however. Patents may expire if the inventor does not commercialize the patent within two years of its issue. Obtaining a patent usually takes about two years.

Product-patent protection under the new law is available for chemical products, pharmaceuticals, animal foods and agrochemicals, which until now could apply only for process patents. Product protection for these items under the old legislation was not scheduled until 1997. Furthermore, vegetable varieties, micro-organisms, metal alloys and food and beverages for human consumption, which were not scheduled to be covered as of 1997, will now also enjoy full patent protection. In addition, importation of patented products or of products developed by a patented process now constitute exploitation of a patent.

The government can institute compulsory licensing in the case of a national emergency or for reasons of national security, aside from failure to exploit a patent. Under these conditions, the Secretariat of Commerce must decide that without compulsory licensing, production or distribution of basic goods will be impeded, harmed or made more costly. Under the previous law, failure to fully exploit domestic and export markets could result in the application of compulsory licenses.

Trademarks. Trademarks, service marks, commercial names and commercial phrases are protected for 10-year renewable periods, up from the previous five-year renewable period. The new law also provides that a simple sworn statement or affidavit attesting to uninterrupted use is needed for renewal, instead of the former requirement that periodic evidence be submitted. A trademark will be canceled and will not be eligible for renewals if it is not commercially exploited within the first three years of its issue. The application process for trademarks usually takes four to six months.

(Continued)

Mexico is a signatory to the Berne Convention, the Universal Copyright Convention and the Inter-American Convention on Copyright and Literary Property.

Copyright. Changes in the Law of Authors' Rights in 1991 extended copyright protection—previously limited to composers, writers and performers—to producers of sound recordings. The law also grants protection for computer programs, which were previously covered only by an administrative ruling. (The computer industry, however, has said that the new protection appears to be insufficient.)

Inventors' certificates. With the widened scope of protection, inventor's certificates—designed to provide some legal protection for unpatentable products such as pharmaceuticals and metal alloys—were eliminated in 1991.

Industrial designs and models. The new legislation grants industrial designs 15 years of protection, up from seven years previously. Utility models—tools, instruments and other objects that have undergone minor improvements—are now protected for 10 years. They were not previously recognized under the law.

licensing agreements between parent and subsidiary said they planned to revamp contracts in order to ring them in line with their worldwide licensing policies.

Strengthen licensing ties by securing an equity link. Some firms maintain that taking an equity stake in a prospective licensing partner can solidify the relationship and enhance the chances for success. It also can open up business opportunities in other areas in which the partners may have complementary strengths. Furthermore, the equity link can act as a strong deterrent against any unfair infringement or use of the technology.

Emphasize the win-win elements. Executives say the best way to protect a firm's technology is to make the deal equally worthwhile to the licensee. Although this axiom applies in all countries, it is especially applicable in Mexico, where the potential to exploit weak intellectual-property laws is acute. If licensees feel cheated, they may not hesitate to extract more from the technology—through unauthorized use—than agreed. Also, structure the agreements—i.e. the confidentiality provisions—so as to show why it is in the best interest of the licensee to safeguard the technology. Otherwise, improvements will not be forthcoming, and the product and licensee may lose a valuable competitive edge.

Avoid merely convenient alliances. Once a licensing agreement is signed, it is difficult to enforce or escape. Companies with grievances—nonpayment of royalties, poor quality, etc.—are limited to civil court procedures, which often can be time-consuming, expensive and frustrating. Consequently, firms emphasize the need to take the time and energy to investigate a potential partner thoroughly. For instance, screen potential licensing partners for compatibility, commitment to the venture, importance of the technology or licensing deal to their business, resources (financial, managerial, technical, sales and marketing, etc.), reputation among other MNCs, previous licensing experiences, links with the government and similarities in management style. In any event, try to foresee the divorce at the time of the marriage by making the agreement as clear and self-executing as possible.

Develop internal resources to monitor and confront any piracy. Insufficient government resources and labor power to enforce the laws place greater responsibility on corporate management. Several firms develop their own teams to police any potential infringement or abuse. They train personnel in how to scout for possible problems and detect warning signals. Signs of piracy can often show up in obscure places, so the more eyes and ears a company has, the better. One food company, which has had problems with competitors who try to copy the design and packaging of the products in order to mislead the consumer, teaches all sales personnel how to identify and deal with various forms of piracy.

Once a firm does uncover a problem, executives suggest contacting the violator directly to resolve the matter through discussions and negotiations. Most firms first try to avoid court procedures because they can be expensive and time-consuming. The courts may also be biased in favor of the local firm. Furthermore, the public image of an MNC can be damaged by a legal battle.

Adopt a hands-on approach. Some firms suggest managing a technology partnership more as a franchise than as a license. In other words, the licensor can take a more hands-on approach to the operations and activity of the licensee. Problems in licensing deals, says one executive, often crop up because the licensor thinks it can transfer the technology and then sit back and wait until the profits start to roll in. Trying to get something for nothing, he adds, usually results in a very short-term benefit; however, the lack of involvement may do irreparable long-term damage to the brand or trademark. Instead, his company takes a very communicative, open approach with licensees by asking for three-year business plans, for instance, or actively participating in the formulation and implementation of marketing strategies. In Mexico, however, close involvement may entail a delicate balancing act. Excessive intervention in a licensee's business may run afoul of the technology law and *reglamentos,* as well as foreign investment legislation.

Spell out what technical assistance entails. In addition to the designs and blueprints conveyed in a formal technology transfer, a substantial amount of technology is transmitted through an exchange of technical information, know-how and direct contact between technical experts. Executives warn, however, that firms need to spell out clearly the payment terms and precise conditions for providing information, training and guidance. Otherwise, a few phone calls here and there can add up to an expensive amount of engineers' time and erode any profitability from the deal.

4
Venezuela

The developed countries have constantly called on the less developed nations to provide stronger and more efficient protection of patents, trademark and copyrights. This discussion has certainly been heard in Venezuela. In the last 10 years there have been no fewer than four proposed bills to reform the current Industrial Property Law (IPL), which dates to 1955. The common theme of all these projects has been the reformulation of Venezuelan law on the basis of international industrial-property norms.

Government officials and private-sector groups have urged legislators to improve patent and trademark rights and protection to eliminate pirating. However, the proposed bills have run up against a psychological barrier: Most Latin American governments, including Venezuela's, are not very interested in adopting laws similar to those in the US. While local businessmen by no means favor pirating, they are also not much in favor of reforming trademarks, patents, copyrights and industrial-property laws primarily for the benefit of foreign firms. Consequently, discussions on proposed intellectual-property bills always reach a high pitch. Proposed reforms to the IPR law await congressional approval.

A new economic environment—with radical modifications in the nation's trade, tariff and development policies—has started to emerge in Venezuela. More and more officials have begun to realize that the country cannot continue to repel foreigners with weak intellectual-property laws, which also restrict the productive capacity of local manufacturers by failing to protect the latter's intellectual property as well. In fact, one of the most pressing needs is to reform the IPL code with respect to expropriation: Art. 16 expressly states that the government, by decree, may expropriate an invention or discovery when the state deems it of public or social usefulness.

Moreover, when the Industrial Property Law was passed in 1955, its authors did not recognize the direct connection between strong intellectual-property laws and economic development. Consequently, little was done to assure adequate protection for ideas. Inadequately copied from the laws of other nations—including the US—Venezuela's IP code has been losing validity ever since its creation and has increasingly represented a major obstacle to economic growth. Yet it is only recently that local lawmakers have begun to realize the nation's urgent need to adequately protect intellectual property as a means of spurring economic development.

During the oil boom of the 1970s the economy was characterized by a high volume of imports and a single lucrative export—petroleum. High oil prices brought in enough currency to pay for the import of everything the nation needed, including technology, and lawmakers gave little thought to IPL reform.

As the boom turned to bust in the 1980s, the interest of international companies waned in proportion to the nation's mounting economic problems and legal insecurity. Among the main difficulties were $33 billion in public- and private-sector foreign debt, currency devaluation, the scandal in preferential-rate dollars and the government's refusal to recognize B70 billion in letters of credit drawn by the private sector in late 1988 and early 1989 at the preferential rate of B14.5:$1.

The nation's economic problems, however, have yielded one positive by-product: The realization (albeit belated) by government officials and lawmakers that strong industrial-property laws have a desirable effect on foreign investment in a nation and on a nation's international economic relations. Prominent government officials are also urging Venezuela to study the feasibility of joining organizations such as OPIC (the Overseas Private Investment Corp) and MIGA (the Multilateral Investment Guarantee Agency), and to sign international agreements, such as the New York Agreement of 1958 on international trade arbitration and the Washington Agreement of 1965 on foreign investment arbitration, in order to boost the nation's international image and attract foreign investors.

Foreign-Investment Regulations

Concrete steps the government has recently taken to attract foreign capital have rekindled international interest in local business opportunities. The government actions include passage of Decree Law 727 (see the box on p. 51), which revamped the foreign investment code; negotiations to enter GATT; and a restructuring of the public-sector foreign debt. The government has assigned top priority to the promotion of investments and technology in tourism, agriculture, agro-industry and manufacturing. Furthermore, Venezuela has begun vigorously to promote its policy of extending tax incentives to foreign companies willing to set up shop locally and invest in designated priority areas. The nation has also undertaken to actively seek joint-venture partners abroad for local projects on the downstream side of the petroleum, petrochemical and aluminum sectors. Government officials woo foreign investors by touting the nation's direct air and sea access to key markets in the US, Canada and Western Europe and its location as an excellent staging ground for enterprises with plans to penetrate the small and medium-sized markets in Latin American and the Caribbean. Officials also point to the recently approved regulations that allow *maquiladoras* (cross-border assembly plants based on the Mexican model) to set up shop in Venezuela: With prior authorization, those firms are now allowed to import goods and raw materials duty free, manufacture products from them and then reexport the output to other markets.

Of course, whether a foreign firm establishes an operational base in Venezuela through a subsidiary or chooses instead to enter into distribution or licensing contracts depends on the plans and size of the company in question. Several noted local investment specialists agree that licensing has usually been the preferred method for small and medium-sized firms for penetrating the Venezuelan market, while larger firms have preferred to establish joint-venture subsidiaries. However, the specialists add that passage of Decree Law 727 has made direct distribution and the creation of a wholly owned subsidiary equally attractive alternatives for investments of any size.

Most experts believe that licensing still offers major advantages in Venezuela, since it avoids the added problems of opening a subsidiary in Latin America—labor difficulties; increased fixed costs; and the significant inconvenience of doing without the services of a valuable executive (the local licensee) who knows the market, the language and the ever-changing economic situation. Smaller firms, especially, would rather not give up that kind of local expertise. Licensing technology to a local business, which then manufactures the product in Venezuela—and may distribute it as well—often makes more sense.

Unfortunately, Venezuela's current industrial-property laws afford inadequate protection for intellectual property, and firms are not inclined to export their valuable intellectual property, much less license it, to nations with inadequate protection. Indeed, most of the licensing agreements reached in Venezuela—as high as 95% of the cases, according to one legal consultant—are for older, sometimes even outdated, technology. Because of this inadequate protection, state-of-the-art technology is rarely licensed to Venezuelan firms. The consultant adds that the patents licensed to companies in Venezuela contain little innovative know-how relative to other technologies already on the market. Foreign firms that do license technology in Venezuela, he adds, are usually seeking to carve out a market niche for themselves.

Decree Law 727 now makes direct distribution possible. In effect, the internal commerce of goods has now been opened to foreign equity investment of up to 100% of total corporate capital. Direct distribution offers an attractive alternative to licensing in view of the progressive reductions in tariff rates. The first step in the process began in end-March 1990, when the top rates were lowered from 80% to 50% ad valorem (for finished goods). (Tariffs under the 1990 regime were scaled in 10% increments ranging from 0% to 50% and depend on the amount of value added to a particular product.) This liberalization will continue through 1993, when maximum import tariffs will be cut to 20%: The ceiling was lowered to 40% in March 1991; it was further lowered to 30% in March 1992, and will be dropped to 20% in March 1993.

Technology Imports

Venezuela imports technology from around the world and has no preference, or reservations, concerning its origin. There has been a tendency to import more technology from Europe, but not because European technology is preferred over that of the US (more than 50% of the foreign investment in Venezuela comes from the US). Much of this direct investment is in subsidiaries, which for a long time did not sign contracts with the parent companies because of regulations that prohibit the payment of more than 5% in royalties. Importation of the technology went on, but was associated with the direct investments. European investment in Venezuela, however, has been characterized by more of a tendency to enter into licensing and technology-assistance agreements.

Except in petroleum, petrochemical fields and plastics, Venezuela is a net importer of technology. SIEX (the Superintendencia de Inversiones Extranjeras, or Superintendency of Foreign Investment) is in charge of registering technology contracts entered into by Venezuelan firms, but no office keeps records of technology exports.

Currency unification—the free rate and the preferential rate were consolidated in March 1989—caused a marked decrease in contract totals, since technology-assistance contracts were no longer eligible for preferential-rate dollars. The US has been the main supplier of technology.

Legal Context

The Industrial Property Law of 1955 and the Copyright Law of 1963 are intended to protect most types of intellectual property in Venezuela. Nevertheless, protection is admittedly inadequate owing to the existence of outdated laws, a ponderous judicial process and sometimes indifferent law enforcement.

Proposed reforms to the IPR law include an extension of patent terms to 15 years (from the current 10); patent protection for chemicals and pharmaceuticals; and provisions to register and protect service marks, which are currently unprotected.

The Industrial Property Law

The Industrial Property Law (Ley de Propiedad Industrial) protects patents and trademarks as well as industrial models and sketches and *denominacion comercial*, or company names. Promulgated on Sept. 2, 1955, it is a combination of two earlier laws—one on patents (1927) and one on trademarks (1930)—that were approved with little reform.

The office responsible for patent and trademark registration is the industrial-property registrar's office (Oficina de Registro de la Propiedad Industrial), a division of the Development Ministry, with headquarters in Caracas. Patent and trademark applications and all pertinent matters that require dealing with the IPL office must be channeled through a duly registered industrial-property agent (who must also be either a lawyer or an economist).

The law has 50 classifications; the first 49 are specific, and the last one addresses all other products that do not fit into any of the other 49 classifications.

Exclusions from the Industrial Property Law

Under the IP code, pharmaceuticals, chemicals and food products may not be patented. The US is one of the biggest critics of Venezuela on this ground. Particularly because of the lack of patent protection for pharmaceutical products, the US trade representative has placed Venezuela on a watch list of countries with questionable intellectual-property laws. In fact, in 1990 the US refused to renew an agricultural-assistance agreement because Venezuela had not updated its Industrial Property Law.

The same problems cropped up during Venezuela's negotiations to join GATT. As a result, Venezuelan laboratories that import raw materials for the manufacture of pharmaceuticals must source from companies outside GATT (such as Hungary and China), where protection for chemical and pharmaceutical patents is equally lax.

Proposed reforms to the Industrial Property Law include explicit protection for these now-excluded products. They have engendered heated debate, however, because domestic laboratories have already started to claim that passage of the legislation would mean bankruptcy, with its attendant loss of jobs, for many local drug firms.

Patents

Patent protection is granted for 10 years and is nonrenewable. Proposed reforms include an extension to 15 years. Several stages are involved in the acquisition of a Venezuelan patent, including a preliminary analysis and testing by the industrial-property registrar's office. This process is not very thorough, according to experts, mainly because the registrar's office works with a limited budget. When an application is finally approved, the decision must be published in the monthly bulletin of the registrar's office. Any interested party may request a review of a patent or trademark to make sure there is no visual or phonic resemblance to something already registered or in the process of being registered.

A person who acquires a patent abroad receives preferential rights to the same patent in Venezuela for one year from the date of the foreign registration. After that, any individual may apply to register the patent in Venezuela. While the local applicant will not necessarily be awarded the patent in such cases—normal administrative channels must still be followed—the possibility exists that someone other than the legitimate owner can register an international patent in Venezuela.

Trademarks

Trademark protection is granted for 15 years and is renewable for successive 15-year periods. Applications for renewal must be made within the six-month period prior to the expiration of the trademark. A key clause in trademark legislation states that to maintain rights, a trademark owner must market a product at least once every two years after the registration date or forfeit all rights to the mark.

Know-how

Venezuela, like the other countries in the Andean Pact (the trade agreement among Bolivia, Chile, Colombia, Ecuador and Peru signed in 1969 and joined by Venezuela in 1973) does not recognize or protect know-how. Once transferred to licensees, the know-how becomes their property.

Licensing restrictions

The new foreign investment code elaborated in Decree Law 727 replaces most of the cumbersome rules and regulations found in its predecessor, Decree Law 1200. While most technology contracts and patent and trademark licenses are exempt from prior approval (but not from registration) by SIEX, there are legal limitations on licensing. All trademark, patent, technical know-how and technical-assistance contracts, for example, must provide for a training program for employees (except in the case of contracts for "occasional or specific" services; see the box on p. 52).

Decree Law 727

Decree Law 727, promulgated on Jan. 26, 1990, contains Venezuela's foreign-investment code and replaces Decree Law 1200. The new code offers foreign companies a wide opening into the nation's domestic market and does away with many cumbersome rules. The most positive aspects of Decree Law 727 are the elimination (by discarding approval requirements) of the arbitrary powers previously vested in government bureaucrats and the removal of most limits on reinvestment and repatriation of profits and dividends. The law also removes most restrictions on technology contracts. It now requires only that the contracts be registered, after the fact, with SIEX. As a result, the new code also lessens the time spent on lobbying to get paperwork approved.

Investment is still off limits in a few areas, including finance, insurance, petroleum, petrochemicals and mining; security services; radio, television and Spanish-language newspapers; and "basic industries" as defined by the president and his cabinet. While Decree Law 727 maintains reporting requirements similar to those that existed under Decree Law 1200, prior SIEX approval is no longer necessary for most foreign investment transactions. Except for the off-limits sectors mentioned above, a foreign investor may now, for example, organize a wholly owned subsidiary or branch in Venezuela and have the local entity enter into a trademark or technical-assistance agreement with the parent company as long as the royalty does not exceed 5% of net technological sales. Again, the only requirement is that the transactions be reported to SIEX within 60 days of their initiation. (Prior SIEX approval is required only if royalties from a wholly owned subsidiary to a parent firm exceed 5%.)

Trademark and patent licenses and technology transfers are divided into two categories under Decree Law 727: (1) pure technology-license agreements (including most normal technology-license and technical-assistance agreements and trademark and patent licenses); and (2) contracts for specific, occasional or one-time services.

For pure technology-license agreements, no approval is necessary, even if the Venezuelan company is classified as a foreign entity. These agreements must, however, be registered with SIEX within 60 days. Decree Law 727 places no limitation on the duration of licenses

(Continued)

and agreements, and confidentiality provisions may survive the termination of the agreement for a period equal to the original length of the agreement. All contracts except those for "specific and occasional services" (see below) must contain a clause outlining a training program that transfers the technology to employees of the licensee.

By definition, contracts for "specific and occasional" services are for the delivery of technology or technical assistance that was not foreseen by the recipient of the services. The payment is classified as a fee rather than a royalty. Such contracts must be registered with SIEX within 60 days of their signing, and notice of payment of the fee must be filed no later than 60 days after the payment is made. "Specific" services refer to those that are "nonrecurring," including professionally prepared studies and opinions, e.g. on feasibility, marketing or economic and geological matters. The service must be performed within a term of six months. The compensation is classified as a fee rather than a royalty.

Registration requirements and payment notices for "specific" services are the same as for specific and occasional contracts. Specific-service contracts may be extended automatically for an additional six-month period, but SIEX must first be notified.

Both Decision 24 of the Andean Pact and Venezuela's Decree Law 746 of 1975 (promulgated by current President Carlos Andres Perez during his first administration and still in force) list 10 restrictive clauses—or "tying in" provisions—that may *not* be included in licensing contracts. The three that appear on the Andean Pact list are (1) clauses that require royalty payments for unused technology; (2) clauses that commit the licensee to turn over to the licensor any technical improvements derived from use of the licensed technology; and (3) clauses that require the licensee to sell its output to the licensor.

The other seven prohibited clauses are (4) prohibitions on the production and sale by the licensee of products manufactured under the technology agreement after the contract expires; (5) bans on the continued use of the technology once the contract ends; (6) requirements regarding the use of specific quality controls as a proviso for employing the technology; (7) prevention of the use of trademarks similar to those of the licensor after the contract terminates; (8) calls for royalty payments when the technology is transferred to the user through a sales contract; (9) stipulations that the user must pay the local tax on the licensor's royalties and fees; and (10) requirements that the user give irrevocable authorization to the supplier of the technology to sell the products.

Copyright Law

The Copyright Law (Ley Sobre El Derecho de Autor), which dates to Jan. 3, 1963, protects creative works of a "literary, scientific or artistic nature." Because of this wide spectrum, the law is sometimes used to protect other things that are not normally copyrighted.

Protection is granted for the life of the author plus 50 years. No preliminary testing or analysis is necessary to acquire a copyright; one simply registers an application with the public registrar's office (Oficina de Registro Subalterno), which records it with the stipulation that there is a "claim of authorship" (*presuncion de autoria*) of that work. No proof of its usefulness is necessary.

Venezuela's copyright law is similar to the Inter-American Commission Agreement on Copyrights to which the nation subscribes. Local copyright experts say the main weakness of the law is that it was taken over from the laws of other nations: It was not created in response to the specific needs of Venezuela, but is the product of an international trend to provide copyright protection.

Software

Software protection is an especially confusing area in Venezuela. Local software companies usually utilize the copyright law, mainly because it is the simplest way of acquiring some legal protection. In practice, however, this approach does not offer much real security because unauthorized copying of software programs is as much a way of life as the stealing of satellite signals—and most people who own satellite dishes in Venezuela do not pay for the programs they pick up.

As an alternative, several companies have gone through the arduous process of acquiring a patent on a particular piece of software because the IP code affords better protection and recourse in the courts. Thus, a precedent has been established. However, according to most experts, patenting software under the IP law is not the most appropriate way of protecting it. In theory, they say, it should be protected under the copyright law, which claims to protect "any work of creativity by an author, whether of a literary, scientific or artistic nature." The confusion emanates from the language of the patent law, which also explicitly protects works of "creativity."

Registration Expenses

Even though the fees have been raised recently, registration is still extremely inexpensive in Venezuela. The total cost of getting a patent or trademark registered, for example, including the requisite announcements in newspapers and the registrar's fees, is about B1,500 (B64.9:$1 in May 1992). Because of the low cost, many unscrupulous individuals try to register pirated international trademarks with the intention of bargaining with the legitimate owners to obtain some economic gain.

Royalties and Fees

Under Decree Law 727, royalty payments to a foreign licensor may be freely made. Technology or service fees received by the subsidiary may not be excluded from its taxable income, however; they are both treated as profits for tax purposes.

Royalty or fee payments from a majority foreign-owned subsidiary to its parent company or affiliate are limited to a maximum of 5% of "net technological sales," defined as the aggregate net sales price of the licensed products less the f.o.b. price of imported inputs provided by the licensor.

Payment is also permitted for technical assistance in cases of specific "occasional" or "one-time" services (as defined by Decree Law 727), even when provided by a parent company. The payment calculation may not, however, be based on production, sales or any other aggregate that could cause the compensation to be construed as a royalty in excess of the 5% limit.

Royalties and fees are not tax deductible if the patent involved has expired or if the technology has become public knowledge (as determined by the Ministry of Finance in a tax audit). Technical-assistance fees must be backed by tangible proof of the aid received; the request must usually come from a local company; and the payments to technicians or managers who provide the service must be in line with "normal" compensation abroad.

The foreign investment regulations specified in Decree Law 727 generally allow the licensor and the licensee to work out their own payment arrangements. For several years, though, royalty limits of either 5% of net technological sales or 3% of net profits derived from the licensed product have become established as guidelines for new contracts. Since net profits derived from the sale of a licensed product can be practically impossible to calculate, many licensors choose the 5% option even though the netting of inputs makes the latter less desirable. Other payment schedules are equally acceptable, however—as long as they do not exceed the 5% limit on contracts between a parent and its subsidiary.

Proposed Bill on Monopolies and Cartels

Venezuela has no antitrust laws, though the Congress has currently tabled proposed legislation (Ley Anti-Monopolio) on monopolies and cartels. Discussion of the proposal is not expected before the congressional session that begins in the fourth quarter of 1990.

The bill is not intended to limit the sharing of technology by firms in the same industry, though it would outlaw "acts or agreements leading to a monopoly position that would eliminate competition or raise or lower prices artificially." (Public utilities, however, are considered natural monopolies under the bill.) If the bill ever becomes law—the original proposal was introduced in the late 1970s—it is likely to affect local companies more than foreign firms, which are already subject to specific legislation.

Currently, many companies occupy a dominant position in the market. Since the Venezuelan government has itself encouraged monopolies and restricted free competition for the last 40 years, monopolies are the norm in many sectors and free competition is the exception. With economic liberties and guarantees "suspended" since the early 1960s (when the Venezuelan Congress authorized the president and his cabinet to dictate economic measures by decree), the state exercises broad powers over the private sector.

International Legislation

Venezuela is not a signatory to any international legislation, except for the Bolivarian Agreement of 1911, nor a member of any international group on intellectual-property rights. The 1911 agreement (whose signatories also include Colombia, Peru and Panama) has very little application today and is, in fact, almost never used. In general, it states that anyone who obtains a trademark or patent in one of the "Bolivarian" nations has preference to register the patent or trademark in any of the signatory nations for a period of two years, during which time no one else may register it.

Practical Matters

Venezuela's intellectual-property laws are sound, though they are limited in scope and enforcement is poor. Also lacking are special courts to deal with intellectual-property matters. The fact that a protracted number of court appearances is necessary before a decision is reached in an industrial-property dispute generates a lack of confidence in existing intellectual-property laws.

Unfortunately, there is also some corruption in the Venezuelan government, encouraged partly by the excessive amount of bureaucracy in the ministries, especially the planning ministries. According to legal consultants who must deal with it on a regular basis, the bureaucratic wrangling at the Development Ministry can be especially daunting.

The Venezuelan chapter of the Licensing Executives Society (LES)—an association of executives in licensing with approximately 6,000 members worldwide—believes that protection of know-how and trade secrets, which are ordinarily part of technology contracts or licensing, is weak or nonexistent in Venezuela. LES estimates that 65% of contracts in Venezuela are not protected by the Industrial Property Law but only by their use of trade secrets.

As noted earlier, one of the most pressing problems is that the existing IP law prohibits the patenting of a variety of products, including chemicals, pharmaceuticals and food products, biological, genetic-engineering and microbiological processes, and plants. With the acceleration of developments and discoveries in these fields, the country's difficulties will only increase.

The most immediate problem is in agriculture, which is basic to national development. At present, the country imports a great number of agricultural goods that could be produced locally in comparable quality and quantity. Since protection of the processes used to produce the items is unavailable, however, many international concerns prefer not to license the technologies in Venezuela.

Another area of concern is that of well-known brand names—which Venezuela does not legally recognize. Theoretically, anyone can come along and register a brand of shoes called "Ford," and the registration would be legal. Only the legal interpretation of the law by the industrial-property registrar prevents this from happening. The registrar, Haydee Maradei de Garcia, who has served in her post since the late 1970s, is strongly aware of the problem of pirating in Venezuela and has generally interpreted the law in a manner intended to eliminate the problem. For example, one applicant wanted to register the name

"Canon Data" for a company in data processing, but the request was denied on the grounds that Canon is a well-known brand name.

To prevent possible pirating of brand names, some companies register their trademarks or brand names in 10 or 15 of the 50 classes of products available to make sure a third party does not come along and register the same mark under another class of products.

Patent and Trademark Protection

Patents and trademarks must be registered to be protected, and trademarks in particular should be registered as soon as possible to prevent piracy. Registering a patent in Venezuela, however, may take as long as two or three years. Consequently, economic considerations sometimes force companies to put their product on the market before ownership is clearly established, thus running the risk that someone else has already registered a similar patent or trademark. (Penalties for infringement of patent and trademark rights are light, however, usually involving fines of B50-2,000 and prison terms of one to 12 months.)

Firms must also be thoroughly familiar with Venezuela's trademark, patent and copyright regulations and must comply with them strictly—particularly with the two-year clause regarding trademark use—in order to be legally protected. Some companies that have been careless about this have been obliged to pay pirates thousands of dollars as trademark "ransom."

But proving piracy can be difficult. Since Venezuelan courts may require the plaintiff to post a bond in order to obtain an injunction to halt violations, much damage can be done before a case is settled. Because legal recourse is costly and time-consuming, many foreign firms prefer out-of-court settlements. Still, some companies that have gone through the complete court process have found the protection adequate. Sterling Drug's Venezuelan affiliate, for instance, won a court case that successfully halted production of one of its trademarked products by a local pharmaceutical laboratory.

Renewal of trademarks can also be a problem, and companies must pay strict attention to deadlines for renewal applications, submitting documents as soon as possible within the six-month period before the expiration dates. In addition to cases of local companies registering a trademark before the foreign owner got around to it, there are numerous examples of local competitors grabbing a mark once its registration has expired. In such instances, one recourse has been to buy out the local producer; another—rarely used—has been to enter into a joint venture with the new holder.

Payment Instruments

Payments can be indexed to compensate for currency fluctuations, and licensing contracts in currencies other than the bolivar have always been permitted. However, the relationship between the payment currency and the accounting currency must be clearly designated; a licensing contract, for example, may stipulate payment of a percentage of sales translated into dollars at the current exchange rate.

SIEX approval is not necessary if the percentage of royalty payments does not exceed 5% of net technological sales (see the discussion above). If the payment is a fixed amount in a foreign currency, however, royalty payments at the stipulated exchange rate may exceed the 5% maximum; in those cases previous approval from SIEX would be required.

Other Problems

Since there is no clear distinction between what is protected by the Industrial Property Law and what is protected by the Copyright Law, some overlap exists. As a result, some court cases have come up that called both laws into play—in the area of software litigation, for example. Subsequent well-meaning resolutions have occasionally added to the confusion.

A 1974 government resolution, for example, states that "with the previous authorization of the IPL registrar in the Development Ministry" copyrights, trademarks and patents can be mortgaged (i.e. used as collateral to acquire loans). In other words, the IPL registrar can authorize the mortgaging of copyrights even though they are not within her jurisdiction—as copyrights fall under the jurisdiction of the public registrar's office.

Tax Consequences

The 1991 tax reform significantly trimmed corporate tax rates, providing a much-needed boost for foreign investment. Under the previous code, rates had been generally high by Latin American standards, due to a 1986 measure which raised corporate taxes, limited the range of certain tax breaks and lessened fiscal dependence on petroleum revenues.

Tax morality among Venezuelan companies has been low, and the practice of keeping several sets of accounts is common. In general, however, large companies handle taxes quite legally, but as there have been many tax breaks, loopholes and incentives, their tax liability has been

Patents and Trademarks in Venezuela

Conventions and laws. Convention of Caracas. Industrial Property Law of 1955, Decree 746 of 1975, Decree Law 727 of 1990.

Patents

Types and duration. Patents of invention, introduction (importation), improvement, industrial model or design; 10 years from date of granting.

Novelty. Not known, patented or put to use in Venezuela; not already in the public domain because of its use, sale or advertisement inside or outside Venezuela prior to the date of filing an application.

Unpatentable. Foods and beverages; medicines and chemicals (but processes are patentable); financial, speculative, commercial or publicity schemes; inventions with no industrial application; working methods or manufacturing techniques; inventions contrary to Venezuelan law, public welfare or order, morals or state security.

Application procedure. Application must be made to the Industrial Property Registry. Applications must be published at applicant's expense in a Caracas daily newspaper three times in 30 days and once afterward in the *Industrial Property Bulletin*. Opposition has 60 days from the last advertisement to enter its claim.

Fees. Application: B100 (B50 when patent is related to agriculture or health; B200 when related to luxury items), plus a minimum B9 for processing. Annual fees are the same as the basic application fees.

Compulsory licensing is possible under the 1955 Industrial Property Law. The state can also expropriate a patent, but only in conjunction with the expropriation of a company.

Trademarks

Duration. Fifteen years from date of registration; renewable within six months of expiration.

Legal effect. Registration is not compulsory, but validity of trademark may not be contested later than two years after its registration. A trademark may be forfeited if not used for two consecutive years or if a renewal request is not entered within six months of expiration.

(Continued)

Not registrable. Immoral marks; political symbols; geographic names; insufficiently distinguishable marks; caricatures or illustrations ridiculing persons; names of real people, except when used with prior consent; unsubstantiated claims of awards or achievement.

Application procedure. Application to the Industrial Property Registry. Examination is undertaken only in case of opposition.

Fees. Application, B20; registration and renewal, B50; stamp taxes and verification fees, B9 minimum; transfer of title, B1,000.

Industrial designs and models

Coverage for drawings and models is on the same basis as patents, and application procedures and fees are the same. Coverage extends only to products made in Venezuela within two years of the date of granting; it may be revoked if product is imported afterwards.

relatively low. Among foreign-owned firms, also, tax morality appears to be high.

The Finance Ministry periodically sends auditors to inspect corporate accounts without giving advance notice; most companies are visited about once every three or four years, and the audits are quite thorough.

Royalty Remittances

Decree Law 727 allows all types of technology contracts with no prohibitions except for the 5% limitation on technology contracts between a parent company and subsidiary.

Government officials, however, have been wary of contracts between parent companies and subsidiaries drawn up for unnecessary, obsolete or even nonexistent technologies in order to get around the 5% limitation. Licensing contracts must be for technologies that "are not easily obtainable in the country." Given the relaxed rules on foreign investment contained in Decree Law 727—whereby a local firm can remit up to 100% of profits or dividends—the only remaining advantage to the practice of setting up false licensing contracts would be the tax deduction (see below). However, the Finance Ministry can invalidate the deduction if it considers the technology unnecessary or easily obtainable in Venezuela.

Before Decree Law 727, the approval process through SIEX served to demonstrate that the technology in question was, indeed, necessary and not easy to obtain in Venezuela. Under Decree Law 727, however, virtually all contracts are automatically approved. In the future, if the government begins to see a tendency toward contracts for unnecessary technologies, officials may urge the Finance Ministry to audit tax returns more closely.

Royalties and fees are normally subject to corporate income tax rates (see below) when the licensor is a legal entity. For nonresident recipients, the tax is withheld at the source. The withholding tax is 90% of gross receipts on royalties paid for the use of trademarks, brand names, etc.; 50% for use of technological services (e.g. patents, models, industrial drawings and designs, formulations); and 30% for technical assistance (e.g. engineering services, transfer of technical knowledge, consulting, project research and development).

Royalty payments to nonresidents are deductible as an expense of the licensee only if the taxes are withheld at source. Payments to a foreign parent from a Venezuelan licensee that is considered a foreign enterprise (i.e. one in which foreign investors own more than 49% of the equity) are permitted under Decree Law 727. (They were not allowed under the earlier foreign-investment regime, Decree Law 1200.)

Corporate Income Tax Rates

A long-awaited tax reform bill went into effect in September 1991, introducing a simplified two-tier rate for corporations. Firms with net incomes of up to B2 million pay a 20% tax, and those with net earnings over B2 million pay 30%. Companies engaged in the mining or petroleum industry pay 30%. The bill significantly reduced taxes, particularly for larger corporations. In the previous schedule, firms with income over B5 million paid 50%, less B850,000.

Branches of foreign firms pay income tax on the same basis as local corporations, but their net income after this tax is subject to an additional levy of 20%, whether or not the income is remitted to the home office.

To reduce tax evasion by so-called convenience firms, holding companies are liable for tax if more than 50% of their gross income is in dividends. Mining and petroleum concerns, firms registered on the stock exchange, *financieras*, insurance companies and regional investment corporations that hold shares in state enterprises are excluded. Certain income earned abroad is subject to tax at special rates.

A 10% tax is imposed on net income (calculated as 30% of gross receipts generated in Venezuela) of insurance and reinsurance companies not domiciled in the country.

Licensing Experience in Venezuela

Large US, European and Japanese companies usually have in-house lawyers at headquarters who concentrate specifically on patents and trademarks. At the local level they have little at all, especially in countries such as Venezuela, with a relatively small market (19.5 million) in world terms. Thus, while other management decisions may be handled locally after consultation with the head office, business executives and lawyers who handle multinational clients insist that technology is different. MNCs may consult with the local general manager, but the decision to file a patent or register a trademark in Venezuela is usually made at headquarters. There are a number of reasons for this, but in many cases it boils down to the fact that a company may not manufacture or distribute a particular product in Venezuela that it does market abroad. However, the firm may still wish to protect its right to make that product in Venezuela.

In fact, MNCs may not even advise the local general manager of what they're doing in Venezuela. One example is that of a large US multinational with its Latin American headquarters based in Caracas—complete with a local in-house legal department. Despite this structure, patent and trademark decisions are still made at US headquarters.

A committee at headquarters usually meets to look at new products coming out of the pipeline and decide which they'll protect and where. (Participants generally include the new-product manager, the research and development representative and the patents and trademark lawyers.) With current costs at approximately $600-700 per trademark, per class, per country, the decision must be weighed carefully. (The cost to register trademarks is even higher in Venezuela since they must be registered in multiple categories to be effective.) Patent costs in Venezuela alone can run between $2,000 and $3,000 to file and follow through until final approval, which sometimes takes years. (The standard fee listed in the agents' code is $700-1,200, but complex and protracted registrations can easily double or triple this amount.) And even then, patents are rarely enforceable—since 1955 there have only been two cases of patents that were enforced by the legal system in Venezuela. Nonetheless, the threat of a lawsuit can still be the strongest deterrent against patent and trademark piracy, since the legal expenses can be exorbitant. Because headquarters usually handles patents and trademarks issues, very few local MNC representatives have a stake in the matter. This is obvious when a large organization such as the Venezuelan-American Chamber of Commerce and Industry (VenAmCham) holds a patents and trademarks seminar.

"You're lucky if you get two or three of the large companies to attend," says one prominent patents and trademarks attorney. He adds that when VenAmCham held a patents and trademarks seminar in 1989, seminar panelists were mostly international experts who confined their discussions to theory. Most participants, on the other hand, wanted a discussion of how to protect their patents and trademarks in a country where very little protection actually exists.

Since trademark registration takes approximately two to four years, this is a particularly acute problem for companies involved in licensing. Among the most affected firms is York Andina SA, a company that licenses the use of some 200 trademarked goods in Venezuela for Walt Disney and other companies. Except for long-lasting images such as Mickey Mouse or Donald Duck, most of the products licensed by York Andina in Venezuela (such as spin-offs from the E.T., Batman and Rambo movies) have short life spans. Licensing agreements for these products are promoted in conjunction with the corresponding movies.

The Batman movie (a Warner Brothers product and not a York client) released in 1989 and the more recently released Dick Tracy film (Walt Disney Productions) provide two of the best examples of what can and does happened in Venezuela.

Batman (i.e. the bat logotype) was registered in Venezuela under current trademark and copyright (the logotype) laws. Prior to the movie's local release last year, the local Warner Brothers representative signed "between 10 and 12 contracts" licensing the rights to use Batman and the Batman logo on everything from ice cream cones to beach balls. Nevertheless, while the Warner Brothers office licensed the rights to use Batman to these dozen companies, up to three times that number used Batman and the Batman logo without paying for any licensing rights.

Unfortunately, the law offered very little protection to the legal owners or licensees. In fact, in May and June 1990, the legal system began taking up the Batman pirating cases initiated in September and October of 1989. In the meantime, according to a former Warner Brothers spokesman, the pirates took advantage of the boom, col-

(Continued)

lected their money and ran. While it's difficult to estimate the damage incurred, it includes lost income and the inappropriate use of the image in question (such as a T-shirt with the image of Batman—or Mickey Mouse—with a beer mug in his hand).

Pirate production

According to York's managing director Ricardo Weisz, there are two principal types of pirates in Venezuela: artisan pirates and industrial pirates. The artisan is the one-man business who—because he is either unfamiliar with the law or just doesn't care—uses the image of a trademark product on his goods. The industrial pirate, on the other hand, is a large scale lawbreaker with a large production capacity who is fully aware he's breaking the law but knows the legal system is slow to react.

Under the circumstances, Weisz says his experience is that the most effective means to deter pirating in a reduced market such as Venezuela's—and really one of the few available to business there—is to apply pressure—peer-group pressure—on pirates. Companies usually don't threaten pirates with lawsuits, at least not initially. They simply advise pirates that what they're doing is illegal and demand that they cease. If the pirate refuses, York advises the pirate's competitors and all other related companies, including the media, of his transgressions. This makes it more difficult for the pirate to conduct his business later on.

Learning from Batman

Given the slow legal system, York and its licensees are also learning to outflank potential pirates by being first on the market with licensed products. The summer 1990 Dick Tracy movie is an example. Though it was released locally in August, licensees were gearing up for a heavy promotional campaign months before, in hopes of a boom similar to Batman's. To deter pirates, they coordinated their promotional campaigns for the movie based on the comic-page detective. The logo for the movie was still a closely guarded secret in June, and was not made public until a few days before the official promotional campaign started.

With this strategy, the best the licensors can hope is that the campaign is successful and the movie a hit. If licensees sell all their licensed production, the promotion is considered a success. Only in extreme cases, says Weisz, will York suggest that Disney initiate legal action against pirates in Venezuela.

Tax Treaties

Decision 40 of the Andean Pact is a double-taxation convention. In addition, Venezuela has subscribed to several air- and sea-transport tax conventions with European countries. Venezuela is now seeking additional tax treaties, particularly with the US, to make its rules regarding taxation of foreign-sourced income effective.

There is no special tax regime for headquarters operations that do not earn income. Those receiving income from abroad must pay the appropriate tax based on the presumed category of the income. Thus, the net profits of certain types of businesses (mainly those with international operations) are calculated as a percentage of gross income whether or not the actual profit in Venezuela can be determined. For example, the net taxable income on sales of merchandise on consignment is calculated as 25% of gross income from that source; for film producers and distributors, 25%; for international news agencies, 15%; and for international transportation companies, 20%. The net taxable income on foreign technology revenues is 90% for revenues from royalties, 50% from technological services and 30% from technical assistance. The law clearly defines what can be considered technical assistance and technological services. For contracts combining both technical assistance and technological services, 25% of income is defined as technical assistance and 75% as technological services. If the contract includes services contracted partly abroad and partly in Venezuela, 60% of the income is considered foreign sourced, and 40% Venezuelan.

5 Japan

By the beginning of the 1980s, the transformation of the Japanese economy into a major international competitor was complete. To many in government and business around the world, "Japan Inc" has grown into an economic behemoth, playing a formidable role in international trade, manufacturing and finance. At the same time, foreign companies that were trying to sell their products or operate businesses in Japan frequently complained that the Japanese market was extremely difficult to penetrate. This criticism was heard especially from businesses that had failed to crack the difficult Japanese distribution system. The US government has even gone so far as to classify the Japanese distribution system as one of the "structural problems" of its economy.

Unlike in the US, for example, the Japanese wholesaler network usually involves several layers of sales and a series of mark-ups between supplier and end-user. In addition, many distributors place a premium on long-term relationships with suppliers, which makes it difficult to introduce new products of either Japanese or foreign companies. Goods perceived to be unsuitable for the Japanese marketplace are simply ignored, finding no acceptance from the wholesaler or the thousands of small independent retail outlets around the country. Few foreign companies have been willing to invest the time, effort and large financial resources necessary to adapt its products or create its own distribution network to reach the Japanese consumer. (Amway's direct-sales-force strategy is the significant, successful exception.) But with half again as many retail stores as in the US (250,000 vs 180,000, according to the Japan External Trade Organization) concentrated in an area the size of California, the Japanese consumer market holds significant potential for foreign companies.

This increase in consumer spending has also been encouraged by the trickle-down effects of the success and prosperity of Japanese trade and industry. The market has not grown indiscriminately, however. While Japanese consumers are exceptionally demanding, they are also sophisticated with regard to products, and tend to be very sensitive to cost vs product benefit. Consumers attach stronger importance to corporate images than to brand names in making purchases. Because of the relatively high education level of the Japanese consumer and the wide range of product choice available in the market, the importance of product image and differentiation cannot be ignored.

In order to address the particular needs of Japanese consumers, many foreign companies have found it necessary to modify or adapt their products to meet local market requirements. Coca-Cola (Japan) was originally established in 1945 to supply soft drinks to US military personnel stationed in Japan after the end of World War II. Seeking the local Japanese market as well, the company granted franchise rights and licensed its bottling technology to a Japanese food wholesaler and retailer. Shortly afterwards, in 1955, Coca-Cola (Japan) was formed as a fully owned subsidiary. Coca-Cola took advantage of its early market leadership and created a dominant brand image for the Japanese public. In 1988, Coca-Cola enjoyed an overwhelming 93% share in the Japanese cola market (according to *Tokyo Business Today*). Capitalizing on its strong corporate image, Coca-Cola then succeeded in developing canned coffee, Oolong tea and other soft drinks to compete with domestic Japanese rivals like the Ueshima Coffee Company. Today Coca-Cola's Georgia brand canned coffee drink outsells similar products in the Japanese market.

Against the twin obstacles of a complex and difficult distribution system and the particular tastes and requirements of Japanese consumers, licensing in Japan can represent a strong alternative. As the Coca-Cola example shows, this can be an important first step into the Japanese market. In such a strategy, the license arrangement can precede a more permanent presence in Japan—either a joint venture, a company acquisition (sometimes the licensee), or the start-up of a Japanese subsidiary. Aside from Coca-Cola, other companies that have used this tactic include Imperial Chemical Industries (ICI).

Another course of action is to use licenses as a means of establishing links with the powerful Japanese distribution system. By licensing products to a local company the licensor can avoid or minimize the resources of time, people and money that would otherwise be necessary to bring a product onto market through the wholesaler network.

Transfer of Technology

From 1946 to 1980, the import of foreign technology through licensing and technical-assistance contracts played a very important role in the development of the Japanese economy. For most of the post-war era, technology flowed almost exclusively from the US and Europe to Japan, as Japanese corporations and government agencies strove to catch up with Western production and technological advances that had been created during the Second World War. According to the Ministry of International Trade and Industry (MITI), Japan engaged in some 42,000 deals and paid over $2.15 billion to foreigners as royalties for imported technology between 1950 and 1969, while the country received only $180 million for exported technology in return. In many cases the Japanese industries used the licensed technology to develop and market even more sophisticated products than did the licensors themselves.

As measured in the balance of royalty and fee payments made and received in the 1980s, Japan was still a net importer of technology last decade, though the gap has been closing. The pattern of increased Japanese technology flow to the US is clear: In 1975, US companies paid only $6 million in royalties to Japan while they received $227 million in return (according to *Tokyo Business Today*). Total royalty payments to all foreign countries in 1975 were $846 million, compared with royalty receipts of $173 million. Japanese firms were more active in exporting and licensing technology to developing countries in Asia, Africa and South America (notably Brazil) during this period, but had still not made any inroads to the United States. By the late 1980s, however, the ratio had narrowed considerably; in 1987, American firms paid $100 million and received $767 million from Japan.

These figures only tell part of the story, however, as many Japanese businesses have favored broader cooperative agreements, like joint product development, instead of direct technology licensing. An example of this type of technology transfer is the New United Motors Manufacturing (NUMMI) joint venture established by Toyota and General Motors.

The Legislative Framework

A business wishing to license products or technology in Japan is protected by a well-codified set of national laws regarding industrial- and intellectual-property rights.

Statutory requirements and licensing regulations are specified in the Japanese Patent Act, the Utility Models Act, the Design Act and the Trademark Act, all of which were ratified in 1959. Since then, the government has amended these laws in order to bring them up to date with changing technology. In addition, Japan has been an active member and signatory to various international conventions, including GATT and the World Intellectual Property Organization. The *keidanren*, Japan's big-business federation, has strongly endorsed international agreements over bilateral treaties for the protection of industrial- and intellectual-property rights.

Even so, federal legislation for the protection of intellectual-property rights has not reduced criticism and concern over their enforcement in Japan. During the 1980s, high-tech companies such as IBM, Digital Equipment and Intel fought long and sometimes unsuccessful court-room battles with Japanese firms over charges of copyright violation and infringement. Texas Instruments, for instance, was awarded a favorable decision in late 1989 in the patent courts regarding its patent rights for a basic semiconductor. This verdict came only after many years of litigation, however, and long after the damage had been done.

Much of the conflict lies in differing interpretations of the nature of patent and copyright protection. The Japanese Patent Office has been criticized for allowing patent claims to be based on minor or insignificant variations to the original idea—such as a bicycle with *red* pedals as a patentable variation of the standard bicycle.

In 1990 the US Trade Representative Office removed Japan from its "Special 301 watchlist" of IP rights violators. Japan has been criticized for its slow processing of patent and trademark applications and lack of effective protection from illicit rentals of foreign recordings.

Patents

In practice, Japan's patent system is similar to the German and Dutch "deferred examination" schemes, and the patent law closely parallels the provisions of the European Patent Convention. In 1988, the single-claim filing system was changed to a more efficient multiple-claim system, which provides protection for a group of associated inventions from one patent application. The same revision also extended the patent term to 20 years from the date the application is filed, and the grace period (the time allowed between making an invention public and filing the application) was lengthened from six to 12 months. The Patent Act provides that a patentee may grant an exclusive or nonexclusive license on its patent. Since a patent right comes into force in Japan when the issued right has been registered in the Patent Register, the laws concerning licenses apply only to issued and registered patents.

The key elements of the patent law are as follows: public disclosure of the application 18 months after the filing or priority date; formal examination, made on request by the applicant or a third party up to seven years from the filing date (during which time the patent receives preliminary protection); and reexamination, which may be requested within 30 days of refusal by the Patent Office.

Trademarks

In Japan, a trademark right commences when the mark is registered in the Trademark Register. It does not result from the actual use or the filing of a trademark application. Under the same law, the owner of an unregistered trademark does not have the right to exclude others from using the same mark, even if the trademark application is pending before the Patent Office. Further, there is no service-mark registration system in Japan, so firms wishing to protect company service marks must rely on the fairly cumbersome measure provided by the Unfair Competition Prevention Law.

Company logos trademarked in Japan for one type of product may not necessarily be trademarked for other types of products or uses. This lesson was learned recently by Evian, the French bottled-water company. When it trademarked its logo for use on its bottled mineral water, a distributor in Japan printed T-shirts with the Evian logo for promotional purposes. Evian learned that it did not own the right to use its own logo on clothing, but that in fact that right belonged to another firm. Likewise, registration of a trade name in the Commercial Register only provides protection for that name in the city where it was registered. If an *un*registered trade name or service mark is well known in Japan as an identification of a service or product, the Unfair Competition Prohibition Act may entitle the enterprise to prohibit others from using the identification (especially if it could cause confusion in the market).

FECA coverage

Patents, copyrights, and trademarks are all subject to licenses in Japan under the legislation of the Foreign Exchange and Foreign Trade Control Act (revised FECA), which went into effect in December 1980. The previous law, the Foreign Trade Investment Act, had controlled a certain class of technology import, but was abolished in 1980. The revised FECA applies to the licensing by a foreign licensor to a Japanese business both industrial-property rights and "other rights concerning technology." It is generally understood that the latter term covers "know-how," including secret formulas, processes, or other specialized technical information. The courts have held that know-how and other intellectual property may be the subject of licensing agreements in Japan.

Under the terms of the revised FECA, prior notice of intention to enter an industrial-property or intellectual-licensing agreement must be submitted to the Ministry of Finance and to the ministry that has jurisdiction over the industry concerned. The parties entering into the license are prohibited from concluding any agreement on the license for 30 days thereafter. If the proposal is thought to threaten national security or the sound management of domestic industries, the authorities may recommend revision or cancellation of all or part of the agreement, after hearing opinions from the Foreign Exchange Council. If the foreign licensor and local licensee do not accept the recommendations, the respective ministers are authorized to order them to comply.

The Fair Trade Commission (FTC) also reviews licensing agreements and suggests any changes it deems necessary, even if the license is already officially approved. The FTC can also review longstanding pacts upon request from other companies. Under the Anti-Monopoly Act Guidelines for International Licensing Agreements (formulated in 1968), the FTC must be notified of all international contracts and agreements within 30 days of signing. The guidelines stipulate that no restrictions be applied to the area, price or quantity of the licensee's export sales unless the licensor has registered patent rights in the area to which the licensee's export is restricted; is selling patented goods in the restricted area; or has granted to a third party an exclusive license to sell in the restricted area.

Under the same guidelines, foreign licensors are expressly forbidden to restrict licensees from handling competitive technology (unless the licensor grants exclusive rights to the licensee and does not restrict products already handled by the licensee); require the licensee to buy raw materials from the licensor or his designee; oblige the licensee to sell patented goods through the licensor or a person designated by the licensor; restrict resale pricing of the licensed products; require the licensee to share technical innovation with the licensor on the licensed product, unless the licensor reciprocates with its innovation on the same; or impose charges (e.g. payments for patent rights or know-how) on products not involving use of the licensed product, unless necessary for the licensor's trademark reputation or the effectiveness of the technology that is being licensed.

An exclusive license does not take effect until it has been registered in the Register at the Patent Office. The application for registration of a license usually takes two or three months to complete after the date of filing. Unlike recording procedures in the US Patent Office, the application for registration at the Japanese Patent Office must be filed jointly by the licensor and the licensee (with the exception that the licensee may apply for registration in its own name under a separate agreement with the licensor). While it is legal to grant a license for a limited period within the life of the patent, it is illegal for the licensor to receive royalties or other countervalue after the expiration of the patent. If the license agreement covers both a Japanese and non-Japanese patent, the licensor can request royalties only on the exported products after the expiration of the Japanese patent, and not on products manufactured and sold within Japan.

Royalty Payments

Under Japanese law, a contract does not require a royalty payment in order to be effective. Therefore, a unilateral contract under which a licensor grants a license without any money payment or exchange of rights may be thoroughly legal and effective. Prior to 1968, imports of foreign technology under licensing agreements were carefully controlled and regulated by the government, especially with regard to the type and amount of royalty payments made to foreign licensors. Sometimes the licensors were requested by the government to reduce the amount of royalties to be paid. With the liberalization of the regulations for imports of foreign technology starting in 1968, there have been no administrative controls or limits to the amount of royalties and types of payments permitted. MITI has suggested that it considers 5% to be an ideal maximum for royalty rates, but in practice more than half of all the licensing agreements now provide for royalties of 5% or more. Some royalties of more than 8% have been successfully negotiated.

On the other hand, disclosure fees are common in Japan, and provisions for minimum royalties are often included in licensing agreements. The number of licenses offered gratis is also rising. Many of these are part of cross-licensing deals or represent the supply of technology to foreign joint ventures in Japan. Technical agreements calling for the licensor to provide on-site technical services usually stipulate the maximum number of man-days to be provided and the per diem rate to be used. Before technical personnel are sent to Japan, the Ministry of Finance requires at least a month's notice, a rèsumè listing their skills, and justification for their services.

Tax Consequences

The Japanese licensee is required to withhold taxes on gross payments made to the foreign licensor. Japanese tax authorities interpret this regulation as covering reimbursed expenses as well, including travel costs and salaries paid to engineers or technicians provided by the licensor. Japanese definitions of industrial property are wide, and income from contracts that involve any form of technology—even if services are performed outside of Japan—may be subject to withholding tax. The standard withholding rate on royalties and fees for licensing of patents, trademarks, copyrights, know-how and technical assistance is 20%, though this is variously reduced from 5% to 15% under tax treaties with different countries. Income received by nonresident companies (e.g. branches of foreign firms) for personal services, including technical and managerial skills, is also subject to the 20% withholding tax.

Generally, a licensing agreement does not result in a permanent business operation in Japan. If it involves construction, installation or assembly activities and the foreign licensor provides supervisory personnel for such activities for a period of more than one year (or more than two years for construction and installation activities under a US-Japan treaty), the licensor is deemed to have a permanent establishment in Japan and, therefore, subject to corporate tax.

Corporate taxation of a foreign-owned subsidiary can be quite high in Japan. In addition to the national corporation tax (at a basic rate of 37.5%), companies must pay an enterprise tax and inhabitants tax, both of which vary by location and size of firm (with rates ranging from 6.6% to 13.2% of taxable income). Finally, a foreign-owned subsidiary that wishes to distribute dividends to the parent company is subject to a 20% withholding tax, the same as the withholding for a royalty payment from a licensee.

Practical Matters

Despite well-established and updated Japanese legislation governing licenses, there are still many problems and obstacles for a foreign company wishing to license products or technology in Japan. Foreign firms continue to have major problems with the Japanese patent system. The Japanese system for patents is based on a "first-to-file" philosophy as to the priority of competing inventions (as opposed to the "first-to-invent" system in the US and elsewhere). The narrow scope of claim interpretation in Japan encourages large numbers of patent filings based on minor or insignificant variations of the prior art (the previously mentioned "red-pedal" syndrome). As a result, the country's 1,000 patent examiners receive over 500,000 applications per year, less than half of which are actually reviewed. (By comparison, the US Patent and Trademark Office employs 1,500 examiners to review about 140,000 applications received annually.)

Naturally, the volume of applications also slows the approval process. It takes an average of 37 months after applying for a patent for an inventor to receive notice of acceptance or rejection in Japan, compared with 30 months in Europe and 20 months in the US. Applications in languages other than Japanese are generally not accepted; if an application written in English is accepted, the review process takes longer. Foreign applicants also complain that rejection notices are inadequate and that Japanese patent examiners do not meet with them to discuss reasons for rejections.

The Pharmaceuticals Case

The difficulties faced by foreign pharmaceuticals companies trying to introduce medicines approved in other countries to the Japanese market provides a good example of the problems of getting products through the patent process and into the distribution system in Japan. Tests and trials, often taking years to complete, must be reproduced in Japan to the satisfaction of local authorities. The Japanese patent office has particular problems with new biotechnology products, where the breadth of rights is still to be determined. Finally, because of the close relationships among manufacturers, wholesalers, hospitals and physicians, most foreign companies must license their medical technology to established Japanese health-care companies to get into the distribution system.

Prior to 1975, the Japanese government restricted the ownership and direct presence of international pharmaceuticals companies in Japan in order to protect and encourage the development of domestic Japanese firms. Established European and US companies—such as Merck, Ciba-Geigy, Hoffman-LaRoche and Eli Lilly—all used licensing and joint-venture arrangements to get their products into the Japanese marketplace. The procedure was similar for all the foreign companies: a product-licensing agreement enabled the Japanese partner to steer the pharmaceutical compound through the trials and clinical studies necessary for domestic regulatory approval, and a joint venture permitted the product to be marketed by the foreign company while distribution was handled by the local Japanese partner. In some cases, to maximize the value of a compound or product, the Japanese partner would share in the product-development process and take charge of local regulatory approval requirements.

When the law changed in 1975, foreign ownership of pharmaceuticals companies was possible for the first time in Japan. A few companies, notably Merck, made the effort to acquire their partner's interest in the joint venture or actually acquired a Japanese firm in order to have a wholly owned subsidiary in Japan. While ownership of a subsidiary brings control of the product, many pharmaceuticals companies have preferred to maintain their licensing arrangements with Japanese partners because of the better access to Japanese technology and product development, and the advantage of a Japanese distributor in the market. For smaller pharmaceuticals companies that have entered the Japanese market relatively recently, a licensing agreement with a Japanese firm is the only way to succeed.

In order to enter the Japanese market, Syntex Pharmaceuticals entered into licensing agreements with three Japanese pharmaceuticals companies in 1971. Four years later, Syntex established a joint venture with Tanabe Pharmaceuticals to register and distribute Syntex's principal product, Naproxen. Afterwards, Syntex formed its own wholly owned subsidiary in the country, but since the process and pipeline of new products has developed slowly, the firm still depends on its licensing agreements to register and distribute both existing and new products in Japan.

In the field of telecommunications, AT&T began operations in Japan in 1897, when one of its subsidiaries, Western Electric, set up there. Both as a means of obtaining access to Japanese technology and as a conduit for bringing its own products to the Japanese marketplace, licensing has been an important part of AT&T's strategy in Japan. In the mid-1980s, AT&T brought a computer-linking device to the market by having modifications made under license to a Japanese company. For the future, the telecommunications giant believes that it is important to have access to Japanese technology and developments, and this is also served by its cross-licensing agreements.

International Disputes

Disputes between the US and Japan over the use and protection of advanced technologies (notably biotechnology and computer software) have increased in recent years, and these threaten to emerge as another source of friction in economic relations between the two countries. In 1986 Japan amended its copyright legislation to further protect the copyright of computer programs and "new media" information services, such as two-way cable television. But actions of this sort, while welcome, were not thorough enough to answer demands for increased protection of intellectual-property rights.

Patents and Trademarks in Japan

Conventions. Paris Union 1883–1967; Arrangement of Madrid 1891–1967; Agreement of the Hague 1961; World Intellectual Property Organization Convention (WIPO) 1967; Patent Cooperation Treaty 1970; Strasbourg Agreement 1971.
Basic laws. Patent Law (No. 121); Trademark Law (No. 127); Utility Model Law (No. 123); Design Law (No. 125); all effective 1960. Amendments to Patent Utility Model and Trademark Law (1975), effective 1976. Revised Patent Law (1987), effective 1988.

Patents
Duration. Twenty years.
Application procedure. File application with Director-General, Patent Office, Tokyo, specifying title of invention, investor's and applicant's full names, domiciles and nationalities. Attach specifications in Japanese, drawings and technical papers.
Examination procedure. An application is examined only if a request is filed within seven years of the original filing date. After payment of fees, the patent is published in the Patent Register, and patent letters are issued.
Unpatentable. Substances made by nuclear transformation; products contrary to public health, order or morals; and inventions lacking industrial utility or inventive merit.
Fees. Applications, Y5,400; annual fees, Y4,000 in first year, rising to Y48,000 in last three years; examination, Y19,000, plus Y3,000 per claim; opposition, Y3,200; appeal, Y16,000.
Compulsory licenses may be granted after three or more consecutive years if the patent in question is unworked; if patent is deemed necessary to public interest; or if a second patent is needed for the first, and the second patent owner is uncooperative.

Trademarks
Duration. Ten years, renewable for like periods.
Legal effect. First user is entitled to registration and exclusive use, but a trademark may be registered without previous use. A mark unused for more than three years may be canceled.
Not registrable. Trade names and marks that might be confused with existing ones.
Registration procedure. File six specimens with Patent Office. Include applicant's name (if juridical person, the representative's

name), domicile, agent or attorney, description and class of goods on which mark will appear.
Fees. Application, Y10,000; registration, Y32,000; renewal application, Y10,000; renewal registration, Y60,000; appeal, Y16,000; opposition, Y3,200.

Industrial designs and models
Utility models are protected for up to 10 years from approval but no longer than 15 years from filing. The application is withdrawn after four years unless an examination has been requested. Fees are Y4,000 for application and Y12,000 for examination. Industrial designs may be protected for 15 years from date of registration.

Today Japan competes with the US in virtually every area of technology, with few notable exceptions (such as aircraft engines). Even though Japan still lags in basic research in most areas, Japanese companies have created technological innovations that set the pace for progress in many industries. Technological progress, however, has not made the debate over protection of intellectual-property rights any easier.

How the US and Japan manage technology issues will be a critical factor in future bilateral relations; this in turn will influence corporate decisions on future licensing arrangements in both countries.

A timely example of this debate is the controversy over the development of the FSX fighter, in which Japanese and US firms would share advanced defense technology. Many of the technologies involved in the development and production of the FSX will have significant application in industries other than defense. Failure to reach a satisfactory solution to cooperate on this project could cast a cloud over US-Japanese political ties, and could strain licensing attitudes of companies in both countries at a time when cooperation, mutual trust and understanding are critically needed.

It is clear that Japan has now become a major player in world technology and that product-focused research and development has been the stimulus for the rapid economic growth of the last two decades. Though some critics have argued that Japan is still lacking in basic research, there is no disagreement that commercial research and development have thrived in Japan's corporations. As Japanese companies have prospered, technology licensing from Japan to other developing countries will grow. The expectation is that technology licensing will become more of a two-way street, with cross-licensing agreements between foreign companies and their Japanese counterparts becoming more common. Because efforts by the Japanese government to encourage imports still face the obstacles of getting products through the market to the consumers, product licensing and distribution agreements will be dominant strategies for many foreign companies trying to enter the Japanese market.

The next major impetus for change and further movements in cross-licensing may result from the creation of the European Single Market in 1992. The formation of an integrated economic and trading community in Europe has already caused great concern in Japanese business circles. In addition to increased Japanese direct investment in plants and production in Europe, many business leaders predict an increase in industrial cooperation between the regions, primarily in the form of joint ventures and technological links.

The outcome of further cross-licensing and technology transfer will be more trade and further commercial integration of both foreign and domestic Japanese companies, resulting in access and opportunities in Japan's enormous consumer market.

6 South Korea

Korea and its ethnically homogeneous people have a rich history that dates back over 4,000 years. Because of its geography and culture, the country has traditionally served as a natural bridge for trade and ideas between China and Japan. Resuming its status as an independent nation in 1945 after 40 years of Japanese colonial rule, Korea was almost immediately embroiled in internal problems and political conflict developed once again, with full civil war erupting in 1950.

The Korean War left the country devastated and economically close to the bottom of the international income scale. Without the benefit of primary natural resources, South Korea launched a bold series of economic development programs in an effort to transform the economy from a marginally subsistent agricultural base into one of Asia's major industrial nations. That these dramatic changes and industrialization programs succeeded was due largely to the fact that the country was led by two successive military governments in the period 1962–88. General Park Chung-hee became president following a 1962 military coup; he in turn was replaced by General Chun Doo-hwan in another coup in 1979. Both administrations held to the policies of technological and industrial development for Korean business. The government encouraged higher-quality, low-cost production through export incentives, and carefully selected and controlled the accumulation of foreign technological capability.

In 1980, under the administration of President Chun, South Korea began to adopt a more liberal policy toward foreign investment and technology as the country pursued three major objectives: price stability, high growth led by exports, and improvements in domestic income distribution. The government took steps to loosen previously restrictive foreign investment regulations, and encouraged joint ventures that would help increase exports and introduce foreign technology, ultimately contributing to the country's international competitiveness.

Since 1982, the government has continued to liberalize its foreign-investment policy, opening more industries to foreign capital and in some cases even ownership.

With the election in 1988 of President Roh Tae-woo, the first popularly elected leader in the country since 1960, the government accelerated this policy of liberalization, amending the Foreign Capital Inducement Act and scrapping protective measures for various technology imports. In 1991 the Korea Intellectual Property Office drafted a trade secrets law defining violations as "unfair competition," which will allow firms to seek injunctions.

Although these changes show a growing response to pressure from abroad to eliminate technology-protective barriers, the US and other countries criticize the inadequacy of South Korea's intellectual property protection. The US Trade Representative's Office placed Korea on Special 301 IPR "watch list" in 1990, maintaining that IPL "penalties are often light and insufficient to deter future violations." Moreover, US officials complain that Seoul offers no protection for designs of semiconductor chips and still has not amended its 1987 patent law to upgrade protection for pharmaceutical firms. The Union des Fabricants in 1990 labeled South Korea the world's foremost producer and exporter of counterfeit goods.

The most significant characteristic of the modern South Korean economy is its rapid development since the reconstruction programs began in the 1960s. Industrialization took place at a speedy pace. Since 1966, real gross domestic product has increased at an average annual rate of nearly 9%.

In 1990 President Roh shook up the cabinet in his government, which now includes members from two of the former opposition parties that merged with his Democratic Justice Party early in 1991. The primary effect of this reshuffling will be a correction of economic policy in order to get the economy—particularly exports—back on track. The new Ministry of Trade and Industry (MTI) program will focus on exports, ahead of domestic programs aimed at price stability and more equal distribution of wealth.

Attracting Foreign Technology

In its remarkable journey from poverty to wealth, South Korea has borrowed many ideas from the Japanese growth model, not least of which is the desire to gain access to foreign technology and know-how. Through the 1960s and 1970s, the South Korean government was very selective and highly conscious of its licensing approvals, as the main concern was to protect and encourage the growth of developing domestic industries. Licensing of foreign technology during this period was primarily focused on the production of brand-name products from foreign companies by South Korean manufacturers. But starting in the early 1980s the government's policy was to place greater emphasis on the quality of the technology being transferred and its usefulness in spurring exports. As the pace of dropping controls and regulations for investment accelerated in the 1980s, more foreign companies used the opportunity to license their products and technology in South Korea, both to reach the growing domestic market and to take advantage of the lower cost of production in South Korea for export to other countries. (The table on p. 82 shows the historical trend of royalty payments in this period.)

In 1986 the Ministry of Science and Technology identified six areas in which the government will encourage technology transfers and licensing over the 15-year period from 1987 to 2001. They are

(1) computers, software, semiconductors and information networks;

(2) fine chemicals and biotechnology;

(3) technology for designing, engineering, developing, automating, molding and testing product quality;

(4) energy conservation and alternative energy development;

(5) health, environmental protection, and other social services; and

(6) marine and aeronautical industries.

At the same time, the government began efforts to diversify technology sources and thus reduce dependence on the US and Japan. Korean companies have introduced new technologies from France, Britain, Canada, Denmark, Italy and Sweden. Royalty payments to these countries in 1988 reached a combined \$94.5 million, almost 14% of the total royalties paid that year.

The trend of the government's program can also be seen by industry segment. Since the late 1980s, the leading payer of royalties has been the electrical/electronics sector, followed by machinery, energy and power, and petrochemicals. In contrast, royalties paid by metals firms and shipbuilding have fallen considerably.

These figures indicate that the sectors targeted by the Ministry of Science and Technology for the introduction of advanced foreign technology are making efforts to improve their international competitiveness. These levels of royalty payments represent almost 30% of the total expenditure for research and development in the country (according to the Ministry of Finance), compared with 0.2% in the US (1986), 6.8% in Japan (1986) and 7.6% in China (1984).

South Korea's Royalty Payments by Country
($ millions)

Country	1962-76	1977-81	1982-85	1986	1987	1988
US	29.7	159.8	411.1	191.6	239.9	330.0
Japan	63.7	139.8	194.2	129.5	181.4	214.7
Germany	8.2	14.0	29.9	19.1	18.6	22.1
France	1.6	14.3	17.5	17.2	25.1	47.9
Other	10.4	124.1	121.2	53.6	58.7	61.6
Total	113.6	451.4	773.9	411.0	523.7	676.3

For foreign companies considering investment in South Korea, the country has become a very attractive target. Strong economic growth has built a sound infrastructure, a steadily improving financial and legal environment, political stability and a growing middle class with a rising level of wealth and living standards. Unlike Japan, South Korea has a less complicated distribution network and has not hesitated to duplicate foreign marketing programs or to adopt ideas that make the economy grow faster. In fact, the government's stated policy is to "effectively induce and protect foreign capital conducive to the sound development of the national economy and the improvement of the international balance of payments." The legislation promulgated in the last five years demonstrates the government's commitment to more liberalization and an opening of the country to foreign investment.

Foreign-Investment Preferences

Over the past two decades the government's favored foreign-investment program was the joint venture. Limits on the levels of foreign ownership and control made it possible for domestic Korean companies to benefit from the new technology and capital investment in the country. The problems for foreign companies that formed joint ventures usually concerned management of the business, financing the operation locally, and differences in cultural and business philosophies with the Korean partner.

As the rules for foreign ownership have been liberalized and the restrictions have become looser, some foreign firms have opted for direct ownership of their own subsidiaries in South Korea (when allowed by the government) in order to overcome some of these difficulties. Many companies have found, however, that carefully prepared technical agreements and product licenses can often accomplish the same business objective in a much less costly and more efficient way. The rationale for the government's liberalization policy is to encourage, and gradually force, domestic Korean firms to compete on an even footing with MNCs, both in the domestic market and in the international marketplace.

The results of this policy have not always been harmonious, however. In a celebrated case in the mid-1980s, Bristol-Myers (now Bristol-Myers Squibb) filed suit against Dong-A Pharmaceuticals, South Korea's largest pharmaceuticals manufacturer, over the alleged patent infringement of one of its best-selling antibiotics, amikacin. Bristol-Myers also claimed that the government-funded Korea Advanced Institute of Science and Technology had been involved in "reverse engineering" and had provided research to Dong-A to enable the company to copy the product. In 1984, Dong-A succeeded in getting patents from the Korean Office of Patent Administration (OPA) for two innovative techniques it had developed to manufacture amikacin. Bristol-Myers sought a court injunction to suspend production and sales of the amikacin from Dong-A, claiming that the company had infringed on its patent rights and that the new manufacturing process did not represent an improvement of the technology. In the suit the OPA was urged to invalidate Dong-A's patents, but because there was no law at that time protecting product patents in South Korea, Bristol-Myers lost the court cases. The case was not dropped, though, as Bristol-Myers later demanded invocation of Section 301 of the 1974 US Trade Act, a law that allows the US to retaliate against countries engaging in unfair trade practices.

The pressure from the US Trade Commission resulting from this case and others from the pharmaceuticals industry resulted in a bilateral agreement between the US and South Korea in 1987. The agreement gave retroactive patent protection to over 900 US pharmaceutical and chemical products, and recognized product patents as legally binding in South Korea. Although South Korean law protected patents, trademarks, designs and utility models, foreign governments believed that the country still had some way to go before it could provide adequate protection for technology and intellectual-property rights.

As a result of the considerable pressure from the US as well as the European Community, South Korea began a program in 1987 to bring its property-protection laws in line with international standards. At the root of the problem for South Korea is the cultural belief that copying is not wrong, and the attitude that the knowledge of one belongs to all if it benefits society. The government has taken steps to begin using international rules for patents and copyrights, and South Korea has since joined the Universal Copyright Convention (1987), the Geneva Phonogram Convention, which covers sound recordings (1987), and the Budapest Treaty regarding patents (1989).

Patents and Trademarks

South Korea's Patent and Trademark Laws were substantially amended effective July 1, 1987, and have been subject to further revisions and clarifications since that time. The most important change of the 1987 amendments was the extension of patent protection not only to the process involved in making a patented item, but to the item (product) itself. Coverage includes pharmaceuticals, the methods of formulating two or more drugs into a new one, new substances produced by chemical methods, and inventions using chemical substances. Foods, beverages and other consumable items, and plants may not be patented, however. The new patent law extends the previous patent term from 12 years to 15 years from the date of publication of the patent application, no longer calculated from the filing date. Furthermore, the 1987 law established a patent-restoration system that effectively extends the patent term by up to five years for products that were subject to delay in marketing due to unusually long statutory testing periods. Also under the amended law, a holder of a dependent patent may now be granted a nonexclusive license only if the dependent patent represents a substantial technical advance over the prevailing one. For cases of compulsory licensing, Korean companies applying for nonexclusive license to work an unused patent must now negotiate directly with the patent holder.

Prior to 1987, many foreign companies could not register their trademarks in South Korea, or chose not to, because the trademark law required that registration be tied to technology transfer. Under the amended trademark legislation, the requirement for technology transfer or inducement as a condition for accepting trademark-license applications has been dropped. In addition, export requirements for goods covered by trademark licenses have been repealed, and royalty restrictions, such as amount and duration, have also been lifted. There are still problems in this area for foreign companies, though, as the government permits the foreigner to license its trademark only when the firm has either a majority equity position in a Korean venture, an approved joint venture, or a technical-assistance agreement with a South Korean company. The Unfair Competition Law states that foreign owners of trademarks who have formal residence or commercial establishment in a member country of the Paris Convention are given equal protection against trademark infringement, including counterfeits. But given the current number of violations, enforcement of this law is obviously lax.

In September 1990 the Trademark Law was amended. Under the new law, "use" is more difficult to prove for products that require special import or manufacturing permits, such as pharmaceuticals, food products and agrichemicals. Non-use of a trademark for one year or more is

Patents and Trademarks in South Korea

Conventions. World Intellectual Property Organization, Paris Convention, 15 bilateral pacts.
Basic laws. Law 950 of 1961 (amended 1963); Law 71 of 1949 (amended 1958, 1963); Patent Law 2505 and Trademark Law 2506 of 1973 (amended 1980, 1982); Trademark Law 3892 of 1986 (amended 1990); and Patent Law 3892 of 1987.

Patents
Duration. Fifteen years from day after publication or registration. This may be extended by five years if other laws require additional approval involving long testing periods.
Novelty. Not known in Korea by publication, public use, exhibition or experimentation. Not known in other countries through publication.
Unpatentable. Food and drink; medicines; articles manufactured by chemical or nuclear processes; and articles detrimental to public order, good morals or health.
Application procedure. Application to Patent Bureau must include notarized power of attorney; notarized certificate of nationality of corporation; specification with claims; certified copy of basic application in the home country; and deed of assignment of invention.
Examination procedure. Examination as to form, unity of invention, novelty and patentability. On rejection, applicant may amend or request consideration. If still rejected, applicant should appeal within 30 days to Appeal Trial Court of the Patent Office.
Fees. Applications, W15,000; examinations, W56,000; publication of applications, W23,000; registrations, W15,000 p.a. for first to third years, W28,000 p.a. for fourth to sixth years, W56,000 p.a. for seventh to ninth years, W71,000 p.a. for years 10-12, W150,000 p.a. for years 13-15 and W280,000 p.a. for years 16-20.
Compulsory licensing. A patent must be worked within three years of being granted—or one year in case of exportation—unless "due reasons" can be shown.

Trademarks
Duration. Ten years from date of registration; renewable.

(Continued)

Unregistrable. The 11 categories of unregistrable trademarks include those similar to national flags, offensive to public order, or similar to other trademarks.
Application procedure. Applications should be accompanied by notarized power of attorney, notarized certificate of nationality, an electrotype and 10 printed facsimiles.
Fees. Application, W42,000 for up to 10 trademarks, plus W5,000 per item on excess; registration, W180,000 (for 10 years) plus additional charges on excess; renewal, W180,000.

Industrial designs and models
Protection is for eight and 10 years. Application procedures are similar to those for patents. Fees are as follows: application, W41,000; registration, W10,500 p.a. through the third year; W21,000 p.a. for years four to six; W33,000 p.a. for years seven and eight (designs) and W41,000 p.a. for years seven to nine (models); and W50,000 p.a. for the 10th year (models).]

grounds for deregulation. Those trademarks that do not require Ministry of Health permits usually can be protected by annual publication of the mark in an advertisement.

The Corporate Response

Even with the new amendments, foreign companies sometimes have difficulty getting trademark protection. Italy's Benetton SpA cites the lack of effective protection in South Korea as the reason it won't take a competitor to court over the use of its logo. A Korean company, Non No Inc, markets a line of brightly colored casual clothing through a chain of boutiques named Pastelton. The Pastelton logo uses a similar typeface as Benetton, including the distinctive "t" that only has a right branch. Benetton claims the government regulations do not protect it from this type of trademark infringement. In the famous Itaewon shopping district of Seoul, the South Korean capital, stores are well stocked and openly sell products with the trademarks and logos of famous designer items such as Louis Vuitton bags, Reebok shoes, Polo shirts and Rolex watches. Similarly, Pizza Heart, a Korean restaurant chain competes against PepsiCo's Pizza Hut franchise, and Bory soap and Juicy Fresh gum are found on store shelves next to Proctor and Gamble's Ivory brand and Wrigley's Juicy Fruit label gum. In 1989 the Ministry of Trade and Industry dismissed a suit filed by Yoshida of Japan (better known as YKK) regarding the approval of the Korea Property Office

South Korean Royalty Receipts and Payments, 1972–87
(W millions)

Year	Payments	Receipts
1972	4,032	—
1973	4,577	—
1974	7,124	—
1975	12,845	—
1976	14,725	—
1977	28,099	—
1978	41,172	145
1979	45,464	920
1980	65,136	3,945
1981	72,941	8,036
1982	84,578	13,306
1983	115,982	14,662
1984	171,860	13,540
1985	257,083	9,831
1986	362,276	10,294
1987	430,800	7,945

SOURCES: Ministry of Science and Technology; Korea Industrial Promotion Association.

for Korea Zipper to use the YKK trademark. The ministry ruled that the Property Office was correct in its approval, as Yoshida had not been active in its supply of raw materials and technical assistance to Korea Zipper since 1980.

Korea's former copyright law, which had not been amended since its enactment in 1957, provided protection only for domestic copyright owners. A foreign writer had no legal basis under this law to prevent outright copying of his work. This changed in 1987, when South Korea joined the Universal Copyright Convention and amended its own copyright law. Now all works covered by the convention, whether authored or published in South Korea or abroad, are legally protected against unauthorized reproduction, translation and distribution. The amended law protects works authored by individuals for a term of life plus 50 years, as is the case in other countries that are members of the convention. Works authored by juridical entities, such as corporations, are protected for a period of 50 years from the time of their first publication in the country of origin. Sound recordings also receive protection in conformity with international standards, as the term of protection is extended to 20 years and requires local manufacturers to obtain permission in the form of licensing contracts with foreign copyright owners for domestic reproduction. The definitions and scope of "fair use" of copyrights for public purposes have been clarified and limited to such noncommercial purposes as education and government administration.

Foreign companies have been quick to put the amended copyright laws to the test. Hoffman-LaRoche, the Swiss pharmaceuticals group, successfully blocked an allegedly pirated product by convincing South Korean authorities that documentation used by the local company to win approval to sell the drug constituted a violation of its copyright. But not all the cases have been so clear cut and favorable to the foreign copyright holder. Shortly after the copyright law was amended, the Economic Planning Board (EPB) released guidelines entitled the "Scope and Criteria of Unfair Trade Practices in International Agreements." The purpose of these guidelines was to give notice to the kinds of terms and conditions that the EPB would not accept when reviewing international agreements. Specifically mentioned were copyright license agreements, as this was considered to be a rather new and uncharted area of international trade for South Korea. The government's plan is to develop experience with copyright licenses in the context of international trade, and the guideline was an alert for both licensor and licensee that the allowable parameters were not yet solidly set.

Taking a proactive approach to another area of intellectual-property protection, South Korea enacted a separate Computer Program Protection Act (CPPA) in 1987. Prior to the enactment of the CPPA there was some controversy about the methods then available to protect computer programs in South Korea. This had been handled by the Copyright Act, the Patent Act and the trade-secret clauses in commercial contract law. Under the CPPA, the term "computer program" refers to a series of commands to be employed directly or indirectly in a computer to obtain a specific result. A computer program created by a foreigner that meets the requirements of the Universal Copyright Convention is entitled to legal protection in South Korea under the CPPA. Computer programs are therefore protected under the same basic principles as other literary works, including term of protection and compulsory licensing provisions.

Since the major changes to the Patent Act and Copyright Act in 1987, the Office of Patents Administration (OPA) has continued to strengthen the legislation regarding property protection. In 1989 the OPA announced revisions to the Designs Law, covering industrial designs, graphic and industrial art, and product designs. In 1990 new legislation was enacted to protect designs for semiconductor-chip circuits in response to mounting US pressure and the threat of the Section 301 trade statute. These newer laws, a result of bilateral negotiations between the US and South Korea, have not gone down well with South Korea's other major trading partners, notably the European Community and Japan. The EC was quick to end special tariff benefits on imports from South Korea in 1988 following the retroactive patent protection given to US pharmaceuticals companies, as mentioned above. Claims that local companies have changed their concentration to copying Japanese and European products after signing bilateral agreements with the US regarding intellectual-property protection have tarnished the efforts the government has made to improve its property-rights program.

To address this problem and demonstrate the government's unequivocal commitment to intellectual-property protection, President Roh created a permanent interagency Task Force at the end of 1988. All issues of intellectual-property-rights protection fall under the jurisdiction of this task force, and all foreign enquiries can be made directly to this group. Foreign companies have responded favorably to the measures taken by the government, including the new legislation and the stricter enforcement measures. The number of applications to register intellectual-property rights—particularly for trademarks—made by foreigners has grown substantially.

Legislation

The principal government document that spells out the legal and administrative guidelines for licensing in South Korea is the Foreign Capital Inducement Act (FCIA), which was created in 1966 and last amended in 1983. The enforcement decrees and working rules for the FCIA have been updated more frequently, having been amended nine times since 1985, with the most recent revisions becoming effective Jan. 1, 1990. Licensing is specifically defined in the FCIA as a technology-inducement contract, in which a national or juridical person of the Republic of Korea purchases property rights or other technology (i.e. know-how) from a foreign national. Implicit in the definition is the concept of royalty payments for the transferred technology. In theory the approval process for a technology-inducement contract, or license, is fairly straightforward: A report of the license and any requested supplemental material is submitted to the Ministry of Finance at the time of execution. Approval is considered automatic after 20 days unless the ministry orders modifications. An approved report becomes effective within six months of its acceptance, but if it is not used within the six months it is considered null and void (unless an extension has been approved by the ministry). Technology supplied to a joint venture as part of the foreign partner's contribution to the investment does not need this separate approval if the technology is specified in the overall joint-venture arrangement.

In practice, however, the review and approval of a technology license that is longer than three years and includes a royalty greater than $100,000 is a much more detailed process. The license will be reviewed by the relevant ministry of the industry involved, and be checked for term, amount of royalty, and the contents and method for transfer of the technology. Licenses regarding low-quality or obsolete technology and those that restrict exports are likely to be rejected directly. Contracts that are deemed to lead to excessive competition among domestic producers or present too great a challenge to Korean technology are also officially discouraged. If there is any uncertainty regarding the proposed technology transfer, the agreement is sent to the Foreign Capital Project Review Committee for further deliberation. Specific conditions that prompt a review from this committee include the following:

- when a project has connections to more than one ministry and agreement cannot be reached between them;
- when the technology is deemed to have serious impact on the national economy; and
- when the relevant minister decides that a review by the committee is necessary.

In addition to the circumstances listed above, the following stipulations are considered "restraint of trade" under South Korea's Antimonopoly Law: (1) requirements that the licensee purchase basic parts or raw materials from the licensor or from suppliers designated by the licensor; (2) territorial restrictions on sales of products containing the licensed technology, except where the licensor already has a patent, is engaged in normal sales activity, or has granted exclusive rights to a third party; (3) limits on the use of sales agents, or the volume or price (including resale price) for items produced by the licensee; (4) clauses preventing the licensee from handling competitive products or using competitive technology; (5) unilateral royalty impositions that are not explicitly provided for in the contract; and (6) obligations on the part of the licensee to pay for promotional expenses set by the licensor. For copyright contracts, restricting the handling of similar publications after the expiration or termination of the contract is also considered restraint of trade.

Overseas remittances of royalties to be paid under a technology-inducement contract are guaranteed under the FCIA, in accordance with the approved contract terms. While no formal guideline sets the limits for royalty payments, a local licensee must justify royalty fees above a running rate of 2-3% of net sales. Recent royalty contracts indicate that this does not appear to be a hindrance to approvals:

- Hyundai Motor Co paid Y160 million in a lump sum, plus Y10,000 per vehicle for technical information from Mitsubishi Motors.
- Korea-Pacific Chemical Co paid $5.8 million, plus 3.9% of net sales to Union Carbide for technical services and data transfer.
- Yukong Ltd made a down payment of $4.66 million to Institut Francais du Petrol (France) for 10 years of production technology.

The Ministry of Trade and Industry also acts on an industry-by-industry basis when considering royalty contracts. In 1989 it ruled that a royalty rate around 7% of sales was too high for domestic personal computer producers to pay for technology, and cited the high level of royalties as the main reason smaller companies that could not afford to pay for the software resorted to illegal copying. MTI also stated in this ruling that six Korean firms that held property rights for hardware from IBM were only paying 1-3% of sales in royalties, an apparently acceptable level.

Tax Consequences

Prior to 1988 all foreign-technology suppliers were eligible for a five-year exemption from both income and corporate taxes in South Korea. The tax exemption was changed in March 1988, and the Ministry of Finance now only accepts applications for the five-year exemption if the license is in one of seven high-technology industries: machinery, electronics, aerospace, defense, precision chemistry, biotechnology and new materials.

Royalties associated with technology transfer now receive special scrutiny from the Office of National Tax Administration (ONTA) in South Korea. To eliminate deals that provide for disguised royalty payments, or double payments in the form of raw-material mark-ups, ONTA checks the terms and conditions of the formal contracts approved under the FCIA. ONTA may also confirm that data, designs and formulas have actually been provided from the licensor, and compare the licensee's import prices with ordinary procurement costs of similar materials. Foreign technicians' costs, such as travel and living expenses, must be covered by the royalty fees and not by separate payments.

Technology transfers between a foreign parent and its Korean subsidiary do not escape review by ONTA. Transfer prices are tested for legitimacy, and the technology received is expected to contribute to the subsidiary's business performance, including sales growth and profits. ONTA also determines whether the licensing arrangements are subject to export obligations, and reports failures to meet export commitments to the proper ministry. The regulations currently state that exports must be 50% higher than the imported raw materials, but this may be withdrawn by the Ministry of Finance in cases of high-tech agreements or those that cause trade friction. Regarding other tax concessions and related exemptions, ONTA makes the final determination that all requirements of licensor and licensee under the FCIA application are being met.

The Road Ahead

The basic conditions of South Korea's current policy and restrictions regarding licensing, including technology requirements, royalty terms and tax considerations, are part of the government's five-year program for industrial development. The country's economic goals for the 1990s include a continued emphasis on industrial development and growth, as South Korea hopes to join the ranks of the OECD by 1993.

Since 1987 the country has made great progress in improving the local business climate for foreign investment and technology transfer, highlighted by the laws and regulations discussed above. Under pressure from its major trading partners, particularly the US, South Korea has begun to ease restrictions on imports, opened more industries to investment from foreigners, and improved measures to protect intellectual-property rights. But in the process of learning to play by international rules, South Korea has learned that it cannot solve its problems by only signing bilateral agreements; it needs to enact laws and stick to national programs that make the playing field even for all foreign investors and the diversity of technology they offer to the country.

As the South Korean economy continues to grow and the industrialization goals for the 1990s are met, the government will need to take measures to diversify its sources for exports, and satisfy more than the US and Japan in trade and technical agreements. This will involve expanded measures to open markets and establish trade relations with the European Community, Eastern Europe, the Soviet Union and even the People's Republic of China. To this end, the actions taken by the government in the last three years to join various international conventions on trade and property-rights protection have been significant. In the longer term these actions should help strengthen local industries as well as improve the climate for further foreign investment in technology and industry. As a sourcing site for world trade, a growing domestic market in its own right, and a potential competitor among the major industrialized nations, South Korea should continue to be one of the important economies of both Asia and the world over the next decade.

7
Taiwan

In recent years, changes in the political, economic and legal structure of the Republic of China (Taiwan) have resulted in new opportunities in licensing. Factors underlying the enhanced licensing environment include improved protection for intellectual property; relaxation of foreign exchange controls; increased spending power of consumers, industry and government; and a growing recognition of the importance of technology for Taiwan's transition from a mainly offshore manufacturing site to an industrial power with an indigenous technology base.

The ongoing trade talks with the US are also a major factor. By law, the US is required to identify, and in some cases retaliate against, trade partners that do not adequately and effectively protect the intellectual-property rights of US individuals and businesses. Many of the recent licensing developments in Taiwan—such as the passage and enforcement of intellectual-property legislation—follow aggressive lobbying efforts by US industry (via the US Trade Representative) to pressure Taiwan to provide better protection of intellectual-property rights.

Licensing in Taiwan may take place within or without a government-regulated setting. The elements that will determine which setting is chosen include the subject matter of the license agreement, the parties involved, the form and method of compensation, and the tax consequences.

A typical licensing transaction in Taiwan involves no more than a grant of the right to use an older technology that happens to be under patent in a country to which an ROC (Republic of China) company exports. No actual transfer of technology takes place, and the offshore payment of royalties can be arranged. The transaction would then take place without the need to secure government approval or other government involvement. A large-scale investment, however, may include several license agreements concerning technical cooperation, capitalization of patents and know-how, and trademarks, all of which may be subject to extensive regulations and require government approval.

The advantages to licensing in Taiwan can include better market penetration, control of infringement by allocating resources to licensed competitors (rather than undertaking the expense and uncertainty of litigation), trademark protection, and tax benefits for both the licensee and licensor. Foreign licensors may use licensing at the same time as other forms of business presence, such as direct distribution.

The ROC government actively promotes technology by means of tax incentives and by having its trade offices abroad locate and facilitate the transfer of new technologies. Furthermore, various government agencies may either directly assist foreign owners of intellectual property in licensing their technology to local companies or may act indirectly by providing "advice" to trade associations.

The agency in charge of administration of the Copyright Law is the Copyright Committee of the Ministry of the Interior. Appeals of the ministry's decision are made to the Executive Yuan, and, as with patent and trademark matters, the Administrative Court of the Judicial Yuan is the tribunal of last resort in administrative matters. The Copyright Office appears to be somewhat more progressive than its counterpart in patents and trademarks. Public hearings concerning proposed copyright legislation have been held on several occasions.

Except for nationals of the US, foreign authors must register their works to enjoy copyright protection. Registration of works by foreigners is only allowed, however, when the work is first published in the ROC or where ROC nationals are accorded protection in the country of the nation seeking protection in the ROC. Only nationals of the UK, and in some cases Spain, enjoy protection upon registration. No protection is available to foreign authors, including US authors, for translations of their literary works.

Injunctions and damages are available in civil suits, but criminal actions are more prevalent. Prison terms range from six months to five years; fines, from NT$15,000 to NT$150,000. As with patents, criminal actions for copyright infringement can only be brought upon complaint of the injured party. In practice, criminal charges are often filed in an attempt to induce the counterparty to settle quickly.

In July 1989 Taiwan initialed a bilateral copyright agreement with the US. Earlier in the year the parties signed an agreement concerning audio-visual works. Taiwan also began a comprehensive revision of its Copyright Law last year. The third version of the draft revision was completed just before the March 1990 trade talks between the ROC and the US. While further changes are anticipated before the law goes to the legislature, the new law will ultimately include new or revised articles in the areas of neighboring rights (rights of performers, producers and broadcasting organizations), moral rights, term of protection, limitations on rights, compulsory licenses, and translation rights.

There are currently no provisions in the Copyright Law for voluntary licensing. There are provisions for compulsory licensing of sound recordings. Copyrights may also be licensed within the framework of an investment or technical-cooperation agreement (see below) under the rubric of "know-how."

Technical-Cooperation Agreements

When licensing is mentioned in the ROC in the context of an international transaction, the Statute for Technical Cooperation (STC) comes to mind. The STC refers to the licensor as the "technician" and the licensee as the "Cooperator." Technical cooperation is defined as the transfer of patented (ROC) technology or "know-how" from a foreign or overseas Chinese person to a local natural or juristic person or government entity. Local juristic persons may include wholly owned ROC subsidiaries of the licensor.

With the relaxation of foreign exchange controls, however, one of the primary reasons for licensing under the STC has disappeared. Nevertheless, when licensing know-how (as mentioned above), it may still be necessary to license under the STC when trademarks are involved. In some circumstances, there are tax advantages to licensing under the STC as well.

Other practical considerations when licensing under the STC include the following:

Disclosure of other licenses. The law requires the licensor to provide copies of agreements concerning the licensed subject matter that have been entered into with parties in other countries. The Investment Commission—the agency in charge of handling applications filed under the STC—no longer requires this.

Royalties. As of 1987, the amount of royalties to be paid under the agreement is not to be a factor in approving or withholding approval of an application.

Arbitration. The law states that parties shall submit disputes to arbitration. Arbitration clauses, however, are not required by the Investment Commission.

The Investment Commission may require the parties to amend provisions that require minimum amounts of royalties, tying arrangements, terms in excess of five years, or limitations on the market of products manufactured under the license.

Technical-Cooperation Agreements

Country	Number	% of total
Japan	1,996	62.0
USA	729	22.6
Europe	410	12.7
Other	87	2.7
Industry	**Number**	**% of total**
Electronics	885	27.5
Chemicals	658	20.4
Machinery*	427	13.3
Basic Metals	370	11.5
Other	882	27.4

*Includes instruments.

Intellectual-Property Laws

The ROC recognizes the traditional forms of intellectual property: patents, trademarks and copyrights. The IPR situation in Taiwan is improving, steadily but very slowly. Following (and in anticipation of further) negotiations with the US, Taiwan government officials periodically reexamine the patent and copyright laws, but so far have made only minor adjustments. In both the short and medium term, intellectual property protection will remain a troublesome area.

Still pending in late 1991 were revisions to the Patent Law, which should extend the time inventors have in which to register their patents, lengthen protection periods, reduce delays in the appeals process and amend compulsory-use regulations. The government has promised to introduce new legislation, including the right of priority and patent protection of microorganisms.

In December 1990, the cabinet drafted revisions to the Copyright Law that would extend protection for foreign works. The amendments enshrine respect for international codes and agreements, reciprocal protection for local and foreign works and compulsory licensing of translations. Protection will be for the life of the author plus 50 years, and fines for violations will be sharply increased. Jail sentences for repeated or large-scale offenders range up to seven years. In September 1991 draft Trademark Law amendments went before the Yuan, and a draft design law was also pending.

Other recent legislative and judicial developments may provide indirect protection for foreign licensors. The Fair Trade Law, which took effect in February 1992, provides indirect protection of trademarks under a clause prohibiting "unfair competition." For the first time, a Taiwan court enforced a US District Court's decision against a Taiwanese company in 1991.

A major ongoing obstacle is the lack of a central body to coordinate IPR policy, legislation and enforcement. Under the present system, the National Bureau of Standards handles patent and trademark registration; the Ministry of the Interior has an anti-piracy task force and a Copyright Committee; the Ministry of Economic Affairs (MOEA) prescribes enforcement rules for the Patent Law, and has an anti-counterfeiting task force; the Government Information Office is active in issues such as illegal rental and broadcast of videotapes; the Board of Foreign Trade negotiates with Washington over Super 301 sanctions related to piracy and legislative reforms; the Judicial Yuan has a special IPR court; and the Ministry of Justice is responsible for prosecution. While the implementation of cabinet-level office to coordinate and control policy research and implementation has been proposed, no action has been taken.

Patents and Trademarks

The original version of the Patent Law currently in use became effective in 1949. Since that time it has been amended or revised five times. The last major revision occurred in 1986, when chemical-product patents (as opposed to the previous limitation of process patents) were added to the list of patentable subject matter.

The original version of the current trademark law became effective in 1933 and was last amended in May 1989. The most significant aspects of the May 1989 amendments are the addition of a "proof of use" requirement and the provision for confiscation of counterfeit products regardless of ownership.

The authority in charge of the administration of patent and trademark matters is the National Bureau of Standards (NBS), an agency under the Ministry of Economic Affairs.

Although the Patent Law calls for the establishment of an independent patent agency, these plans have not been implemented. This structural problem is something of an impediment to effective administration of patent matters. The patent office is thought to be understaffed, resulting in an "outside examiner" system whereby persons not regularly employed by the NBS are retained to examine patent applications. Although these examiners are in principle to be selected from noncommercial enterprises such as schools or public research institutions, many have connections with private industry, which increases the chances of breaches of confidentiality, and may in some cases even have an impact on the decision regarding patentability of the subject matter.

Dispositions of patent and trademark matters by the NBS may be contested by appeal to the Ministry of Economic Affairs, reappeal to the Executive Yuan, or, as a last resort, by filing an administrative lawsuit with the Administrative Court of the Judicial Yuan.

Use of local agents

Applications for patents owned by non-ROC nationals must be filed by a local patent agent. Several categories of persons may qualify as patent agents. Engineers may qualify through examination; no formal legal training is required. There are also a number of "back doors" open to qualifying as a patent agent. Lawyers and accountants, for example, may qualify automatically as patent agents with no examination and no demonstration of technical expertise. Retired patent examiners may also qualify as patent agents, again with no requirement of formal legal training.

Trademark applications can be filed by any person resident in Taiwan. Many local companies do all of their administrative trademark work in-house. Foreign companies tend to use law firms or other companies specializing in patents and trademarks. Laws governing the qualification and duties of patent agents currently before the legislature would require patent agents to be trained in both legal and technical aspects of patent practice. The May 1989 Trademark Law amendments provide that only registered trademark agents may prosecute applications and related matters.

Subject matter

Three kinds of patents are recognized under the Patent Law: inventions, new utility models and new designs. Generally speaking, inventions and new utility models are of the same nature and roughly correspond to the "utility model" patent specified in the Paris Convention. New designs broadly correspond to the design patents in the US.

Three types of trademarks are recognized by Taiwan law: principal, associated and defensive. Designs, words, drawings and symbols, as well as the name of the mark, may be registered provided they are distinctive and do not fall within one of the 13 categories of unregistrable subject matter. Service marks are also registrable. There is currently no provisions for collective or certification marks, although the NBS is considering adding these to a future revision of the Trademark Law. The doctrine of secondary meaning and the importance of consumer identification with trademarks—familiar to trademark lawyers in the US—are relatively unimportant in the NBS examination practice. Complaints from foreign registrants upon rejection of an application often arise from the failure to appreciate the requirement under ROC Trademark Law that a mark be distinctive to be registrable.

Foreign nationals—both corporate and individual—may apply for trademarks and patents in the ROC where their country grants reciprocal rights to ROC nationals. In 1989, nationals from 38 foreign countries were granted ROC patents.

Application and issue

Patent applications generally take 12–15 months for disposition; trademarks take two to four months. The patent or mark is published in the *Patent Gazette* and *Trademark Gazette* respectively. Publication marks the commencement of a three-month period during which an interested party may file an opposition.

Prior to the disposition of an application, the NBS may issue an "office action." In patent-of-invention cases the letter issued by the bureau frequently suggests amendment of the application, which is often an indication that the patent will be granted only if it is "downgraded" to a new-utility-model application. Rather than risk rejection and the cumbersome appeals process that ensues, patent agents frequently suggest acceptance of the downgrade despite the fact that new utility models have a shorter period of protection and contain lighter penalties for infringement.

During the period 1951–89 a total of 314,645 patent applications were handled by the ROC patent office. Of this amount, just over one third, or 109,322, were filed by foreigners. In 1989 a total of 32,103 patent applications were filed, 2,592 more than the previous year. Of these, 14,186, or roughly 44%, were filed by foreigners. The top three foreign countries were Japan, with 3,860 applications, the US, with 2,577, and West Germany, with 452.

The number of approved trademark applications grew at a fairly steady rate, from 1,897 in 1955 to 9,406 in 1977. The figure jumped by more than two thirds, to 15,977, in 1978. The number of approved trademarks in 1989 was 45,838, or 79.6% of all applications.

Agent's or attorney's fees vary depending on the length of the specification and claims. The major expense is for translation. Total application costs generally range between NT$20,000 and NT$60,000. Companies are advised to spend a little extra on monitoring translations. Errors in translation are common, even in applications filed by large, established firms, and although the NBS has copies of the original foreign specification, they are under no obligation to review anything but the translated version.

Working/use

Patents that are not "worked" in Taiwan may be subject to compulsory licenses, or in some cases to cancellation. As a practical matter, these measures are rarely taken; still, the presence of compulsory-license provisions in the Patent Law is one of the major concerns of foreign companies with patents (see below).

Registration for a mark will be canceled if the mark is not used for a continuous period of two years. Advertisement of the product or service covered by the mark or use of the mark on exported products is considered use for these purposes.

Infringement

The Patent Law and Trademark Law provide civil and criminal remedies for infringement. Criminal suits are much more common due to the difficulty of proving damages and the lack of adequate discovery procedures available to plaintiffs in civil actions.

Criminal charges in patent cases can only be brought upon complaint of the injured party. In trademark cases, the prosecutor may bring the suit with or without the injured party's participation. Foreign persons may bring patent or trademark infringement actions regardless of their lack of a formal presence in the ROC.

As part of its effort to demonstrate improvements in protection of intellectual-property rights, the ROC government regularly prepares statistics on enforcement measures.

Trademark licensing

Trademark licensing is subject to several restrictions under the Trademark Law:

- The licensed use must be under the strict supervision and control of the owner of the trademark;
- the license must be necessary for the ROC's economic development;
- the license must be approved by the NBS; and
- the licensee must indicate the fact of the license when using the trademarks.

Trademarks owned by foreign nationals must comply with an additional set of regulations in order to obtain NBS approval when being licensed in the ROC. These regulations are known as the Criteria Governing the Licensing of Trademarks Owned by Foreign Enterprises. Under the criteria, licenses may be approved by the NBS when the competent investment authority, the Investment Commission of the Ministry of Economic Affairs (MOEA), has previously approved either (1) a technical-cooperation agreement to which the trademark owner is a party or (2) a foreign investment application whereby the foreign owner of the ROC-registered trademark, its parent or subsidiary, establishes an ROC subsidiary or obtains at least 20% equity in an ROC company.

Art. 5 of the criteria also provides for licensing when the trademarked goods are of superior quality, have an international market and where the production of the goods is under the supervision and control of the trademark owner such that the licensed goods are of identical quality to the goods produced by the licensor. After many years of enforcing stricter standards in Taiwan, the current trend is to approve license applications based on this provision.

A trademark-license application takes two to four months for approval. In 1989, 2,462 trademark licenses were approved by the NBS.

Royalty rates for trademark licenses are set by the NBS and are generally limited to 1% of gross sales.

Patent licensing

Patent rights can be licensed through capitalization in a so-called foreign investment application. The amount of capitalization cannot exceed 20% of the paid-in capital of the invested enterprise. The patent must be registered in the ROC to qualify under this provision.

Patents can also be licensed under a technical-cooperation agreement. Again, "patent" here refers to a patent registered in the ROC.

Patent licenses must be registered with the NBS within three months to be effective against third parties. In 1989, 134 patent licenses were registered in Taiwan.

Agreements for licensing invention and new utility-model patents may be null and void if tying provisions or excessive royalties are included in the agreement.

Know-how may be licensed in a similar manner as patents, except that the valuation may not exceed 15% of the paid-in capital. Know-how is also specified as licensable subject matter in the Statute for Technical Cooperation. Unexpired foreign patents and copyrights may constitute know-how.

Pressure for Change

Foreign companies, individually and through organizations such as the Pharmaceuticals Committee of the ROC American Chamber of Commerce, have led a sustained lobbying effort, both in the US and the ROC, to revise the Patent Law. Pressure is applied through frequent meetings with, and letters to, local patent and trade officials, the United States Trade Representative and other international bodies. The Pharmaceuticals Committee is one of the most active in the American Chamber of Commerce in Taiwan. Its efforts are credited in part for having chemical product patents included in the 1986 amendments to the Patent Law.

The main areas of current concern are as follows.

Burden-of-proof responsibilities. Under the current law, persons that sell products for which a patented process is outstanding in the ROC bear the burden of proving that their product was not made with the patented process. This burden of proof does not apply, however, when the product is imported and the importer can show the identity of the manufacturer and supplier. Critics assert that this restriction unfairly protects local industries and does not agree with international practice.

Term of protection. The pharmaceuticals industry is lobbying for a longer term of protection on pharmaceuticals due to the long interim period between the filing date of a patent application and the date on which the product makes it to the market.

Compulsory licenses. Economies of scale do not permit the local manufacture of many patented products. Foreign companies would like to see the compulsory licensing system abolished, or at least modified to include in the definition of "working" the "import and sale of a patented product in an amount sufficient to meet the ROC's needs."

Subject matter. With the growth of biotechnology industries, pressure is mounting for deletion of "microorganisms" from unpatentable subject matter under the current law.

Interpretation of claims. Current practice is to limit the grant of a patent to products for which actual working examples are provided. For reasons of time and expense, this is untenable in most patent cases, and applicants are often forced to reduce the scope of their claims.

Interviews. Although the possibility for application interviews exists by law, they are rarely granted. Many applicants are of the opinion that a system granting regular interviews could improve the overall performance and effectiveness of examiners.

Copyrights

The Copyright Law was first enacted in 1928. It has been revised or amended five times since, including the most recent comprehensive revision of 1985. Key points of the 1985 revisions include specific protection for computer programs, the abolition of registration as a condition of copyright and the introduction of a "leasing" right.

Three articles were amended and one was added in January 1990. These amendments primarily affect the rights in audio-visual works owned by the US motion picture industry.

Registration is no longer required as a condition for protection or as a prerequisite to filing an infringement action. It is still recommended, though, to facilitate police action in infringement cases.

The number of copyright registrations has grown dramatically in recent years. The percentage of copyright registration applications filed by foreigners, however, is far lower than the corresponding figures for patents and trademarks. In 1989, a total of 12,938 applications were filed; 11,983 were approved. Of the approved registrations, 704, or just under 6%, were for works of foreign authors.

Enforcement of Intellectual Property Rights

The legislation on civil and criminal sanctions for infringement of intellectual-property rights is generally considered to be adequate; the problem is enforcement. Complaints and even news reports of the occurrence of "leaks" from the police in advance of anticounterfeiting actions are common. There are also complaints that judges, police and prosecutors are insufficiently trained in intellectual-property concepts and lack appreciation of the value of such property. This lack of understanding and resolve, the argument goes, is then reflected in the lax approach to investigation and prosecution of alleged infringements.

Most incarcerations for criminal infringement are for periods of six months or less. In the vast majority of these sentences the defendant may convert the sentence to a fine by paying a nominal penalty fee.

Recent educational campaigns have been launched to help correct these inadequacies. The judiciary and prosecutors' offices frequently circulate memos instructing police, prosecutors and judges to take a more aggressive position on intellectual-property matters; enforcement statistics are published regularly, and the curriculum of law schools, police and judicial training now includes coursework on intellectual property. Publicity campaigns have also been undertaken through the mass media to educate the public on the importance of intellectual-property protection.

In defense of Taiwan's record on improving the environment for protection of intellectual property, various agencies within the government cite cases of foreign companies that lack the commitment to carry out a

Intellectual Property Laws

Conventions. None.
Basic laws. Patent Act last amended December 1986; Enforcement Rules 1947-87; Trademark Law last amended May 1989; Copyright Law last amended January 1990.

Patents
Types and duration. Patents of invention, 15 years from publication date or 18 years from application date, whichever comes first; patents of addition, valid for the remaining (unexpired) term of the main patent (of invention); utility models, 10 years from publication date or 12 years from application date, whichever comes first; new design patents, five years from publication date or six years from application date, whichever comes first; associated patents, valid for the original term of the main (new design) patent.
Novelty requirement. Not published anywhere in the world; no public use in the ROC. Publication or public use for research or for display at government-recognized exhibitions excepted from the novelty requirement if an application is filed within six months. Not a novelty if product has been manufactured for any reason other than experimental purposes.
Unpatentable items. Foods, drinks, habit-forming substances; plants, animals, microorganisms; diagnostic, curative and surgical methods; scientific principles; items harmful to public order, morals or health; and models of a shape identical or similar to that of the ruling Nationalist party, national or military flags, the national emblem or any government medal.
Application procedure. Foreign applicants must apply for a patent through an authorized ROC patent agent. Applications are filed with the Patent Office in the National Bureau of Standards, Ministry of Economic Affairs. Foreign applications must include the following (all in Chinese): petition, stating full particulars of patent and inventor; power of attorney, signed by applicant; oath, signed by inventor, legalized certificate of applicant's nationality, in duplicate; specification, in triplicate, describing nature, object and usefulness of invention (plus construction and manner of use, for mechanical inventions and for chemical inventions, details specified above) and ending in one or more claims; drawings, in triplicate; and filing fees.

A model or specimen may be required. Power of attorney and specification must be filed with application; other documents may be filed at a later date.

Examination procedure. Examination as to value of productive utilization; there may be an examination as to novelty. Applicants must defend themselves within specified period or the application will be canceled. When patent is published, opposition has three months to file protest with Patent Office.

An invention must have industrial value in order to be patented. It must be both practically workable and developed to the point of being utilized industrially. Items in the research and development stage are granted an automatic six-month grace period from the date the article is first published or working.

Compulsory licensing. A patent must be worked within four years of the date of grant to avoid the possibility of compulsory licensing or revocation.

Fees. Application for invention NT$1,500; addition, NT$1,200; utility model, NT$1,200; new design, NT$2,100; associated design, NT$2,100; opposition, NT$1,500. Annual fees, NT$900 for first three years; NT$1,800 for fourth through sixth years; NT$2,700 for seventh through ninth years; NT$3,600 for 10th through 12th years; and NT$4,500 for years 13 through 15.

Trademarks

Duration. Ten years from date of registration, renewable for additional periods of 10 years.

Legal effect. Rights based on first registration (not use); rights may be canceled if mark is not used within two years of registration or if use is discontinued for two years or more.

Registrable. Distinctive words, drawings, symbols or combinations thereof; service marks.

Application procedure. A separate application is necessary for each group of goods (there are 95 classes) and services (12 classes); application must be made by a resident of Taiwan. Documents required include application (similar to that for patents) stating date or expected date of first use in Taiwan, power of attorney, certificate of nationality stating type of business and its objects, and 18 specimens and a printing plate of the mark.

Fees. Application, NT$2,700; opposition, NT$1,500; renewal, NT$2,700; authorization, NT$1,500; examination, NT$2,100.

(Continued)

Industrial designs and models
Coverage is available for 10 years on industrial models and five years on designs. No separate legislation applies; industrial designs and models are primarily covered in patent law under "new design."

Copyrights
Duration. Individual authorship of audio-visual works, photographs, compilations, translations and computer programs are protected for 30 years; other works are protected for the life of the author. Works authored by juristic entities are protected for 30 years.
Subject matter. Categories covered by the copyright law include literary works, oral works, translations of literary works, translations of oral works, compilations, artistic works, pictorial works, musical works, motion pictures, sound recordings, video tapes, photographic works, lectures, computer programs, maps, and technical and engineering drawings.
Legal effect. Ten rights are specified under the law: reproduction, compilation, translation (ROC authored works only), lease, adaptation, public recitation, public broadcasting, public presentation, public performance and public display.
Registrable. Original works.
Application procedure. Applications must be filed with the Copyright Office of the Ministry of the Interior. Two copies must be deposited, and a power-of-attorney statement and certificate of corporate good standing or nationality papers must be filed.
Fees. Official fees vary with subject matter: literary works range from NT$600 to NT$3,600, depending on the retail price of the work; pictorial works run NT$600-1,200; scientific or engineering design drawings are NT$6,000; sound recordings, NT$600 to NT$1,200; and motion pictures and videos, NT$1,200.

consistent registration and enforcement program for their intellectual property; of local lawyers or patent agents who are too quick to place the blame on government agencies; and of deal-making between plaintiff and defendant that leaves the police or prosecutors feeling that their efforts are in vain.

Enforcement is also a major topic in the regularly scheduled trade talks between Taiwan and the US. With the specter of a Super 301 action hanging over Taiwan, the ROC will continue to give additional attention to the US in the area of enforcement. Some of the key industries in the US that are affected by lack of enforcement in Taiwan are computer software and distributors for the major US film producers.

Legal Matters

The concept of the rule of law is not well established in the ROC. Until very recently the judicial branch was viewed as an arm of the executive, which is controlled in turn by the ruling party.

The legislature has also been viewed as an agency that merely rubber-stamps laws and policies put forward by the executive. Opinion polls regularly show low public esteem for judges and prosecutors, and several major scandals involving alleged corruption of judicial officials have dealt further blows to public confidence in the judiciary. Political considerations and bribes affecting the outcomes of court decisions are not unusual.

There are fewer than 3,000 lawyers who are admitted to the local bar in Taiwan. Many partners in the major firms have not been admitted to practice law in the ROC. The bar examination is extremely competitive and generally only 10-20 out of more than 2,000 candidates are successful each year. The 1989 examination was an exception: More than 280 persons passed.

Problems faced by companies such as breach of confidence, theft of trade secrets or unauthorized use of customer lists, etc., by employees derive at least in part from this lack of a strong legal tradition.

International Conventions

Since its withdrawal from the United Nations in 1971, Taiwan's participation in international organizations has been fairly minimal. To some extent, this trend is beginning to reverse itself now, with the ROC's formal application to rejoin the General Agreement on Tariffs and Trade on Jan. 1, 1990. Resistance to Taiwan's GATT application from mainland China as well as other political factors are expected to delay the entry into for several years, though.

Taiwan is not a member of WIPO, the Berne or Paris Unions, or any other international treaty for the protection of intellectual property. In addition to bilateral agreements on audiovisual works and copyrights, the US and Taiwan are discussing a bilateral agreement on industrial property. Taiwan has recently publicized its interest in entering into more such bilateral agreements, particularly with European nations.

Licensing Outside the System

Notwithstanding the licensing formalities described above, a substantial amount of licensing occurs outside the parameters of government-sanctioned licenses. With the relaxation of exchange controls, a business or individual may remit royalty payments up to US$5 million annually. Many local companies now have offshore operations from which royalty payments to licensors may be made. In many licensing situations these factors render the STC superfluous. Important exceptions are trademark and tax considerations. It should also be kept in mind that the environment, although drastically liberalized over the past three years, could easily revert to the days of strict foreign exchange controls and other restrictions affecting licensing. For licensing arrangements that involve long-term commitments, therefore, it is advisable to license under the STC for in-bound transactions.

When parties to licenses arranged under the STC encounter resistance to their terms from the Investment Commission, they often enter into side agreements intended to supersede the official accord on file with the Investment Commission. No cases have been reported as to whether and under what circumstances such a side agreement would withstand a legal challenge.

The government agencies handling foreign-investment-related licensing and technical cooperations are straightforward in their approach. Personnel within the Investment Commission are accessible and responsive. Because the agency's mandate is to promote foreign investment it is more adept at dealing with foreign businesses than may be the case with the other agencies handling licensing agreements.

Practical Matters

Royalty payments can be made in any way agreed upon by the parties involved. If the remittance is made from Taiwan, or if receipts are issued in the ROC, there are tax consequences to consider. When royalties are to be paid on a continuing basis, the parties may agree that payment shall accompany or be made within *x* number of days of, for example, the quarterly or monthly report. Payment by wire transfer is convenient and popular.

The local labor force is well educated, highly skilled and competent enough to participate actively in technology transfer. Large numbers of middle- and senior-level engineers have received advanced training abroad or worked for major international companies.

No technology per se is off limits; however, there are industries in which foreign investment is prohibited or restricted. These are identified in the so-called Negative List and include agriculture-related industries, telecommunications, real estate brokering, broadcasting and transportation. Licenses with ROC enterprises involved in these industries, however, are common.

There is a 20-year guarantee against expropriation for foreign-invested enterprises whose ownership share is 45% or more foreign. Other foreign-invested enterprises are guaranteed reasonable compensation.

Depending on the counterparty, it is usually advisable to develop a good relationship and to move the transaction into a partnership mode as early as possible. Local parties, including large, established companies, often do not use outside or in-house counsel in negotiating license agreements.

Companies and individuals in the ROC are simply not as legally oriented as their foreign counterparts. There is often a surprising amount of inattention by the local party to the details of an agreement. This is particularly true after the parties have reached agreement on the fundamental terms. It is important, therefore, that the licensor spend the extra effort to make sure that the licensee fully understands terms in the agreement.

Tax Consequences

When licensing payments are received and a receipt is issued in Taiwan, a stamp tax of 0.4% of the amount paid is assessed. Royalties remitted to a recipient abroad who has no domicile in Taiwan and maintains no office in the country are subject to 20% tax. The tax is withheld by the licensee.

Under income tax laws and rulings of the Ministry of Finance, exemptions from the withholding tax may be obtained in the following circumstances:

- when using ROC-registered patents that are licensed for a government-approved technical-cooperation project;
- when using ROC-registered trademarks that are licensed in agreement with an trademark license approved by the National Bureau of Standards; and
- when using know-how related to plant construction, manufacturing or product design, where such know-how is part of an approved technical-cooperation project, and where the technology will be used in a "strategic industry."

A number of foreign parties have licensed their foreign patents in Taiwan as "know-how" and have been exempted from the withholding tax after obtaining approval under a technical-cooperation agreement.

There is also a tax advantage to the licensee in obtaining approval of a technical-cooperation project. Without MOEA approval of royalty payments, the tax authorities will not recognize the payments as an expense. The typical tax rate for a local licensee would be 25%; thus, with approval of a technical-cooperation project the licensee's tax burden will be substantially lightened.

8
Thailand

Licensing, particularly of technology and trademarks, is playing a rapidly expanding role in Thailand's economy. The country is enjoying one of the highest growth rates in the world—over 12% in 1989 and 10% in 1990—and while industry develops and consumer incomes increase, demand for technology and for foreign brands is growing rapidly. Overseas royalty-fee payments totalled $127.5 million in 1989.

Underlying factors bode well for further development of licensing as a business strategy in Thailand. Importantly, the recent surge in investment and growth was in large part due to foreign interest in the country; however, this is matched by a dynamic domestic business community that seeks equity control of joint ventures. In many cases the foreign interest will license technology to the Thailand-registered joint-venture company. While industrial development (the manufacturing sector grew over 15% in real terms in 1989) demands foreign technology, high income growth, particularly in the urban sector, stimulates demand for high-quality foreign brand-name products.

Development of licensing will be constrained in several areas, however, due to a legal environment that has yet to reach international standards in many aspects. The inherent value of intellectual-property rights has yet to be recognized in Thai society; in international trade negotiations, revisions of deficient laws are discussed only as a quid pro quo. Thus, patent law does not apply to such items as computer software and pharmaceuticals, while legal protection of many other items, such as clothing trademarks and copyrights for textbooks, manuals, and video and music recordings, is not enforced adequately.

For the time being, increasing discipline in the use of intellectual property from foreign sources is driven by development of the market, as business strives to cultivate long-lasting partnerships with foreign corporations, and as increasingly discerning consumers demand genuine brand-name products. It is likely that Thailand will bow to international pressure to upgrade its laws, however, in order to ensure continued access to foreign technology. This development is expected within the next three to four years. Adequate enforcement, though, will take longer to evolve.

Industrial development has created demand for a wider spectrum of technology. Increasingly, Thai manufacturing is moving upstream, away from simple assembly. Machining technology to produce components of higher accuracy is in high demand. Heavy industry is beginning to be developed, particularly on the Eastern seaboard, requiring foreign technology.

The Board of Investment (BOI) promotes industry, with technology and technology transfer an important criterion. The most important development for technology imports in recent years was the reduction in machinery-import duties across the board from 40-50% to 5%, effective Oct. 1, 1990.

In addition to the demand for technology, several other features of the business environment encourage licensing technology. The government actively promotes majority Thai equity in joint-venture firms. It is a requirement for listing on the securities exchange in most cases, and often for promotion by the BOI, if not at the outset, then within a set period of years. The alien business law prohibits the granting of business licenses to many types of business; this does not include most types of manufacturing. However, the vast majority of foreign investors in Thailand finds it most convenient to set up a joint-venture company registered under Thai law, with Thais holding majority equity. Under these conditions, foreign companies often find it in their best interests to separate the intellectual-property aspect of their contribution through licensing.

In addition, foreign interests, whether in joint-venture companies or in wholly owned subsidiaries, generally find a tax advantage in paying royalty fees to the overseas parent as opposed to repatriating profits. Business profits are taxed at 30% for listed companies, and 35% for all others; a further withholding tax of 15-20% is applied to dividends remitted abroad. Royalties remitted abroad are subject to a 25% withholding tax, reduced to 15% under double-taxation treaties in force with 24 trading partners, including all major partners except the US (though negotiations are under way). While the royalties withholding tax allows no deduction for expenses, and the Bank of Thailand may rule payments to be excessive in cases and mandate a reduction, in the majority of cases there is a clear tax advantage to remanding profits through this mechanism.

Licensing compares favorably with direct distribution in many cases. Thailand's business community is dynamic, offering good opportunities to form relationships with domestic businesses that enjoy the home-team advantage in marketing. Certainly, licensed domestic production holds a strong advantage over direct distribution of imported goods, given trade barriers in a country that has adopted a strategy of export development but has not completely abandoned notions of import substitution.

Moreover, in the rapidly industrializing environment, imported goods will find it difficult to compete with domestically manufactured products. Those companies that do not move to gain a foothold in domestic production, whether through a joint venture or licensed production, or a combination of the two, will often find themselves beaten to the punch by competitors. Those companies that choose a strategy of setting up production facilities in the country and distributing directly will often realize their profits through licensing agreements with the parent company, for the reasons listed above.

The structure of the marketing environment leads many manufacturers to distribute through trading companies that are able to develop economies of scale in the unique terrain, structuring their relationships through licensing agreements. Thailand has a vast hinterland and a very complex metropolis in Bangkok, with a diverse marketing system still dominated by small independent dry-goods shops. The wholesaling tradition is weak, with suppliers waiting for proprietors to approach them with orders rather than going out and nurturing their marketing skills. While a number of supermarkets have become popular with upper-income groups, and convenience stores such as 7-11 have begun to gain a presence, the dry-goods store will remain the dominant force in marketing for the foreseeable future.

In this environment, several large trading firms have made their mark, with long-established foreign firms most prominent. A major trading house may service thousands of minor shops, keeping track of inventories of their product lines, recalling unsold stock, soliciting orders and offering credit. Manufacturers of all but the highest-volume products find it more efficient to distribute through these trading houses. These specialists are better equipped to manage sales forces and stocks, and to offer and manage credit to small retailers.

However, these retailers are increasingly diversifying into licensed manufacturing of the products they sell. This is used as a tactic to bond manufacturers with proven products to them. Furthermore, these companies often diversify their business for traditional reasons; by entering licensing agreements with quality-conscious multinational manufacturers that have tight quality control and state-of-the-art marketing techniques, they are able to develop manufacturing and marketing quality throughout the company.

Thus, the future of licensing in Thailand looks bright. The rapidly industrializing economy will remain technology hungry, while mounting incomes push demand for foreign name-brand consumer goods. At the same time, an improving legal environment will open new opportunities for foreign developers of intellectual property to reap the rewards of their efforts, particularly in such areas as software, pharmaceuticals, entertainment media and instructional materials. Opportunities for owners of well-known fashion trademarks will improve as counterfeiters are pushed out of the market.

The Legal Context

Thai law recognizes trademarks, patents and copyrights. However, in addition to inadequate enforcement of intellectual-property laws, the law has several deficiencies that are of concern to foreign governments and business. Thai law specifically exempts pharmaceuticals, computer software, agricultural equipment and biotechnology from patent protection. Whether copyright law covers software is a matter to be considered by Thai courts, but it is doubtful that a court decision will resolve the matter, as copyright laws are limited to artistic and literary works. This situation has become a major point of conflict in negotiations between Thailand and its major trading partners, as inadequate protection deprives foreign business of significant revenues.

The US Trade Representative's Office in 1991 cited Thailand as "priority foreign country" targeted for possible trade retaliation, mainly in response to Bangkok's failure to enforce copyrights and provide product protection for chemicals and pharmaceuticals. In addition, the US has pressured Thailand to amend its 1984 Judicial Council ruling in order to enforce stronger protection for the US's computer software, with much success. The US also pressed Bangkok to amend the copyright act by October 1991. Thai-US relations are particularly shaky over copyright protection, particularly for the computer software, music and video industries. Apart from legal shortcomings, a severe lack of enforcement remains the fundamental problem in Thailand.

A single body of law is in force for the whole of Thailand. Specific legislation includes separate acts covering trademarks, patents and copyrights; the Civil and Commercial Code, which governs the terms and conditions of licensing agreements; and the Penal Code, which sets out the remedies regarding trademark infringements. Thailand became a signatory of the Berne Convention for the Protection of Literary and

Artistic Works in 1931; this is the only international intellectual-property-rights legislation to which Thailand is signatory.

Thailand participates in the General Agreement on Tariffs and Trade process, and is a strong advocate of multilateralism. This is due to its position as a rapidly developing exporter—the annual value of Thai exports more doubled from 1987 to 1990, fueling the country's double-digit economic growth of recent years—and its concern to open markets for agricultural commodities, of which it is a major producer. While the Thai government has not taken the initiative to liberalize trade in services, restrictions on such trade is not at a comparatively high level. It is likely to make concessions in this area in a multilateral context, in exchange for reduced protection in markets for Thai goods.

The upgrading of intellectual-property rights to international standards, however, will likely be the result of bilateral pressure applied by the US, through threats to apply sanctions provided for in Clause 301 of the Omnibus Trade Act. Up to the present, Thailand has been successful in buying time to reform relevant laws, and sanctions have yet to be applied.

While the Thai government is extremely reluctant to be seen as caving in to US pressure, especially when so many in Thailand earn their livelihoods through these activities, the US finally is taking a stand through Special 301. The Thai government will not sacrifice trade with its largest market, in order to protect the right to free use of such patents. In 1991 Bangkok proposed new patent protection laws to fend off Washington's threatened sanctions, which would compensate for estimated US losses (about US$200 million annually.) Whether IPR in Thailand will reach international standards within the next few years greatly depends upon the strength of US threats.

Patents

Thailand's first patent legislation was enacted in 1979. The Patent Act only protects patents granted by the Thai Patent Office; thus, foreign patent holders must obtain a separate Thai patent if patent rights are to be protected. However, patents ancillary to a foreign patent must be applied for within a year of the original patent application.

Of key concern to multinationals is the prohibition of patents on key technologies, including pharmaceuticals and computer software; also unpatentable are foods and beverages; agricultural machinery; varieties of plants or animals, and biological processes for their production; scientific or mathematical rules or theories; and inventions that would be contrary to public interest, or that have been proscribed by royal decree.

Applicants must be Thai nationals or nationals of countries offering reciprocal rights to Thais. Rules regarding originality of the inventive step effectively prevent foreign patent holders from applying for a Thai patent after the foreign patent was granted; thus, for patent protection to be effective in Thailand, a Thai patent must be applied for simultaneously with the foreign patent.

Patents are valid for 15 years for a device or process, or seven years for a design. Patent rights may be assigned to another person, which must be done by written contract, or inherited. Employers hold the right to patents deriving from the inventions of employees developed in the course of employment or using resources at the place of work. The employee has the right to remuneration for benefits derived by the employer from the patent; this right cannot be voided by the employment contract or termination thereof. The Director-General of the Department of Commercial Registration has the power to fix such remuneration. Government employees also hold employee rights to remuneration.

Patent fees are B1,000 at application and B1,000 upon receipt. Annual fees apply from the fifth year, increasing annually from B2,000 in the fifth to B30,000 in the 15th year.

Patent holders may grant patent licenses, which must be registered with the Department of Commercial Registration. To date (since 1979) no patent licenses have been recorded.

The Patents Act states that the license may not "stipulate any condition, restriction, or compensation that would have the effect of prejudicing or hindering the development of national industry, handicrafts, agriculture or commerce." Such stipulations were detailed in a 1986 ministerial regulation. The 15 stipulations under this clause of the regulation would have the effect of giving the patentee scope to interfere in how the licensee produced and marketed the patented product, in such ways as setting prices; selecting distributors; limiting production or sales; or encumbering the licensee with requirements to use other patents of the patentee, or source materials from the patentee's designated suppliers, or reserve over half of production to persons designated by the patentee.

The patent law provides for compulsory licensing where there has been no production of a patented product for three years, or in which production does not fulfill demand or is unreasonably priced. The patentee remains entitled to a royalty.

The language of Thai patent legislation reflects the society's attitude toward intellectual-property-rights protection—generally unfavorable. The country is aware that it imports much more technology than it exports, and wishes to pay as little as possible for it, preferably nothing. "Borrowing" of ideas from domestic sources is also rampant.

As it stands, upgrading of patent laws to international standards will require more than amendment of existing law to delete the specific exceptions to patent rights that are such blatant violations of standards in industrialized countries. Beyond this, the process of registering foreign patents will need to be facilitated to give quick recognition to their rights; a new law is clearly needed.

Copyrights

Literary and artistic works in all recording media are protected under the Copyright Act of 1978. Foreign copyrights have been recognized since 1931, when Thailand signed the Berne Convention for the Protection of Literary and Artistic Works. This protects copyrights granted in other member nations. As the US signed the convention in 1988, protection is only extended to US copyrights granted after that date.

Under this framework, Thai copyrights only apply to those works first made public in Thailand, or created by a Thai national, or a person resident in Thailand when the work was created or first made public in the kingdom. There is no provision for registration of copyright; a copy of the work may be submitted to the National Library as evidence of a claim to protection. No copyright mark is required.

While Thai copyright law offers protection up to international standards in most legal aspects, a clause allowing use of copyrighted material without permission for educational purposes has been used as a basis for commercial printing of texts without remuneration to copyright holders. Furthermore, little effort has been made to enforce rights to such materials as manuals and recorded music and videotapes, pirated copies of which are freely available.

In an effort to ward off US trade retaliation under Special 301, however, the Commercial Registration Department of Thailand may establish an information center to help local tape producers directly arrange contracts with foreign copyright holders. This would help curb the illegal copying and distribution of music tapes and videos.

Copyrights are valid for 50 years after the death of the author, or the death of the last joint author. If the author is a juristic person or anonymous, the copyright is valid for 50 years, or 50 years from its first publication. Copyrights for photographic, audiovisual, cinematographic or sound and video broadcasting work are valid for 50 years from the date of creation, or 50 years after first publication. For works of applied art, the copyright is valid for 25 years, or 25 years from first publication.

Unless such rights have been waived by contract, an employee is entitled to the copyright of works he has created in the course of employment. The employer is entitled to publish such work in accordance with the purpose of employment. The right to copyright specifically commissioned works lies with the employer, unless this right has been waived by contract.

The copyright holder has an unrestricted right to grant licenses to use the work. However, the Bank of Thailand may determine royalty payments on use of foreign copyrights to be excessive, and restrict them. This authority has not been used in an unfair manner.

While the legal framework for copyright protection is not seriously deficient, enforcement, again, remains a key problem. Enhancement of the legal code would include regulation to determine reasonable use of copyrighted materials for education that would ensure fair remuneration to authors, and measures to protect pre-1988 works copyrighted in the US. Still, this will depend on the societal recognition of the inherent value of such rights, and the development of a legal environment where vested interests do not find it so convenient to pay officials to ignore existing legal codes.

Trademarks

Trademarks are protected by the Trademark Acts of 1931 and 1961. Laws concerning trademark rights are generally adequate. To be valid, however, a trademark must be registered in Thailand by a party that maintains a permanent presence in the country; a foreign trademark can be registered by a local party, preventing the overseas owner from using the trademark. Beyond sporadic police raids on counterfeit trading booths that are aimed at increasing protection payments, enforcement depends on investigation and litigation by trademark owners; illegal use of trademarks, particularly for apparel and fashion accessories, is rampant. However, if a bill placed before the National Assembly in 1991 is ratified, those found guilty of violating trademarks registered in Thailand will face mandatory four years' imprisonment or a B400,000 fine (B25.6:$1 in May 1992).

Trademarks are applied for at the Trademark Office. If the competent officer decides that the trademark is registrable, the standards being similar to those used globally, the applicant is asked to submit a printing block. Upon receipt of the block, the trademark is published in the official trademark journal. If there is no objection to registration within 90 days, the trademark will be registered. Most foreign applicants choose to register both English and Thai trademarks, to prevent their trademark being copied with Thai lettering. Trademarks are registered in one or more of 50 classes, which are the same as those in the British Trademark Act of 1919.

Registration of a trademark is effective for 10 years, and is renewable.

A trademark registration can be canceled in five years if unused; and some companies make nominal sales within this window in order to guarantee access to the trademark for future sales. While trademark licensing contracts are not registered, they are common and enforceable.

The legal code for trademarks is generally adequate within the domestic context, although a more efficient framework for recognition of international trademarks would be a welcome development for brands that have yet to develop a significant presence in the domestic market. Enforcement is a constant problem, however, for companies that have not developed a large enough presence in the country to take an aggressive stand against counterfeiters. To date, market forces, rather than laws, underlie the significant growth of contractual trademark use, as increasingly aware consumers demand genuine articles while manufacturers value the support offered by overseas trademark holders, and the access they provide to export markets.

Registration of Licensing Agreements

While the Department of Commercial Registration only requires the registration of domestic patent licensing agreements, overseas payment of royalties generally requires the registration of agreements with the Bank of Thailand. Licensing agreements that are part of applications for Board of Investment privileges require approval of the board.

The Thai legal system has no tradition of antitrust regulation. Competition is not yet given a high value as a tenet of free enterprise, and cartels are a prominent feature of several industrial sectors. Thus, such laws pose no barrier to the sharing of technology.

Practical Matters

The huge influx of foreign investment over recent years—foreign direct investment inflows grew by 59% in 1989, after having jumped 480% in 1988—is a salient indicator of the attractiveness of the Thai business environment. Further development of the political and legal systems will enhance the business environment, though development of the upper sectors of the labor market has lagged behind industrialization. Many companies will find it necessary to develop technical staff from within their existing work forces, but overall, the labor situation remains favorable. Government corruption has not reached a level that seriously interferes with business activities, and the legal tradition is adequate to ensure that contracts are taken seriously.

Government Attitude Toward Business

Overall, the government could only be given a mixed rating for its performance on key business issues. However, it has presided over rapid economic growth, and in particular poses no serious obstacles to licensing strategies. At the same time, foreign businesses find their relations with the government greatly improved through the use of Thai partners, a most viable alternative given the dynamism of local business.

Corruption, however, is an entrenched facet of government business. It can facilitate a broad spectrum of activities under government supervision; in most cases, though, it does not block development with unrealistic informal taxes, and is uneven across government offices, with young idealists or other disinterested officials that do not take bribes interspersed with the bribe-takers. The various applications and approvals necessary for licensing do not mandate pay-offs. While timely gifts may facilitate the speed of processing, above-board transactions are not seriously delayed in order to solicit such gifts. Some companies have successfully taken the high road and vowed to make no pay-offs, either in observance of the US Foreign Corrupt Practices Act or their own principles (the latter group including Thai as well as foreign businesses), and have been grudgingly respected by government officials for it.

The regime of economic management features two groups—a political/bureaucratic group, rooted in vested interests and the longstanding elite structure; and a competent tradition of technocrats. While the former group can weigh against development, the latter, which is most influential in the central bank and in the National Economic and Social Development Board but is represented in a number of other ministries, has kept the economy balanced and, throughout the 1980s, laid the foundations for the tremendous growth now being enjoyed.

The Legal Tradition

The legal environment is beset by outdated laws and delays in court processes. While there are few complaints about unfair decisions by the courts, most litigants prefer to settle out of court.

There are no juries in Thailand; verdicts are passed down by panels of career judges. Overall, there is little interference in court decisions, although there have been aberrations in provincial areas and in some criminal cases. Generally, only the most powerful political elites could hope to influence verdicts.

Interference in the legal process usually occurs within executive agencies, such as the police. However, this is not at a level that seriously jeopardizes business activities.

Patents and Trademarks in Thailand

Conventions. None.
Basic laws. Patent Act of 1979; Trademark Acts of 1931 and 1961.

Patents
Types and duration. Patents (except those covering designs—see below) are granted for a period of 15 years from date of filing. During this period, only the patentee has the right to apply the process or produce or sell the patented product. However, a patented product may be used without restriction for study, research or analysis.
Novelty. Patents may be granted or recognized in Thailand only if the invention is new, involves an inventive step and is capable of industrial application.
Unpatentable. Food, beverages and pharmaceutical products or ingredients; machines made for use in agriculture; any variety of animal or plant or any essentially biological process for the production of animals or plants; scientific or mathematical rules or theories; computer programs; inventions whose use would be contrary to public interests.
Application procedure. Patent applications must give the title and a detailed description of the item, a statement of its nature and purposes, a clear statement of claim and any other information prescribed by ministerial regulations. Provisions are made to protect the secrecy of the application during the period between the filing and the granting of the patent.
Fees. Maximum fees are B1,000 for filing an application plus an additional B1,000 on the receipt of the patent. Annual fees are B2,000 up to the fifth year, followed by increasing fees each year thereafter to a maximum of B30,000 in the 15th and final year of registration.
Compulsory licensing may take effect if a patent has not been used for three years, or if production is at unreasonable prices or fails to meet public demand. A government department may also license a patent (paying a royalty to the patentee) for reasons of public consumption, national defense or development of natural resources.

Trademarks
Duration. Ten years from date of application, renewable for like periods.

(Continued)

Not registrable. A mark that is merely descriptive, has geographical significance, is a surname or is otherwise non-distinctive is not registrable.
Application procedure. The proprietor or his agent must establish a place of business in Thailand prior to registration. If not made by trademark owner, application must be accompanied by power of attorney.
Fees. B500 for registration or renewal.

Industrial designs and models
Industrial designs are covered by the 1979 Patent Act. Application procedures are similar to those for other kinds of patents. A design patent is enforceable for seven years from the time of filing the application.

Of more serious concern to multinationals is legal reform. A number of laws remain on the books that mandate criminal penalties for civil offenses, with company directors held liable. There have been cases in which disgruntled employees have not filed mandatory reports and reported the infraction to the authorities in order to bring action against company directors. While this is not common and such laws are generally not enforced, they remain a threat to business.

Overall, multinational business can be confident that contractual agreements will be respected. While there remains significant scope for improvement of the legal system, its deficiencies do not seriously hinder business beyond the lost revenues due to inadequacies in enforcement of intellectual-property laws, and the law itself, as discussed above.

Payment Instruments

The exchange control regime poses no serious constraints or risks to payments for licensing. Thailand has not limited foreign exchange transactions in the current account since the immediate aftermath of World War II. While the central bank has authority to rule that royalty-payment levels are excessive, it has not used this authority to interfere with fair remuneration for services. Foreign exchange rates are stable, with payment instruments adequate for the low levels of currency risk involved.

Overseas royalty-payment instruments are generally simple. Flat fees are usually denominated in dollars or the currency of the licensor's country, while percentage-based fees are denominated in baht.

Indexing fees to compensate for exchange rate fluctuations is rare, as currency movements are not dramatic enough to require adjustment beyond regular revision of contracts.

Baht/foreign exchange rates are set against a basket of currencies in which the dollar and dollar-linked currencies are dominant. Thus, the baht has fluctuated in a narrow range against the dollar since a 1984 devaluation (no further dramatic adjustments are expected), while tracking dollar movements against other currencies.

In this context, coverage of foreign exchange risk has not been a major concern of foreign business, while instruments for managing risk remain underdeveloped. At present, these are limited to short terms and low amounts. The recently inaugurated policy of liberalizing currency controls, however, is expected to facilitate the development of treasury instruments while increasing exchange rate volatility. This is not expected to provoke significant, rapid devaluation or revaluation of the exchange rate, though, which is considered to be at a trade- and demand-appropriate level.

Tax Consequences

Under Thailand's tax structure, licensing offers advantages to multinational companies that seek to gain a presence in the market. For companies entering the market, it offers advantages over direct marketing, while companies with manufacturing subsidiaries in the country can increase after-tax income by repatriating returns through royalty payments. While there are no direct exemptions for technology transfer, BI promotional privileges can be requested by companies introducing technology to the country; these privileges can include tax exemptions.

Business profits are taxed at 30% for companies listed on the Securities Exchange of Thailand and at 35% for unlisted firms, with a further 15-20% withholding tax applied on dividends remitted abroad, which may be reduced slightly under the provisions of tax treaties. Thus, the effective tax on business profits remitted abroad is in the range of 45–50%. This compares with a 25% withholding tax on royalties remitted abroad, with no allowance for expenses; double-tax treaties reduce the burden to 15% or below for many countries. Thus, royalties receive much more favorable tax treatment than repatriation of profits, and can form an important tool of corporate tax strategy.

There are no tax exemptions for technology transfer as such; however, technology transfer increases chances of a successful application for BOI promotion that can include tax exemptions. Technology imports have become significantly less expensive with the Oct. 1, 1990, reduction of capital-goods import duties, which will trigger increased imports of such equipment.

Technology transfer is one of several criteria for approval of applications for BOI promotion. At present, the BOI has divided the country into three zones with varying levels of promotion, in order to encourage the industrialization of areas outside of Bangkok. Tax holidays in these range from three to eight years, with 50-100% exemption of duties on imported capital goods.

A most significant development was the reduction of import duties on capital equipment, from 40-50% to 5%, effective Oct. 1, 1990. This will greatly facilitate the use of foreign technology by promoting all industrial development rather than just those companies promoted by the BOI. It will be easier for smaller factories to expand, without the red tape involved in BOI applications. Licensed use of technology is expected to surge.

Political and Cultural Considerations

While in a few sectors of industry, members of cartels hold enough political influence to interfere with competition, this is not the case in the leading technology sectors. There are no technologies restricted as a result of these pressures, though certain sectors are restricted for national-security reasons. These include radio communications, private aircraft, and weaponry. In some areas, such as satellite communications, the government has granted concessions or has set up state enterprises to provide services, and these may be protected from competition. Beyond this, there is little restriction on technology; to the contrary, the government and society is very much in favor of rapid technological development.

A guarantee against nationalization was written into the latest investment law, promulgated in 1977. There is little risk of hostile expropriation of profitable firms, although the government has taken equity or forced mergers of failing financial companies with government institutions as part of bailout packages. Nor is there precedent for expropriation of foreign-held assets out of nationalist sentiment. However, the government may require majority Thai ownership or listing on the securities exchange of a company applying for BOI privileges.

Many tips on negotiation in Asian cultures are applicable to Thailand, though many of these do not go far beyond matters of common sense; a mature and flexible negotiator will have little difficulty developing a rapport with his Thai counterparts. Foreign businessmen generally find themselves fascinated by those aspects of culture accessible to them as expatriates or temporary visitors, while most Thais share a cosmopolitan outlook and reciprocate respect by ignoring minor gaffes in communication by well-meaning foreigners. On the other hand, negotiators need to do their homework to find the real authority among potential partners, and any encumbrances on them.

Thailand has had sufficient exposure to foreigners to have developed a cosmopolitan attitude, while, as one of the few developing nations never to have been colonized, it has not developed an inferiority complex that could be a hindrance in dealing with foreign businessmen. Thus, it is rare for cultural misunderstandings to deteriorate along racial lines. Across the negotiating table, progress toward mutually beneficial arrangements is much more important than cultural arrangements, although a negotiator would be well advised to emulate his Asian counterparts and not express emotions dramatically, especially if negative.

However, a charmed negotiator who feels that it will be easy to get the smiling man across the table to sign a deal would do well to remind himself of the prevalence of both smiles and foreign businessmen in Thailand. While Thais are noted for their pleasantness and are most hospitable to foreign visitors, foreign businessmen have poured into the country along with high economic growth and good opportunities in nearly all economic sectors. It is likely that a Thai firm identified as a good prospect has also been noticed by other firms, and is involved in negotiations with more than one foreign interest. The cultural pattern of avoidance of negative issues will often mean that the Thai side does not inform the visiting foreigner of imminent closure with a competitor. An intelligence-gathering capability can be a crucial advantage for negotiators.

In this environment, foreign firms would do well to investigate the backgrounds of the companies with which they are dealing, or to retain a local consultant to do so, in order to make sure that they are dealing with the real authorities within the company, and that there are no encumbrances that will interfere with the negotiations or a lasting relationship. Equity holding and real management structures within Thai businesses can be confusing. There remains a high proportion of family business patterns within Thai companies, including many that are listed on the securities exchange. Thus, formal positions of younger family members or outsiders may have significantly less authority than a family patriarch or an older generation of family members.

Furthermore, linkages between companies and financiers can be very close and extend beyond legalistic arrangements. While in some cases this may mean that a highly leveraged company is in fact at little risk of insolvency, it can also imply a high degree of influence by the bank over the company's activities.

Licensing Experience in Thailand

One global name-brand garment company recently signed a five-year licensing agreement with a joint-venture company comprised of a major trading firm and a manufacturer. Royalties of 10% of wholesale price are remitted quarterly. Minimum royalties, denominated in baht, were set at zero in the final quarter of the signing year; $40 million in the first year; $60 million in the second; and $80 million through the remainder of the contract. The licensee is bound to spend 5% of sales on advertising and promotion.

The contract includes exit clauses to allow the brand owner to enforce quality standards and the licensee to escape minimum royalty obligations (with a year's notice) in case the line proves to be unprofitable.

Through this strategy, the brand owner is able to tap a large market with promotional and product-quality standards in line with its global strategy. At the same time, it is able to leave manufacturing and distribution to local specialists. The trading firm gains a profitable product line, while the manufacturer gains access to quality-control development as well as access to a trusted international name in a very competitive market.

In a second case, the local licensee of an integrated consulting agency—offering management and financial consulting, executive recruitment services, audit services and technical studies—operates under a licensing agreement with a major multinational company. The five-year contract stipulates 5% royalties on turnover, with a 10% commission paid on referrals from the head office or other licensees.

A number of multinational agencies of this sort have gained local representation through licensees. The arrangement allows licensors to tap the talent of long-term expatriates who specialize in the country, while licensees gain access to multinational clients, particularly regional and world headquarters offices, where important decisions are made.

9
China

The environment for transfer-of-technology agreements with the PRC (People's Republic of China) has become increasingly difficult in recent years as the country's foreign exchange scarcities have become a permanent feature of the business climate. The central government, which by the mid-1980s had already turned away from expensive turnkey arrangements in favor of royalty- or fee-based technology imports, has turned yet another corner. Now it is screening projects even more carefully, in many cases insisting on "trade and technology" arrangements that minimize hard-currency outlays and/or have built-in hard-currency-generating mechanisms.

The Chinese attitude toward transfer of technology is fundamentally different from that assumed by licensor and licensee under most Western-style licensing arrangements. As implied by the name of the basic law governing these contracts—the "Regulations of the PRC for the Administration of Technology Import Contracts"—the Chinese authorities consider technology a commodity to be purchased, and once paid for, to be used freely by the recipient. This attitude creates a host of procedures and rules to which Western licensors are unaccustomed.

In addition to the funding problem, foreign licensors continue to be vexed by a number of issues that stem from China's still partially shrouded bureaucratic policies; ongoing cycles of centralization/decentralization of decision-making; inadequate industrial infrastructure; and still-evolving legal infrastructure. The impact of these difficulties has been to reduce dramatically the number of such contracts in recent years (see the table on p. 130).

Despite these problems, companies continue to be motivated to enter into technology-transfer agreements for a variety of reasons, such as the following.

- ***To gain or maintain access to the Chinese market in the face of imposing barriers to direct sales.*** The authorities limit imports into the country via high tariffs on nonessential goods and a relatively centralized import-purchasing system (though provinces with hard currency to spend have some autonomy in import decision-making).
- ***As an alternative to direct investment for companies reluctant to commit capital for long terms.*** Most joint-venture and wholly foreign-owned equity arrangements require the venture to generate its own foreign exchange to support profit remittances. Licensing can offer assurance of hard-currency income, faster payback and greater flexibility in the China market than direct investment. (But potential licensors should note that they may come under pressure to invest capital under a joint-venture arrangement, even if they prefer a straight transfer-of-technology deal).
- ***As a means of licensing less advanced technologies that have become obsolete in the West but are still appropriate for China's development*** (though the question of what level of technology is "appropriate" for China can be a highly controversial issue during negotiations).
- ***To create a vantage point for learning more about the PRC market or a potential joint-venture partner.*** For some firms, licensing is one step along the learning curve in preparation for enhancing direct sales or establishing closer equity or other ties.

Finding a Partner

China's priorities for importing technology are set out in a broad way in its five-year plans, which are reviewed and adjusted periodically. In broad terms, the Seventh Five-Year Plan (1986–90) targeted energy, transport, telecommunications, the upgrading of existing enterprises and the development of raw materials sources and semifinished-product industries. Potential foreign licensors can also get a good idea of what industrial areas are being encouraged or discouraged from the various speeches and pronouncements made by high government officials (consumer goods and the light-industry sector, for example, have a low priority at the moment).

In addition, individual provinces, the key cities (e.g. Beijing, Shanghai, Tianjin) and the Special Economic Zones have their own priority lists (and often foreign exchange allocations) for upgrading plants and industries within their jurisdictions.

For high-priority sectors targeted for modernization, ministerial-level Chinese officials often approach Western firms and invite them to be technology providers. Individual Chinese end-users may also contact foreign firms soliciting technology-transfer ties, but licensors should be careful in these cases to ascertain how much clout the Chinese entity has and whether a project will be able to obtain foreign exchange backing.

Other foreign companies interested in licensing their technology have taken the initiative by making a systematic search for business opportunities. Usually, they start by contacting and presenting their credentials to the ministry or group in charge of their industry in China; the Foreign Trade Corporation handling imports and exports of their product; Techimport (the agency that often conducts negotiations on the part of Chinese licensees); the Ministry of Foreign Economic Relations and Trade (MOFERT), or its provincial-level counterpart. The China Council for the Promotion of International Trade (CCPIT) or the China International Trust and Investment Corp (CITIC) can also be helpful. These contacts should be supplemented by visits to Chinese firms involved that will be the actual end-users in the sector. Again, getting official support for a project, along with foreign exchange, is a most important consideration.

Legal Context

Technology Transfer

China has spelled out its transfer-of-technology rules under a series of laws and implementing regulations that were last updated in January 1988. The "Regulations of the PRC for the Administration of Technology Import Contracts" was promulgated in May 1985, followed by implementing rules in September 1985—the "Procedures for Examination and Approval of Technology Import Contracts." These provided the basic guidelines for drawing up and approving technology acquisition by Chinese entities, imposing conditions on both buyers and sellers to prevent unplanned or unauthorized technology deals.

The 1985 implementing regulations were broadened and superseded in January 1988 by the "Detailed Rules for the Implementation of the Regulations on Administration of Technology Import Contracts." The 1988 rules govern technology-transfer arrangements between PRC and foreign entities. Deals between one PRC entity and another are covered by separate 1987 legislation, and technology that forms part of a foreign investor's capital contribution to a joint venture falls under the specific provisions of the joint-venture laws. (But many joint ventures with Chinese partners contain a separate transfer-of-technology contract between the joint venture and the foreign partner that is an integral part of the agreement. Whether or not royalties are payable, these accords also must comply with China's technology-import laws.)

Foreign Technology Purchases

Technology-purchase statistics issued by the Ministry of Foreign Economic Relations and Trade (MOFERT) show that after registering sharp increases every year until 1986, the number and value of contracts fell significantly in 1987 and 1988.

	Number of contracts	Contract value ($ billions)
1981	73	0.11
1982	102	0.36
1983	219	0.56
1984	332	0.95
1985	671	2.96
1986	744	4.45
1987	561	2.96
1988	437	3.55

According to MOFERT, the value of these technology imports usually includes the equipment and products in which the technology is incor-

The 1988 rules provide a clearer definition of the various kinds of contracts governed by the law, including licensing, know-how, service, certain assembly and processing contracts and other varieties of transfer-of-technology agreements. They also specify what kinds of clauses must be included in the contract and spell out the levels of authorization needed for contract approval.

Though foreign licensors should note that many of the basic terms can be negotiated if there is a valid reason, the summary below outlines the salient points included in the overall law and implementing regulations.

Duration. Technology contracts are limited to 10-year terms unless special dispensation is granted. Generally, the licensee need only maintain confidentiality for this period, and may freely use and disclose the technology thereafter, unless a longer confidentiality period can be justified. Several companies have managed to negotiate longer confidentiality terms. In the case of technology contracts associated with joint ventures of longer duration, for example, the confidentiality period has at times been extended. Also, the authorities are sometimes willing to bend the 10-year rule if regular updates and improvements are an important feature of the arrangement.

Renewal of contracts can also be problematic unless they entail ongoing improvements or new technological advances. In general, the Chinese attitude toward these arrangements is that they are *buying,* not leasing, the technology.

Tie-in arrangements. "Unnecessary" purchases of equipment, components and materials in connection with the technology-transfer deal are forbidden. For follow-up items that are considered necessary to the technology-transfer contract, prices charged for sale by the licensor are generally not to exceed international prices. While foreign technology providers are concerned that the Chinese operation may be unable to meet performance standards—which the licensor must generally guarantee under the contract—if licensees incorporate cheaper materials purchased from third parties the authorities will generally accept the idea that a requisite quality of raw materials may be needed for the product to meet these standards.

Performance tests. The contract must specify who is responsible for meeting technology-transfer targets under the contract and what the penalties will be for failure to pass tests that would lead to certification of the technology.

Confidentiality. Confidentiality clauses, which must now be included in each contract, may not generally exceed the duration of the contract, unless the technology provider supplies additional technology improvements.

Dispute-resolution. Mechanisms for the resolution of disputes must be specified in the contract.

Export provisions. The contract may not contain restrictions on the technology recipient's right to export, unless the examination and approval authority specifically waives this rule. Exceptions are permitted for countries where the technology provider already has exclusive licensing contracts and where it has concluded sole-agency contracts.

Negotiating and Approval Requirements

Technology-import contracts must be examined and approved by MOFERT or one of its regional counterparts, depending on the size and value of the venture. In this way, the central authorities maintain a measure of control over what technology is imported and how much is paid for it.

The current rules call for projects valued in excess of $5 million to be authorized by the State Planning Commission and approved by MOFERT; those below that value must be authorized by provincial or municipal planning commissions and approved by a local branch of MOFERT or its designee.

Approval is supposed to be automatic if the application is not acted on within 60 days (it is unclear whether this applies to cases of special dispensations—e.g. longer-than-10-year contract terms, and waivers on export restrictions of the licensed products).

Aside from the basic law and its implementing rules, Beijing has also issued guidelines to establish purchasing priorities when choosing foreign technology. These guidelines specify that the technology should be more advanced than that currently available in China, and be of practical use. It should help toward the goal of self-sufficiency, enhance social and economic development, and contribute to the generation of foreign exchange.

In addition to MOFERT and the end-user, there are several other bodies that can have a say in technology deals. For one thing, only a limited number of Chinese enterprises are authorized to negotiate and conclude technology-import contracts on their own; at end-1987, that number was 240. All others must conduct negotiations through mediators—generally the foreign trade corporations for that particular industry or the ministerial bureaus in charge of specific industry sectors.

State or regional planning and technology commissions, and the banks financing the technology deals, particularly the Bank of China, are also frequently involved in the negotiations. All these institutions are likely to participate in the talks and review the feasibility study that every end-user is required to submit for approval.

Foreign technology providers should be careful to ascertain from the start that the ultimate recipient of the technology has authority to deal with foreigners and the hard-currency wherewithal to pay for the imported technology. They should also confirm that the local planning authorities have given their go-ahead by asking to see the feasibility study and project authorization certificate.

Even after the contract is signed, the 1988 implementing rules give the approval authorities the specific right to require modification of the contract in the event it fails to meet certain, somewhat hazy, guidelines, including a "reasonable" price for the imported technology and a "reasonable" payment mechanism.

Chinese negotiating tactics often include inviting several competing companies to bid for the same technology agreement. Thus, foreign licensors should be prepared to put their best foot forward and to advance ideas that can give them an edge over the competition. Product quality and a strong track record in transferring similar technology around the world are helpful. Proposals for how the licensee can finance the foreign exchange costs are also advantageous. Another tactic that worked for one company was to visit and lobby the end-user (even though it was negotiating with its overseeing ministry); it was able to win over a licensee that had been leaning in favor of the competition.

Practical Matters

Chinese enterprises have built up considerable experience in licensing foreign technology since the early 1980s, and many foreign firms have successfully entered into licensing arrangements, either as part of investment deals or separately. Nevertheless, foreign companies wishing to carry out licensing deals with a developing, centrally planned economy like the PRC will have several hurdles to overcome.

Lack of Funding

China's foreign exchange crunch has hit transfer-of-technology agreements just as hard as imports and other activities involving foreigners. It has become more difficult to convince the Chinese to part with foreign exchange for royalties and other fees, even when the technology is deeply desired and obviously needed to substitute for imports.

Rather than royalty-based licensing deals or large lump-sum payments for the value of the technology, the authorities are trying to steer foreign firms toward "trade and technology" accords. These minimize payment for the technology itself, instead compensating the foreign partner for expenses actually incurred, such as training, the provision of capital equipment, and the supply of materials, components or SKD (semi-knocked-down) or CKD (completely knocked-down) kits. Often these trade-and-technology deals include terms that make them self-funding from a foreign exchange point of view.

The company providing technology under such an arrangement tries to get the best deal it can; sometimes it must build compensation for the underlying technology and know-how into the price of tie-in items like components or kits (as Fluke did—see the case study on p. 140). In other cases, it buys back some or all of the finished product for sale worldwide.

Broader countertrade arrangements are a variation of the above buyback deal that some foreign companies have entered into to make licensing agreements self-funding. Typically, the foreign licensor agrees to purchase, for hard currency, a certain value of China-made product; the foreign exchange payments would then be creditable against the licensee's hard-currency outlays. These kinds of arrangements are fraught with difficulty, however—as outlined in the case study on p. 134.

Countertrade Clauses

When a US multinational, a producer of heavy-duty industrial equipment, entered into an umbrella licensing arrangement that would transfer its know-how to several different Chinese end-users, it hoped to mitigate the hard-currency pressure on its licensees by incorporating a countertrade agreement into the broad structure of the transfer-of-technology package. The fact that the US-based company has a separate international trading subsidiary made such an option feasible.

The idea was to have that subsidiary purchase goods from a variety of Chinese enterprises that fall under the wing of the ministry supervising the licensees, and to credit the licensed factories with the hard currency to enable them to pay for the semi-knocked-down kits, components and some capital equipment needed to implement the agreement. Some of these goods are products that the US licensor needs for its own operations, and some it plans to sell in the world markets through its trading operation. In the latter case, the company would normally arrange for the final sale prior to making the purchase of China goods. Eventually, the licensor even envisaged buying back some components of the licensed product.

As part of the countertrade arrangement, a "central evidence" account was established with the Bank of China where these credits could be accumulated and subsequently allocated to the individual Chinese licensees in conjunction with the overseeing ministry.

But the accord quickly ran into roadblocks. Over time, says a company spokesman, the list of goods available as well as the number of eligible factories that the firm could do business with under the deal continued to shrink. The licensor believes the central ministry was simply "unable to pull some of these things off." Another difficulty for the licensor has been getting goods that are "world class" in terms of quality, delivery and price.

Because of this combination of negative factors, the countertrade arrangement simply hasn't been able to generate the volumes the company would like. For the overall agreement, this will mean slowdowns in production of licensed goods by the Chinese technology recipients—and lower profits for the US technology provider. The US company has already received some up-front payments (which covered the provision of equipment, training, and a number of other expenses it incurred in implementing the deal). But it is also due a royalty, based on unit of output. The supply of components and kits to the licensees is also a money-maker for the company. Thus, the more hard currency available to its licensees, the higher its own earnings stand to be.

Another foreign technology provider says it deals with the hard-currency problem by seeking out licensees only in provinces that have a foreign exchange excess that could potentially cover these costs. It no longer bothers to pursue deals with the others.

Some foreign firms overcome the foreign exchange hurdle by seeking out projects funded by multilateral agencies, such as the Asian Development Bank (although this avenue of financing is temporarily closed, as these agencies have put new China financing on hold after the crackdown on demonstrators in Tiananmen Square in June 1989).

Secrecy

Although the legal foundations protecting intellectual property have been greatly shored up in recent years, enough loopholes remain to worry potential licensors. For example, foreign firms should insist that prospective licensees sign confidentiality agreements, even in the negotiating stage, if sensitive technological information is presented during these talks, and should make confidentiality clauses in the final contract as comprehensive and water-tight as possible. Breaches of confidentiality are often the result of ignorance of international standards, and attention to this point will drive home the message to the licensee.

In fact, PRC authorities have been quick to act for the injured foreign party. A 1987 case involved a Shenyang factory licensed to produce machine tools by a US firm. A PRC employee trained by the US licensor left the factory and used the techniques in his new work unit. The Shenyang municipal authorities forbade the new work unit to make the tools and also forced the employee to return to his old job.

But as a practical matter, it is sometimes difficult to prove there has been a breach of confidentiality. There have been cases of knock-off electronics products found all over China, and even in export markets like Hong Kong, with no clear connection to the licensee.

Payment Terms

Chinese negotiators have a reputation for being tough bargainers on issues of compensation, and most companies say the Chinese are getting foreign technology on the cheap. Valuation questions are among the stickiest to resolve during negotiations. In some cases, third-party valuations have been an effective means of arriving at a figure that both sides can live with.

The method of payment is negotiable, and the outcome can vary enormously, from up-front lump sums to progressive payments, to running royalties, to a combination of the above. In some cases, the licensor may take payment in product produced by the licensee under a buy-back arrangement, but most licensors resist this alternative unless they have a real need for the product.

Another alternative is for the licensor to build its compensation into proprietary components that it supplies to the technology recipient (see the Fluke case on p. 140).

The Chinese try to discourage up-front payments, preferring to spread them out over the course of the contract or to wait until the licensee is actually producing goods. The foreign licensor, on the other hand, is concerned about covering its initial costs, especially when ex-

Progressive-Payments Clauses

One technology provider that negotiated progressive payments in 1989 obtained the following terms: The contract, valued as a lump sum, calls for the disbursement of funds as certain milestones in the agreement are met (e.g. the arrival of equipment, completion of the basic engineering package, start-up of the facility etc.). The total contract value covers the technology itself (e.g. patents and know-how associated with the product), payments for equipment either supplied by the licensor or purchased by it for the project, fees for basic design and engineering services, training and other items. The letter of credit from the Bank of China, the main financing instrument for the contract, extends over 60 months. (As a further guarantee that the licensor will be paid, the credit was accompanied by a letter of commitment from the Asian Development Bank, which cofinanced the deal.)

The Chinese licensee is getting the know-how for making the product, visits to the US plant, detailed sketches and equipment design, engineering services, assistance in the construction phase (although the Chinese themselves are responsible for building the plant), start-up assistance, and training in operations, maintenance and instrumentation.

The travel and living expenses of the Chinese who will be coming to the US for training will be picked up by the Chinese. The licensor will absorb the costs entailed in arranging for the training, instructional personnel and the use of its facilities. (The ADB loan provided for some of the hard-currency expenses for Chinese travel, training and inspection fees.)

tensive training and provision of machinery are important factors. A common formula acceptable to both sides is for the licensee to pay a smaller up-front fee and then progressive payments as various performance targets are met (e.g. upon purchase of machinery, its installation, start-up, training, testing, etc.—as the firm profiled above did).

Running royalties based on production or sales are an option that the Chinese favor, since this can delay their expenditure of hard currency for several years (and if the Chinese end up exporting some of the product, the deal can become effectively self-financing for them). But technology providers have been able in some cases to negotiate a smaller up-front payment to defray some of their out-of-pocket costs. In some deals, the royalty percentage diminishes over time.

When royalties are based on "net sales value," the stickiest negotiating issue is what items will be deducted to arrive at the net. Chinese negotiators generally try to whittle down the basis for the royalty calculation to the bare minimum. In one case, for example, the Chinese negotiators wanted to exclude the value of the packaging, for which the know-how was provided by the foreign licensor, who insisted on its inclusion as an integral part of the product and the technology arrangement. A compromise was reached that included the value of packaging on royalties paid for exported product.

Because of such complications, some companies have attempted to avoid these valuation questions altogether with a fixed royalty per unit of output. But the Chinese authorities are generally reluctant to grant this type of payment formula without tough negotiations.

One US company won this concession by signing a multiple licensing deal in 1987 for the manufacture of tractors and other heavy-duty vehicles. Its royalty, based on unit of output, takes into account the average percentage of local content over the contract period, the unit-output value, the royalty percentage and total plant output.

Chrysler was another successful negotiator. It signed a seven-year agreement in 1987 under which it will supply technical assistance and machinery for two-liter, four-cylinder engines. Its compensation will consist of a one-time fee in US dollars for the equipment sale (which consists of a complete engine line from one of its Michigan plants), plus ongoing US dollar-denominated royalties for the design and manufacturing know-how. Royalties will be calculated using a set rate per engine unit produced.

Though there is no specific limit on the royalty percentage, 2–5% of net sales has been the rule. The Chinese have gone higher only in rare cases, and at this point such a concession would be extremely difficult to secure. Informal guidelines also apply in certain industries, though Chinese officials do not acknowledge them publicly. Usually these guidelines vary by industry and are based on royalties approved under a previous contract by the same Chinese negotiating authority. It is difficult to ascertain what these guidelines might be unless they are divulged by the foreign licensors themselves.

Other Practical Matters

Trademark licenses. Straight trademark licenses unaccompanied by technology are uncommon, though there have been some cases. The right to use a trademark is generally negotiated at the same time as the transfer-of-technology agreement (often in the context of a joint venture) and may or may not be compensated with a separate royalty or fee.

Training. Chinese law requires the technology provider to train the recipient's personnel, and provisions to this effect should be detailed in the contract. In addition to specifying how much training will be provided (e.g. in number of man-days), the contract should be clear on where it will take place and who will pick up what costs (e.g. travel, accommodation, food etc.) in either country. Most foreign licensors report that the training required to implement these transfer-of-technology agreements is far more extensive in the case of China than similar deals elsewhere in the world.

Exports. Most foreign companies see licensing as a means of entering the PRC market. Chinese enterprises, on the other hand, are often keen to boost foreign exchange earnings by exporting licensed products. The conflict of interest can be a stumbling block, especially for foreign firms with already-established markets that the PRC licensee may encroach upon. But the Chinese do allow for reasonable restrictions. The technology-contract rules forbid "unfair" restrictions on exporting, but the 1988 implementing regulations concede exceptions in cases where the licensor has already concluded exclusive licensing contracts or sole agency agreements.

Overlapping jurisdictions. The Shenzhen Special Economic Zone has its own technology-transfer regulations, as do the Xiamen Special Economic zone (SEZ) and Guangzhou Export Trade Development Zone (ETDZ). Their rules are generally more favorable to foreign licensors than those set by the central government, but some provisions can be even tougher. There has been no experience to date as to whether the national law might override local ones on specific contract points permitted under local regulations.

Disagreements over 'appropriate' technology. The licensee almost always wants the most advanced technology (and for a long time the central authorities encouraged this approach), whether or not it has the capability to handle it or the local materials infrastructure is sufficiently developed. Problems can arise if the licensee's work force or engineers are not skilled enough to absorb the technology, which could prevent the licensor from meeting certain performance targets. Foreign companies should be sure to visit the licensee's plant early on and make an assessment of its capabilities. Foreign firms may also be reluctant to pass on their latest technology out of concern about future competition.

Updating. Normally, companies are expected to update the technology over the life of the agreement, especially in cases where running royalties are involved rather than outright payment for specific patents and know-how. Chinese rules provide for reverse update provisions—i.e. improvements made by the licensee can be transferred back to the licensor.

Disputes. A number of legal disputes have arisen in connection with transfer-of-technology agreements. Under a case that went to arbitration last year, the Chinese party claimed that the product was not up to the promised standard. The parties settled through conciliation procedures before a formal arbitration award was rendered.

Patents, Trademarks and Copyrights

From a position of having practically no legislation on intellectual-property rights, China has come a long way in putting into place a substantial body of laws protecting various types of intellectual property via patents, trademarks and copyrights.

Some of these rules are still unfolding, partly under threats of retaliation under the US's Special Section 301. A new copyright law was enacted in 1991, but has been faulted for failing to provide adequate protection of software. The patent law is also expected to be revised in response to certain criticisms of the original law.

China is a signatory to various international conventions. In March 1983 it became a member of the World Intellectual Property Organization (WIPO), and in December 1984 it joined the Paris Convention for the Protection of Industrial Property (the Paris Union). In October 1989, China signed the Madrid Agreement Concerning the International Registration of Marks (the Madrid Union).

The current legal framework protecting intellectual property began to take shape in the late 1970s, after China designated experts to study the intellectual-property protection of other countries. It recognized that the absence of modern laws governing patents and trademarks was a major stumbling block to the entry of the technology it needed for its industrial-modernization drive.

Fluke and the PRC: The History of a Relationship

After a strong start, the Fluke Co's expanding China business and proliferating electronic-instrument assembly deals fell flat several years ago. The US company's experience parallels that of many other foreign firms, whose market-penetration efforts fell victim to China's disappearing foreign exchange resources since 1986. But a couple of well-structured transfer-of-technology agreements are still delivering profits, and Fluke is pursuing new leads and adapting some of its strategies to leaner business times.

For the first seven years of doing business with the PRC (1973–80), Fluke, a manufacturer of electronic testing and measuring devices for the electronics and electrical industry, stuck to direct sales. Meanwhile, it was learning all it could about the market and looking for suitable vehicles for deeper penetration. That opportunity came in 1980, when Fluke entered into its first transfer-of-technology arrangement with the Beijing Radio Research Institute (BRRI) to produce some of its hand-held digital multimeters for the domestic market. Nine other accords quickly followed, some of them with BRRI, and in 1984 and 1985 Fluke struck similar deals with the Qian Feng factory in Chengdu and the Shanghai Electric Meter Works.

All of these technology-transfer agreements hewed to the same basic structure. Fluke would supply CKD or SKD kits, would handle the purchase for the Chinese partner of the manufacturing-process equipment needed to assemble these kits, and would provide extensive training to Chinese personnel to enable them to carry out the manufacturing operation. The technology transferred consisted primarily of manufacturing-process know-how and expertise in plant management and organization.

In return, Fluke would receive a "package" fee covering the purchase of capital equipment, its outlays for training, and a minimum number of kits. On repeat orders for kits, the US company receives a variable payment based on volume. Contracts have typically ranged in value from around $500,000 to $2 million.

While similar to a licensing agreement in some ways, these deals fall under the "trade and technology" rubric. Even in the early 1980s, the Chinese were reluctant to pay royalties outright for technology. This structure also suited Fluke, which wanted to stay away from transferring proprietary-product technology that would allow the Chinese to replicate its products and possibly pose a competitive threat in its key markets in the future.

These agreements give the Chinese partners access to a wide range of sophisticated products that they would otherwise have to import, while upgrading their manufacturing skills and product knowledge. The Chinese partner in turn sells the assembled instruments to a wide range of domestic customers, including electronics factories (e.g. TV producers), computer factories, power companies, schools, oil refineries and shipyards.

In determining what products to transfer, Fluke considers the technical skills of the Chinese partner as well as the kind of restrictions on that technology that will be imposed by the US government and the Consultative Group Coordinating Committee (COCOM). While US export controls over product sales have been liberalized in recent years, actual transfer-of-technology accords must still pass muster with the US Departments of Commerce, Defense and State as well as COCOM because of the potential military applications.

Under these agreements and through sales of both finished product and the kits, Fluke's business with China peaked in 1985 at close to $10 million, when it accounted for some 5% of the company's worldwide sales. This was divided almost equally between direct sales of finished goods and the technology-transfer agreement (including sales of kits). In 1986, when China ran into severe hard-currency problems and began to seriously restrain its imports, the business fell by half, to less than $3 million. After staying flat for several years, however, revenue from China has picked up to over $4 million (2% of Fluke's worldwide sales). Direct sales now account for the lion's share, while kits come to only around 30% of the business.

While China's dwindling foreign exchange was largely responsible for the business contraction, the vagaries of the national government's decentralization efforts also played a role. These policies put more decision-making into the hands of local governments and the manufacturing units themselves, but gave them more responsibility for meeting their own foreign exchange requirements. Whereas the hard currency for the initial agreements was allocated by the central government, this responsibility later devolved to local governments, and to the Chinese manufacturing unit itself.

For several years now, Fluke's China partners have been resorting to the foreign exchange swap markets to meet their hard-currency needs. During the past few years, even local currency has dried up as a result of the official credit crunch, so even this source of dollars is problematic. Not only have Fluke's Chinese partners' own domestic

(Continued)

customers slashed their orders for finished goods, but those that do continue to buy are chronically late in making payment. To help BRRI deal with foreign exchange constraints, Fluke agreed to allow it to export products using "key components" and the Fluke trademark to certain countries (like Japan) and to permit barter arrangements with Eastern Europe, provided the output met its stringent quality-control standards. To date no Chinese-made product has yet been exported—largely, however, because the PRC partners do not yet have the needed distribution and servicing facilities in place abroad.

In 1986, Fluke was in the process of negotiating a host of new cooperation deals, and exploring the possibility of licensing agreements. Today, assembly agreements with only two partners are still functioning: Those with BRRI and another with Qian Feng in Chengdu have been periodically rolled over. The Shanghai arrangement lapsed after a few years when the product being assembled became obsolete and the factory lacked the foreign exchange to embark on a more advanced venture. Fluke still supplies this factory with finished product for resale, however.

A new direction Fluke has just taken seeks to minimize its Chinese partners' foreign exchange outlays (while keeping Fluke's own costs down). It has entered into a consultancy agreement with BRRI for product development. Under this arrangement, the Chinese partner is itself designing a hand-held multimeter, and Fluke provides advice by making suggestions, answering questions and educating BRRI about what would sell in the world marketplace and why. Rather than charging a consultancy fee, BRRI has agreed to buy certain of the parts from Fluke when the product goes into production.

Talks with new partners for other assembly agreements are also in progress. Now, in addition to examining the potential partner's technical qualifications and basic industry compatibility, Fluke looks more carefully at what Chinese entities are supporting the future partner and whether it is likely to have access to foreign exchange.

Because of the close study of foreign systems and advice from international intellectual-property experts, China's laws in this area are considered to be relatively modern. But while China has made strenuous efforts to modernize its legislation, some weak spots remain. Like other developing countries, Chinese rules are more protective of its local industries and of its right to import or copy certain technologies without paying for them. Thus, legal experts view Chinese law as up to international standards in some areas but deficient in others—for example, in its lack of patent protection for drugs and chemical products.

Since only a relatively few cases of infringement have come before the Chinese courts or other bodies to date, it is difficult to assess how well foreigners' patent or trademark rights will be enforced. However, these few cases do indicate that the legal system is trying to give the foreign patent or trademark holder a fair shake.

Many MNCs report that maintaining close relationships with the government agencies charged with enforcing China's IPR laws is the best way to ensure speedy response to complaints. Foreign firms wanting to stop trademark violations must go through a Beijing-designated qualified agent, such as the China Trademark Service in Beijing or Hong Kong-based Novel Technology Development Patent Agency. No corresponding agencies have yet been created to deal with copyright matters, although firms can try the National Copyright Administration in Beijing.

Increasingly, frustrated US trade officials and industry have been putting pressure on China to improve its lax IP protection. In April 1991 US Trade Representative Carla Hills cited China as one of the "priority foreign countries" targeted for possible trade retaliation for inadequate IP rights protection under the Special 301 provisions of the 1988 Omnibus Trade and Competitiveness Act. Because it is the only US trade partner that offers neither product patent protection for pharmaceuticals or chemicals nor copyright protection for US works, China seems a likely candidate for punitive sanctions. The Bush administration has been reluctant to offend Beijing, however. Political considerations—plus concern over the indirect impact upon Hong Kong, which handles over 60% of China's exports—might continue to outweigh US industry concerns.

Patents

In 1980, the State Council established a patent office and assigned to a special committee the task of drafting a patent law. The committee members worked closely with foreign intellectual-property specialists. The results were the 1984 Patent Law of the PRC and its January 1985 detailed implementing regulations, which went into effect on April 1, 1985. In preparing the law, Chinese drafters studied the patent systems of many countries, including those of the US, France, West Germany and Japan. The result was a body of legislation that incorporated elements from the statutes of developed and developing countries alike. Even so, many foreign firms report problems with patent infringement, and complain of similar deficiencies in the laws that are supposed to protect them.

Patents are granted on a "first to apply" basis, rather than the "first to invent" principle that applies to US patent law. Like patent laws in many developing countries, the PRC law requires that the patent right be *worked* in China. If a patentee does not manufacture the patented item or use the patented process in China within three years of the date of the patent being granted—and has no "valid" justification for doing so—the State Patent Office may grant another entity a compulsory license to practice the patent.

The regulations identify three types of patents: for inventions, utility models and designs. "Invention" refers to a new technical solution relating to a product or process. Utility models relate to a new technical solution of practical use in regard to the shape or structure of a product (utility models are sometimes referred to as "petty inventions"). Design patents apply to the aesthetics of a product regarding its shape, pattern and color. Patent rights for inventions are valid for 15 years; in the case of utility models and designs, the patent rights have a duration of five years.

Patents may not be granted for items in the following categories, although they may be granted for *processes used* in producing items in the last four of these categories: scientific discoveries; rules and methods for mental activities; methods for diagnosis or treatment of disease; food, beverages and flavorings; pharmaceuticals products and substances obtained by means of a chemical process; animal and plant varieties; and substances obtained by means of nuclear transformation.

These restrictions are found in the patent laws of many countries, especially developing countries whose governments wish to protect nascent industries from foreign domination and ensure that the production of pharmaceuticals and foodstuffs is as cheap and widespread as possible.

Patent application procedures are spelled out in the implementing regulations. All documents must be in Chinese, although foreign names or scientific and technical terms can be included in the original language.

Practical implementation of the law has revealed loopholes and inadequacies. Chinese patent officials have been studying these with a view to issuing a revised patent law, but none has been ratified so far. The following are among the controversial issues to be considered.

Product patenting. The current law only allows patents for the processes for making chemical substances to be patented, not the products themselves. Foreign drug companies and agrochemical firms are among the most vociferous proponents of change on this front. They argue that lack of protection discourages imports of advanced technology and effectively stalls China's industrial progress.

The upcoming revision of the patent law could contain additional protection for chemicals, though probably not the full protection foreign companies would like. The Chinese authorities are reportedly considering "process to product" protection, which would benefit products made with processes patented in China. Under this intermediate course, the product itself is protected, provided the underlying process is also protected under Chinese patent law.

Computer software. The patent law only offers protection for programs that are so integrated into hardware as to be indistinguishable from it. But proposed drafts of legislation to protect copyrights and computer software have been submitted to the Chinese authorities and are being studied.

The right to import a patented product. Like many developing countries, China does not grant patent holders the right to import the product for which they hold the patent. Foreign firms would like to see a right-to-import clause added to the patent law, but Chinese officials are resistant to any loosening of import controls. A compromise system may be to grant import rights for a product until the time that product is manufactured in China.

Patent protection prior to the grant of the patent. Many advocate the strengthening of legal production in the period between publication of a patent application and the grant of patent rights—for example, by allowing the patentee to claim damages for any illegal use of the patent during this period.

The duration of patent protection for processes used in the manufacture of pharmaceutical chemicals. Because testing new drugs is such a long process, several countries, including the US and Japan, have extended the duration of patent protection in this area. Many argue that China should follow suit, and the patent law revisions may extend such protection for, say, 20 years.

The use of Chinese language in patent applications. All documents submitted in patent applications must be in Chinese, and accurate translation of highly technical documents takes a long time. There have been calls for the patent office to accept some applications in the original language, to be followed by a later version in Chinese. Also suggested has been the extension of the time limit for filing opposition to a patent application, currently three months, to accommodate translation difficulties.

The State Patent office, under the State Council, is the authority that reviews patent applications and grants patent rights. Administrative patent offices have been established by regional authorities and by the official bodies in charge of various sectors of the economy. These offices (numbering 99 by the end of 1987) process applications or handle disputes relating to the patent rights of PRC individuals or enterprises. They are empowered to order offenders to stop patent infringements and to pay compensation to patent holders. If parties involved in patent disputes do not agree with its findings, the case may be brought before the courts.

Foreign applicants must generally go through specially designated agencies. At present there are four:

- *The CCPIT Patent Agency,* a department of the China Council for the Promotion of International Trade (since June 1988 also known as the China Chamber of International Commerce). The agency, based in Beijing, was established in 1980 and formally opened in 1984.
- *China Patent Agent (HK),* a joint venture between the CCPIT and Star Paging (Holding) of Hong Kong. The agency was established in 1984 and now has offices in Hong Kong, Shenzhen and Beijing; and New York, Tokyo and Germany. China Patent Agent (HK) handles the bulk of China's foreign patent business and is favored by foreign clients because of its large and skilled work force.
- *Shanghai Patent Agent,* a Shanghai-based office, is also authorized to handle foreign applications. Another is NTD Patent Agent, a subsidiary of Novel Technology Development Corp of Hong Kong, which is a joint venture between China National Technical Import-Export Corp (Techimport) and the Novel Group of Hong Kong. NTD Patent Agent was established in 1987 and is based in Hong Kong.
- *China Patent and Technology Transfer Co.* is the fourth organization charged with handling PRC applications for foreign patents and with promoting the sale of Chinese technology overseas. Founded in 1987, it falls under the administration of the CCPIT.

Between April 1985, when the patent law went into effect, and end-1989, the patent office received 125,874 patent applications and granted 27,000 patents. Of these, 25,171 applications were from foreign parties. Because most foreign applications are for technical inventions, however, only a small proportion have been granted so far, as they take longer to process than the design or utility models that make up the bulk of domestic applications.

According to foreign lawyers, China's patent-application system is backlogged, but not unusually so. An invention generally takes about two to three years from filing to final approval; designs and utility models are handled much faster, often within 18 months—the simpler process is tantamount to registration and does not involve substantial examinations.

Trademarks

China's trademark law came into force on March 1, 1983, replacing a more rudimentary law that had been on the statute books for 20 years.

Detailed implementing regulations were also promulgated in 1983, replaced by a revised and much broadened set of implementing regulations effective Jan. 13, 1988. Legal sources say that, while some of the trademark rules appear stringent, the Chinese authorities have been liberal in their interpretation and fair about assigning trademarks to their rightful owners, even if a foreign trademark holder has missed some deadlines or not hewed strictly to all the technicalities.

Trademark rights in the PRC are established by registration on a first-to-file basis. However, since China joined the Paris Union in December 1984, nationals of other member nations may claim priority use of trademarks within six months of the date of first filing.

Foreign companies wishing to register trademarks in China must go through an agency designated by the State Administration for Industry and Commerce (SAIC). There are currently two such authorized bodies—the CCPIT and China Patent Agent (HK) (see above). It is likely that the number of authorized agents will grow to meet the increase in demand from foreign applicants.

The implementing regulations make it compulsory to register trademarks for pharmaceuticals and tobacco, thus ensuring some measure of quality control over these products. In addition, the SAIC is empowered to list products for which trademarks are compulsory. On Jan. 14, 1988, the SAIC promulgated one such list, which included unprocessed chemicals and their pharmaceutical preparations, biochemical preparations and blood products.

Registered trademarks must carry a sign indicating that they have been registered. They sign may either be the Chinese characters for a registered trademark or an encircled "R."

Certain words or designs cannot be registered as trademarks—for example, national flags and emblems, generic names of goods or, more subjectively, words or symbols "detrimental to socialist morals or customs or having other unhealthy influences." The 1988 implementing rules also added foreign place names and names of PRC administrative districts above county level to the list of words that cannot be registered as trademarks.

Trademarks are registered according to the category of goods for which the trademark will be used; separate applications must be made for the use of the same trademark for goods in other categories. Under a recent revision, China now conforms with the internationally accepted classification system for trademarks.

Trademark disputes are adjudicated by the Trademark Review and Adjudication Board under the State Administration for Industry and Commerce. The 1983 implementing rules only allow trademark registrants to challenge a trademark registration, and some unscrupulous companies took advantage of this to register the trademarks of foreign

Patents and Trademarks in the PRC

Conventions. Paris Convention (Paris Union), UN World Intellectual Property Organization.
Basic laws. Patent Law of the PRC (March 1984), Implementing Regulations (April 1985). Trademark Law of the PRC (March 1983), Implementing Regulations (January 1988). Regulations of the PRC for the Administration of Technology Import Contracts (May 1985), Implementation Regulations (January 1980). Copyright Law of the PRC (June 1991).

Patents
Types and duration. Patents of invention, 15 years from the date of filing.
Novelty. Inventions must be novel and inventive: No identical invention or utility model can be disclosed or previously filed with the Patent Office prior to the application, and its features must represent notable progress over earlier technology.
Unpatentable. Contrary to law or social morality, or detrimental to the public interest. Also, no patent rights awarded for scientific discoveries; rules and methods for mental activities, methods for the diagnosis and treatment of diseases; food, beverages and flavorings; pharmaceutical products and substances obtained by means of chemical process; animal and plant varieties; substances obtained by means of nuclear transformation.
Application procedure. Application is to the Patent Office of the PRC. The right to apply belongs to the inventor or creator, except in the case of service inventions, when the right belongs to an enterprise. Patents are assigned on a first-to-file basis, unless an applicant claims priority for filing first in a treaty country.
Examination procedure. Applications for a patent of invention are published within 18 months of the date of filing. The applicant must request examination for substance within three years. If not in conformity with the law, the Patent Office will notify the applicant and request observations or amendments. Opposition must be filed within three months, and the applicant then has three months to respond. Appeal may be made to the Patent Reexamination Board within three months of notification, and thereafter to the courts.
Compulsory licensing may apply if, within three years of grant of patent right the patentee fails to make the product or use the process under patent, or to authorize others to do so.

Trademarks
Duration. Ten years from the date of approval of registration, renewable for 10 years.
Application procedure. Application must be made to the Trademark Office (under the State Administration for Industry and Commerce). Foreign companies must go through the agency designated by the SAIC, currently either the CCPIT or China Patent Agent (HK). Separate application must be filed for each class of goods. Any trademark obtaining preliminary approval is published, and objections may be filed within three months of publication; after the final approval of registration, objectors have one year to file.

Industrial designs and models
Procedures for application for utility models or designs are similar to that for patents, except that patent grants are announced and applications are decided without examination as to substance. Duration is five years from date of filing, renewable for three years.

firms. But the 1988 legislation gives the rightful trademark holder recourse by allowing anyone to challenge trademark registration.

Trademarks are valid for 10 years from the date of approval of registration. Trademark holders may authorize the use of the mark to others through licensing arrangements.

One of the features of China's trademark legislation in the 1950s and 1960s was a stress on quality control—a trademark served more as a mark of quality than a symbol identifying a particular manufacturer. The 1983 law retained some of that spirit. For example, Art. 31 rules that the SAIC may impose penalties if goods sold using a trademark are of low quality. These penalties may include fines on the manufacturer and revocation of the trademark registration.

Penalties for trademark infringements are spelled out in the legislation. The 1988 rules introduced a new system of basing penalties on the amount of income derived from the unlawful use of trademarks (however, the authorities have shown themselves reluctant to award damages in cases of infringement—as IBM discovered in the case discussed below).

Foreign firms should note that if no Chinese translation of a trademark is filed with the application, the Trademark Office will supply its own translation.

By end-1987, a total of 187,000 trademarks had been registered in China, of which over 28,000 were registered by foreign companies or individuals, compared with a total of 5,130 foreign trademarks in 1979.

Recent infringement cases

Several trademark cases involving foreign firms have been brought before the authorities in recent years, including the following examples.

Walt Disney of the US successfully acted against a Guangdong candy factory that was using Mickey Mouse and Donald Duck characters on products. Walt Disney was victim of the first-to-file system when a PRC manufacturer managed to register the words "Mickey Mouse" along with a picture of the world-famous cartoon character before Disney's registration had a chance to go into effect. But through "informal persuasion," the authorities convinced the Chinese factory to stop using these trademarks and reassigned them to the US company. Subsequently, Walt Disney filed 350 trademark registrations to guard against similar problems.

Hong Kong Soya Bean Products of Hong Kong, makers of the soybean drink Vitasoy, at first was unable to register the name of the drink as a trademark in the PRC. The trademark office ruled that the Chinese name of the drink (comprising two characters denoting vitamins and one meaning milk) was descriptive of the product and therefore could not constitute a trademark. But, upon appeal, the decision went in Vitasoy's favor. The authorities ruled that, in the case of well-known international names, the general-description rule can be overridden. In fact, the outcome of this case led to a special addendum to the trademark law making an exception for such internationally recognized trademarks.

Sharp Corp of Japan discovered the illegal use of its trademark on video recorders being assembled in the PRC by companies from the Zhuhai SEZ, Guangzhou and Hong Kong. The business license of the Guangzhou company was revoked and the Zhuhai company was fined.

In 1988, ***IBM*** filed complaints against six enterprises located in or near the Shenzhen Special Economic Zone for unlawfully assembling and selling counterfeit IBM products. Through China Patent Agent (HK), IBM approached the Shenzhen Bureau of the Administration of Industry and Commerce (AIC) with carefully compiled investigative and technical reports documenting the infringements. AIC, upon investigating the case (which included raids on the infringing enterprises), immediately ordered the infringers to stop assembling and selling the IBM counterfeits, and when it completed its investigation in early 1989 it found five of the six companies guilty of violating IBM's registered trademarks. The remedies included ordering the counterfeit logos on the sealed machines and parts removed, and manuals, packaging and other accessories burned. The Shenzhen AIC also imposed fines of 18-20% of the illegal turnover, totaling Rmb660,000 ($177,500), and ordered the five violators to promise never to engage in similar infringements.

Copyrights

China's new copyright law became effective on June 1, 1991, but neither the law nor its implementing regulations meet international norms. Particularly problematic is the lack of protection for unpublished foreign works, which draft legislation is trying to ameliorate.

US copyright owners collectively suffer greater trade losses due to piracy in China than in any other Asian country: more than $400 million each year. In 1988 computer software accounted for about $300 million in trade losses, and books for $100 million. The motion picture and recording industries recorded less substantial losses. As a result, the US has threatened to take action under Special 301 unless China makes real progress toward joining the Berne Convention or the Universal Copyright Convention (UCC) by the end of 1991.

The protection offered computer programs and databases by the new copyright rules is vague at best and qualified by exceptions. China had no law protecting software at all until very recently. The recently adopted Regulations for the Protection of Computer Software (which took effect Oct. 1, 1991) fall far short of the mark. The new law provides no protection for software published after June 4, 1991—and seems to suggest that the public is free to copy any software published before the cut-off date. The law seems to require that new software developed outside China be first published in China in order to qualify for protection. The only option would be for firms to simultaneously publish Chinese translations of software in China or involve Chinese citizens in the translation. This does not protect the English-language original.

Traditionally, foreign companies and individuals have been able to protect their works only by writing it into contracts—which is unsatisfactory, since it fails to protect against copyright infringements by third parties. Works published by Chinese authors are protected by regulations issued by the Ministry of Culture in 1984. And China's Civil Code stipulates that individuals and legal persons enjoy copyright protection; this principle has been applied to mediate some domestic copyright disputes in recent years.

The State Copyright Bureau, established in 1985, is responsible for preparing and supervising copyright legislation, dealing with international copyright questions and training PRC individuals and institutions in copyright matters. Local copyright offices have been established throughout the country to handle domestic copyright issues.

In April 1988, the China Copyright Agency opened in Beijing, with a mandate to serve PRC, Hong Kong, Macao and Taiwanese authors on matters of copyright and royalties. Two months later the Copyright Agency of China (Hong Kong) was set up in Hong Kong to offer similar legal services.

Tax Consequences

Foreign licensors with no permanent establishment in China are generally subject to a 10% or 20% withholding tax on the gross amount received from Chinese licensees. The lower rate applies, for example, if the technology falls into certain priority sectors. Royalties or know-how fees may even be subject to a lower tax (say 5%) or entirely exempt from tax (much more difficult to win approval for) if the technology is particularly advanced or if the licensor provides preferential terms. The 10% rate also applies in the Special Economic Zones, coastal cities, and other specially designated areas where foreign business and investment are encouraged. Double-tax treaties with several countries also usually reduce the tax to a maximum 10%.

10
India

Under the British Raj, colonial managing agencies monopolized the import of both technology and goods to India. Through their exports to the colony and their comparative advantage in production, British manufacturers severely hindered the development of indigenous industries in India. As nationalist political organizations—notably the Indian National Congress—emerged, so did the organized boycotts of foreign goods. The "Buy Indian" movement was both an economic campaign and an important step toward political independence.

Under the leadership of Jawaharlal Nehru, who was Prime Minister from 1947 to 1964, India embarked upon a massive program of industrialization. In order to shield basic industries from foreign competition, the government instituted a highly protectionist system of tariffs and regulations to curb imports and restrict foreign equity. Despite the development of local research and development facilities, Indian firms still require essential technology from abroad. Lack of hard currency in the wake of the foreign exchange crisis of 1957 led Indian firms to look to the West for financial support of their technology transfers. During the 1960s, the number of Western joint ventures and foreign equity increased considerably.

By the mid-1970s, however, Indira Gandhi's government had become hostile to the multinationals as well as the large Indian business houses, which had accounted for a large share of foreign collaborations. Antitrust legislation ratified in 1973 severed many links between technology transfers and foreign capital. In 1977, the government shook up the foreign-investment community by demanding that multinationals transfer additional technology at little or no charge. This policy caused IBM and Coca-Cola to abandon their Indian operations altogether.

When he became prime minister after his mother's assassination in 1985, Rajiv Gandhi began to liberalize India's industrial policy, gradually increasing opportunities for the private sector and easing the importation of technology. Opposition parties, as well as the public-sector enterprises and the civil service, criticized the liberalization programs and inveighed against the encroachment of multinational corporations. Reports that a Swedish arms manufacturer, Bofors, had bribed high-level officials severely damaged the administration's credibility.

When Congress lost its parliamentary majority in 1989 elections, the party (and the Nehru-Gandhi clan) relinquished power for only the second time since independence. In order to defeat Congress, the Janata Dal had formed a makeshift coalition with Hindu fundamentalists and Communists. Despite the conflicting interests of the parties, V.P. Singh's coalition government proposed bold policy initiatives, notably in the liberalization of industry.

Violent communal disputes—contention over Singh's proposed caste policy, and fundamentalist campaign to demolish a mosque at a Hindu religious site—brought down the Singh government in November 1990. Although Singh's successor, Chandra Sekhar, was a socialist and a fierce opponent of the multinationals, his administration lessened state control over industry more than any previous administrations. The Chandra Sekhar government lasted barely four months, prompting new elections.

In the May 1991 polling, Congress—which had promoted itself as the only party able to hold India's divergent parts together—stood to profit the most from the growing political instability. The assassination of Rajiv Gandhi shortly before the 1991 elections, though, pulled the keystone from the party structure. In the aftermath, Congress managed to form only a minority government under a little-known party boss, P.V. Narasimha. Due to the economic crisis at home (and to the demise of the planned model elsewhere), economic liberalization has become a buzzword across New Delhi's political spectrum. While the new administration has advanced certain limited liberalization measures, it lacks the mandate necessary to enact far-reaching reform.

Foreign involvement in India's economy remains a highly political issue. In the prelude to British imperial rule, a single English corporation—the East India Company—had established de facto control over much of the Indian subcontinent. Following independence in 1947, India developed a highly autarkic national economy, one in which multinationals and foreign trade have played a conspicuously small role. As a result, US threats of trade sanctions under Super 301 have carried little weight. At issue in the dispute over intellectual property protection in India is national sovereignty, as well as international standards.

Industrial Policy

The Indian government exerts an extreme degree of control over industry through its pervasive industrial policy. In May 1990, however, Industry Ministry Ajit Singh announced the first reform of industrial regulations since 1956. The new policy covers the areas of industrial licensing, foreign collaborations and import policy, and allows many Indian firms the freedom to import technology and to choose foreign partners freely. About 65% of investment proposals will no longer require government scrutiny and approval. Few investments by multinational corporations, however, are small enough to benefit from this program. Nonetheless, it represents an important step toward greater liberalization. Largely because of these liberalized investment regulations, Washington refrained from taking punitive action against India under Super 301.

New Delhi announced in July 1991 that much of the system of business licenses and restrictions will be abolished, including export subsidies, replenishment licenses (which allow exporters to import production units), and licenses for capital goods and raw materials. Since the laws pertain mainly to local operations, the big Indian industrial houses stand to benefit from the liberalization more than multinationals.

India's industrial policy is based on the Industries Development and Regulation Act of 1951, drafted soon after independence. It is also governed by the Industrial Policy Resolution of 1956, which mandates government regulation and planned development in the national interest. Private firms, which are grouped in "houses," are tightly controlled through the licensing regulation, which mandates government approval for capital issues, imports and plant expansion. In addition, the state controls 80% of banking, and thus can almost directly control investment in the private sector. The government maintains control over the private sector by requiring licenses for certain industrial ventures. Because the process of obtaining a license is conducted on a time-consuming case-by-case basis, the Ministry of Industry removes licensing requirements in order to encourage investment into certain areas.

Under the new policy, licenses are no longer necessary for certain industrial ventures (see "Investment Incentives," below), especially those that are located in "backward areas." There is a common application for all industrial licenses. It must contain the full details of the proposed ventures, including projections of cash flow, profitability and production costs for a five- to 10-year period. Applications for large ventures—those involving more than Rs50 million in investment outlays—must be made directly to the Secretariat for Industrial Approvals.

Technology Transfers

In the past, foreign firms have found it quicker to establish a licensing agreement (dubbed "technical collaboration") with a qualified licensee than to arrange a joint venture with suitable Indian firms. Licensing is used as a preliminary step before deciding to a establish a joint venture.

Even though contracts that bind the licensee with regard to tie-in purchases are prohibited, licensing a particular technology can create a market for the licensor to sell corollary components, which can bring greater returns than royalties and fees themselves. In terms of intellectual-property protection, licensing ventures offer better protection than what is available in export sales alone.

The government prefers that foreign companies do business through branches or wholly owned subsidiaries; in most cases, former branches and subsidiaries have transformed into Indian companies, with airlines and shipping companies being the primary exception.

In considering investment proposals, the government looks at the need and appropriateness of the technology as well as the terms of the agreement for either establishing new units or upgrading existing ones. Preferred technologies are new forms of high technology, rather than lower forms duplicating those already available in India. Even though the situation has changed somewhat since the mid-1970s, when many Western firms quit India because of strident government demands, multinationals continue to exercise caution in selecting technology to bring to India.

The government is preparing a new "negative list" of industries that will still require approval. In highly protected sectors such as textiles, the government will certainly continue to ban foreign participation. Sectors dominated by small-scale industries are also protected by Indian law. Production of consumer goods, for example, is permitted only in ventures with certain export obligations.

At present, only public sector firms can operate in the air and rail transportation, communications and power-generation sectors. State enterprises dominate a variety of sectors, including chemicals, steel and banking. In addition, the government can prohibit companies from engaging in industries that it has determined to be already operating at "sufficient capacity," such as automobiles or consumer goods.

A second negative list is also being made of industries in which India will allow no expansion of production. These too will require government approval, and are likely to include India's highly protected automobile industry. Increasingly, however, Indian industries are being privatized. Recently, the petrochemicals sector was opened to private investment. The Mafatlal-Shell joint venture, for example, is now involved in export-oriented production of plastics.

Approval Requirements

All technology-collaboration agreements whose royalty payments do not exceed 5% on sales within India or 8% on exports may be made without government approval.

Under Indian law, a licensing agreement is treated as an investment proposal. Licensing contracts are limited to five years, plus three years for start-up. Generally, agreements can be extended for another five-year period if the licensor provides access to new technology or allows the licensee to export to new markets. After one renewal, the government rarely grants extensions. After the contract expires, the licensee is permitted—without exception—to continue production without making further payments to the licensor, even if the product is still produced by Indian patents.

Although the government permits Indian firms to sublicense technology through the exclusion of secrecy clauses and mandatory nonrestriction clauses in all new foreign licensing contracts, sublicensing requires the agreement of all involved parties (including the foreign firm) and, in practice, occurs only between related companies within the same industrial house.

In addition, the licensee is permitted to export products based upon licensed technology, but only to countries where the licensor has no licensees or joint ventures. Because highly protected Indian industries are very uncompetitive in the world market, licensees generally export only as agents of the licensor.

In evaluating proposals for technical collaborations, the government prefers royalty agreements that offer access to technical know-how and increased research and development over those licenses that merely offer the right to use a patent.

Some firms have found that pledging to form a joint venture with a would-be licensee has helped to soften the government's licensing terms. Foreign share capital consists of cash investment, not equipment or know-how. Portfolio investment in shares and debentures is permitted only for nonresident Indians (NRIs) and, in the case of new companies, for NRIs from oil-exporting developing countries.

Because of the severity of India's foreign debt and the desire for lower capital repatriation, some Indian politicians (including V.P. Singh) would prefer greater foreign equity investment to borrowing abroad.

Under guidelines formulated in 1989 by the Ministry of Science and Technology, the government is encouraging the formation of more research-and-development joint ventures.

Foreign-Investment Requirements

Relative to the size of the economy, foreign investment in India has been low. In 1989, for example, foreign investment in India totaled only $250 million, compared with $2.3 billion in China. The primary reason that foreign investment has been scant is the difficulty of the industrial licensing system. Until recently, all proposals for foreign investment required detailed scrutiny, which often lasted up to three years. Although foreign-collaboration regulations are being liberalized, Industry Minister Ajit Singh affirmed that they will be allowed selectively—only in export or high-tech industries.

During the period 1957–88, over 11,000 foreign collaborations were registered; fully half of these, however, were initiated after 1981. Foreign collaborations can include investment and equity, and those including a share of foreign financing have been increasing. For foreign collaborations (with the exception of ventures involving NRIs), the government requires that the venture involve the transfer of technology. All collaboration agreements last for a term of eight years: three years for start-up of production, and five years to collect royalties on production.

Investment Classifications

While foreign companies and large industrial houses that are regulated by the Foreign Exchange Regulation Act (FERA) and the Monopolies and Restrictive Trade Practices (MRTP) Act were excluded from recent reforms, Industry Minister Ajit Singh has said that the government intends to do more for them in the future.

FERA was designed to stem the encroachment of multinationals into Indian industry as well as to regulate foreign exchange. After it was ratified in 1973, foreign investment fell considerably. All companies in which foreign equity is over 40% are regulated under this law. The MRTP Act was enacted in 1969 to regulate the domination of large Indian business houses, which are defined as enterprises in which over Rs1 billion in fixed assets has been invested. It was designed under the Indira Gandhi administration as part of her populist campaign against the economic might of the large industrial houses, such as the giant Tata and Birla concerns, which hold operations in a wide number of sectors. All firms falling under MRTP criteria require government approval for any investment. As a result, it is generally easier for a foreign company to avoid collaborations with the larger Indian houses that fall under MRTP jurisdiction.

Before losing power, Rajiv Gandhi's administration had actively considered raising the FERA limit on foreign equity from 40% to 51%. Because majority foreign equity is a politically sensitive issue in India, however, a decision on the matter was postponed until after the elections. Under the Singh government, the regulation has remained unchanged. Under the new policy, projects with up to 40% foreign equity receive "automatic" government approval, and FERA companies and MRTP business houses still require government approval. Majority foreign ownership (51% equity or more) is generally permitted only in priority or high-tech industries and for export-oriented projects. Total foreign ownership (100%) is allowed only in projects obligated to export 100% of their production. As a result, many foreign companies keep their equity below 40%, as was the intent of the FERA legislation.

Incentives

In order to spread growth away from the major cities, the Indian government developed a policy to create 100 "growth centers"—equipped with power, water, banking, telecommunications and other infrastructure—in "backward areas" outside India's 21 largest metropolitan areas. Under the new policy, projects with investments up to Rs750 million in fixed assets no longer require government licenses if they are located in backward areas. For ventures located in urban areas, the limit is Rs250 million. Businesses regulated by FERA or MRTP are also encouraged in backward areas, but they still require licenses.

Although export ventures were encouraged by the creation of export-oriented units (EOUs), these got off to a slow start in India. From 1980 to 1988, about 150 EOUs were set up, exporting only Rs5 billion. A more efficient application process, coupled with a depreciating rupee and tax exemptions on export profits, resulted in over 500 applications being made in 1989 alone. Under the new policy, export ventures with capital up to Rs750 million no longer require government licenses. In addition, they are permitted to sell up to one quarter of their production on the local market.

Export ventures fall into two categories: 100% EOUs operating in domestic-tariff areas (in which minimum value added is 20%) and those operating in free-trade zones or export-processing zones, which include customs bonding (where minimum value added is 30%). Export-processing zones (EPZs) exist in a number of states. All produce a variety of products, except the EPZ at Santa Cruz, near Bombay, which exclusively produces electronics.

India's attempt to become a base for offshore electronics assembly will need more foreign investment and technology if it is to be successful. Texas Instruments and Hewlett-Packard, however, are using Indian technicians to write software; since the project combines high-technology and export production, both firms were allowed to hold 100% equity in their units in Bangalore. Such ventures are allowed to import capital goods and raw materials duty free. They are granted a tax holiday of five years for the first eight years of production, with the first three years assumed as a start-up period. Where necessary, licenses for 100% export-oriented units are processed by the Secretariat for Industrial Approvals; those for EPZs are handled by the Development Commissioner of the EPZ.

Intellectual Property Laws

Patents

Patent protection in India is generally adequate for multinational corporations, even though India is not a signatory to the Paris convention. Patents last for 14 years, and they are protected by law. Because of poor protection in certain sectors, however, notably of foods and pharmaceuticals (see below), the US has designated India under its Special 301 trade clause as a country with intellectual-property-rights problems.

Under the Patents Act of 1970, patents fall into three categories: ordinary patents, priority patents and patents of addition. Ordinary patents last for 14 years from the date of filing. Patents on foods, pharmaceuticals, and agricultural chemicals have a duration of either five years from the date of sealing or seven years from the date of granting, whichever is less. Patents of addition expire when the main patent expires.

Filing for a patent first requires the submission of complete specifications in English, drafted preferably in the UK style, to the Controller of Patents and Designs in Bombay, Calcutta or Madras. Within 18 months, the patent is examined to certify its novelty (theoretically, worldwide, but in practice, showing no prior public use in India) and to confirm that it complies with all requirements. The patent application and specifications are published in the *Official Gazette.* If there is no opposition within four months of publication, the patent is sealed two months later. If the patent is opposed and the decision is favorable, it is sealed after final disposal. If a patent is refused, appeal to the High Court must be made within three months. Normally, it takes two years from the date of filing to receive a patent.

Patent protection is ensured by Indian courts, which are empowered to grant injunctions, damages, and delivery or destruction of articles in cases of violation. Nonetheless, a patent by its Indian definition protects only the process of manufacturing a product, not the product itself. As a result, products such as foods, chemicals, pharmaceuticals, alloys, optics and semiconductors remain unpatentable. Foreign companies, notably chemicals and pharmaceuticals firms, have called for greater protection in New Delhi.

The government can issue a compulsory license if it determines that the patent holder has not sufficiently worked or has abused its patent. Moreover, the government can always issue compulsory licenses for food, pharmaceuticals, and agricultural chemicals. If a licensor fails to file against patent infringement within two months, the compulsory licensee can sue in its own names, as if it were the patentee. If a product has not been made available to the public under reasonable conditions three years after a compulsory license has been granted, the patent can be rescinded. From a practical point of view, however, there is no record of any cases in which patents held by foreign firms were revoked for not being worked sufficiently, or taken over by the government.

India has bilateral pacts protecting patents for 12 months and designs for six months with Australia, Canada, Ireland, New Zealand, South Korea, Sri Lanka and the UK.

Copyrights and Industrial Designs

Copyright infringement in India remains a problem, particularly in the widespread unauthorized publication of foreign fiction and textbooks. Although copyright legislation has been revised in order to provide stricter penalties and also to include software, enforcement remains insufficient.

The Designs Act of 1911 (amended in 1970) covers industrial designs. These can be registered for five years and renewed for two additional five-year terms.

Trademarks and Trade Names

Trademarks are governed by the Trade and Merchandise Marks Act of 1958 and Rules of 1959. A trademark is valid for a period of seven years; these can be renewed indefinitely for additional seven-year periods. By law, only the first user is entitled to register a trademark; through registration, the user receives the exclusive right to use the trademark. A trademark must be "distinctive and not deceiving or contrary to law."

Filing requires that applications be submitted to one of the Registrars of Trademarks in Bombay, Calcutta or Madras. After acceptance, it is published in the *Trademarks Journal*, and opposition must be entered within a period of three months.

The use of foreign brand names and trade names for a "consideration"—for cash or other compensation—is prohibited, with exceptions made for certain pharmaceuticals and pesticides. Nonetheless, some Indian companies have hyphenated their domestic brand name with the name of their foreign collaborator; notable examples include Maruti-Suzuki cars and 7 O'Clock-Ejteck razor blades (which uses joint-venture-partner Gillette's brand name). In addition, 100% export-oriented garment projects that use indigenous textiles are permitted to use foreign brand names (such as Benetton and Pierre Cardin). On the other hand, foreign brand names that have been appropriated by Indian firms have little protection; such has been the case with an Indian firm that dubbed itself "Pizza Hut," although it held no franchise arrangement with PepsiCo.

Payment Practices

In order to maintain the confidence of foreign investors, the Indian government has allowed the free flow of remittances abroad, whether royalties, fees, profits, dividends, interest or loan payments. As the nature of foreign collaboration in India has changed over the years, so too has the relative composition of remittances. In 1960, for example, of total earnings remitted by foreign companies, 45.5% was remunerated as profits and only 30.3% as dividends and fees. By 1986, only 1.3% of the total was remitted as profits.

Restrictions on Royalties and Fees

The maximum allowed for royalties and fees cannot comprise more than 8% of the net value of production—the ex-factory sales price, less duties and costs of components. Payments are made for a maximum term of 10 years. Royalties are regulated by the Patents Act of 1970 and are closely monitored by the Indian government.

Some foreign firms have been able to negotiate for royalties to be based on a percentage of the total selling price by offering advantageous prices for components to licensees. In export-oriented ventures or transfers of high technology, the government sometimes allows a higher rate. Royalty rates for sublicenses are lower than rates granted for the initial license. In addition, the government reserves the right to use any patent noncommercially without paying royalties.

Fees are generally paid in three equal payments: the first when the agreement is signed; the next when the documents are transferred; and

Patents and Trademarks in India

Conventions. Reciprocal arrangements for the protection of inventions and designs (12 months for patents, six months for designs) exist with Australia, Canada, Ireland, South Korea, New Zealand, Sri Lanka and the UK.
Basic laws. The Patents Act 1970 and the Designs Act 1911, with amendments passed in 1970; also the Trade and Merchandise Marks Act 1958 and Rules of 1959.

Patents

Types and duration. Kinds: ordinary patents, priority patents and patents of addition. Duration of ordinary patents is 14 years from date of filing complete specifications or priority; for patents on foods, drugs and agricultural chemicals granted under the 1970 act, duration is five years from date of sealing or seven years from date of granting, whichever is less. Duration of patents of addition is the unexpired term of main patent.
Novelty. No prior public use of knowledge in India.
Unpatentable. Patents are granted only on manufacturing processes, not products themselves, for foods, drugs, medicines, agricultural chemicals, and substances prepared or produced by chemical processes.
Filing procedure. Complete specification in English, in duplicate, to controller of patents and designs in Bombay, Calcutta or Madras; claims drafted in the UK style are preferred.
Examination procedure. Examination as to compliance with requirements, patentability and novelty within 18 months from the date of the first examination report. Application and specifications published in the *Official Gazette* and open to public inspection.
Fees. Application fee, when filed with complete specification, Rs50; sealing fee, Rs60.
Compulsory licensing. Patents must be worked within three years of sealing. Compulsory licenses can be granted if patent is not worked, not worked sufficiently, or abused; compulsory licenses can always be requested for patented food, drugs and medicine.

Trademarks

Duration. Seven years, renewable indefinitely for periods of seven years.

(Continued)

Legal effects. First user alone is entitled to registration.
Registrability. Marks must be distinctive and not deceiving or contrary to law.
Filing procedure. Applications in triplicate for each class of goods to the registrar of trademarks in Bombay, Calcutta or Madras. Acceptance is published in *Trademarks Journal*
Fees. Application, Rs40; registration, Rs90; renewal, Rs100.

Industrial designs and models
Designs are registrable for five years, renewable for two five-year periods. Application fee is Rs3; renewal, Rs10.

the remainder when either production starts or 48 months after the signing, whichever is earlier.

Remittance of royalties and fees abroad require the approval of the Reserve Bank and the Foreign Investment Board. For patents on foods and pharmaceuticals, the maximum rate allowable by law is 4%. For consumer goods manufacturing that does not involve technical assistance, the usual royalty is 2.5%. Guaranteed minimum payments not linked to production are prohibited.

When foreign firms negotiate new licensing agreements or ask for extensions of existing ones, they often receive pressure from the government to reduce the level of royalty payments. Also, if a foreign firm holds a significant stake in an Indian firm, royalty and fee payments are normally lower (but regulations that prevented royalties if the foreign share came close to 50% have been relaxed). Many foreign companies with joint ventures in priority industries have negotiated 3-5% royalty agreements.

A lump-sum payment is limited to 50% of the maximum for royalties. Lump-sum payments still require government approval, but now the government promises a decision within 30 days of application. Drawings, documentation and other forms of know-how are eligible for lump-sum payments.

Approval from the Reserve Bank of India is necessary for repatriation of capital. The Reserve Bank of India determines the sale price of the foreign equity holdings by a formula based on historical profits. This procedure generally undervalues the stake being divested.

Foreign Collaborations Approved, 1985–87

By country (Rs millions)				
	1987	1986	1985	% of total
US	2,951	2,937	3,992	29.0
Germany	987	2,016	1,181	12.3
Japan	691	562	1,568	8.3
UK	845	772	371	5.8
Switzerland	885	325	84	3.8
Italy	297	233	695	3.6
France	535	205	236	2.9
United Arab Emirates	0	0	871	2.6
Norway	0	192	650	2.5
Netherlands	101	727	40	2.5
Sweden	109	475	81	2.0
Belgium	275	0	268	1.6
Canada	67	138	247	1.3
Finland	69	360	20	1.3
Other	882	963	399	6.6
Nonresident Indians	2,077	790	1,904	14.0
Total	10,771	10,695	12,607	100.0

By sector (number)				
	1987	1986	1985	% of total
Electrical equipment	183	175	205	19.9
Industrial machinery	132	108	152	13.8
Chemicals	84	107	69	9.2
Transportation	39	53	101	6.8
Instruments	51	34	54	4.9
Metallurgy	29	45	53	4.5
Glass & ceramics	46	28	36	3.2
Consultancy	47	5	23	2.6
Machine tools	10	13	32	1.9
Leather	4	8	19	1.1
Textiles	6	13	10	1.0
Cement	7	11	9	1.0
Medical equipment	10	12	5	1.0
Pharmaceuticals	13	10	5	1.0
Other	212	335	251	28.2
Total	853	957	1,024	100.0

Source: Tata Industries.

Tax Consequences

Tax rates on dividends and interest is 25%; and on royalties and know-how fees, 30%. Lump-sum payments are also subject to Indian taxes. The 1990 budget released left a variety of tax rates unchanged—including those on royalties, know-how, dividends and interest payments. Officials are continuing to streamline the tax structure and allow fewer exemptions. In general, the tax rate for domestic firms fell by 10%, but the rate for foreign firms remained 50%.

After ratification, a new double-taxation treaty between India and the US will provide a maximum tax rate of 15% on dividends from a subsidiary to a parent corporation and 25% on other dividends. Industrial and copyright royalties will be taxable at a top rate of 20% (15% for royalties paid by the public sector) in the first five years after the treaty comes into effect, and 15% thereafter. Presently US firms pay 30% tax on royalties. As a result, US investment in India is expected to increase considerably, while other OECD countries now placed at a relative disadvantage might spur further treaty negotiations.

Export-oriented units receive tax holidays for the five of their first eight years of operation, with three years for start-up. For ventures in backward areas, 20% of profit is tax exempt for a period of 10 years.

11
Czechoslovakia

The purchase of Western licenses is an important catalyst for scientific and technological development in Czechoslovakia. Over the past 20 years, about 1,500 licenses have been purchased, with some 80% coming from Western countries. Currently about 25–30 new licenses are purchased annually, two thirds of which come from the West. West Germany, Japan and the US have traditionally been the leading Western suppliers. East Germany was the country's largest licensor from within Comecon.

The above figures hide the fact, however, that license purchases have been declining since about the mid-1970s, and still remain below levels reached in 1980. The annual volume of goods produced under license agreements reached its peak during the 1976–80 five-year plan period, at K27 billion. During the first half of the 1980s the figure slipped to about K16.5 billion per year. In 1987, the value of goods produced under license recovered slightly, to about K18 billion.

The reduced emphasis on license purchases can be attributed to hard-currency shortages in the country and the sharp drop in investment activity since the late 1970s. In addition, the purchase of Western licenses has been hampered by a reputation for not being cost-effective. The expense of buying equipment and raw materials associated with licensing projects is often exorbitant, in the view of Czechoslovak purchasing authorities. According to one study, for every dollar spent on licensing fees, the user spends between $7 and $50 on associated supplies. This has left many would-be purchasers skeptical of the real advantage in buying a Western license.

But there is evidence to believe that this anti-licensing attitude among some decision-makers has changed in recent years and that license purchases may be regaining their central position in Czechoslovak development strategy. One good sign is that average annual expenditures on license purchases in the 1986–90 plan period ran at approximately double the value of the previous five-year period.

In addition, officials commonly acknowledge that too little use is made of Western industrial capability, and that the application of Western techniques in local industry is not growing fast enough. The State Planning Commission now regularly calls for more cooperation agreements, and admits that Czechoslovakia cannot keep up with rapid changes in technology entirely from its own limited R&D resources. The country also feels that it is losing its technological lead within Comecon to countries like Hungary and Bulgaria.

Licensing is also gaining in stature as import substitution becomes more important. Officials have estimated that for every dollar spent on license fees, equipment and materials, two dollars can be saved on the import of products or other materials. Moreover, the income generated by a license exceeds all associated spending by almost 200%. During 1986–90, the steel and heavy-engineering sectors allocated K400 million for license purchases and another K1–1.5 billion for materials and equipment associated with the licenses. Against these outlays, they targeted an overall income of K7.5 billion, including K1.5 billion in exports.

Problems

But licensing in the country remains plagued by problems. For one, far too many institutions, including state planning boards, ministries and departments, are still involved in the approval process for license purchases. Bureaucratic delays can make a technology obsolete even before it is implemented, depriving the country of truly up-to-date technology. In one recent licensing deal in the textiles industry, the documentation and approval procedure alone took over 12 months.

License purchases are also hindered by regulations that fail to discriminate between deals involving just the purchase of technology and those including the purchase of equipment and materials. Thus, enterprises that wish to make a relatively simple purchase of technology must undertake the same massive administrative effort as those desiring more advanced forms of cooperation. Not surprisingly, many enterprises regard licensing as more of a bureaucratic headache than a means of improving production.

Additionally, there is often a long time span between the acquisition of a license and its final implementation. In some cases, the interval can be three to four years or longer. Delays are frequently caused by late or faulty deliveries by Czechoslovak subcontractors. Nearly everywhere, new technologies are introduced into old organizational and manufacturing structures that are incapable of adjusting quickly enough to realize the license's potential.

Officials have also criticized the arbitrary nature in which licenses are purchased. In some cases, licenses are obtained for investment projects that have been subsequently dropped from the plan, or licenses are bought without adequate preparation or purpose.

Reforms

Beginning in 1985, the Federal Ministry of Finance and the finance ministries of both the Czech Republic and Slovakia introduced new regulations governing spending on science and technology, including purchase of foreign know-how and licenses. Under the scheme, the ministries have attempted to remove many of the legal obstacles and place more of the decision making for technology purchase in the hands of the enterprises. Existing legislation has been simplified, with the number of legal provisions reduced from 31 to 15.

Under the new rules, the rigid demarcation between noninvestment (R&D) and investment spending has been relaxed. As a result, enterprises have had limited success in using unspent allocations at their own discretion. Many of the previous limitations covering the use of technology-development funds have been removed, and the need to submit an advance costing for entire R&D projects to financial authorities has been dropped.

Noninvestment expenditure can, in some cases, be made from an enterprise's own technical development funds. Such money can be used for both in-house R&D and for purchase of licenses and know-how from abroad or from other Czechoslovak enterprises. Unspent sums can theoretically be carried over from one year to the next, and the fund can be topped up from profits. Enterprises are able to apply for bank credits to supplement their technical development funds and to pool funds with other enterprises for joint projects. Enterprise rights to draw on development funds for purchasing instruments or equipment to further an R&D project or to implement acquired technology have also been expanded. This is a significant improvement over the past, when many enterprises and institutes were unable to support research adequately because of the lack of equipment and the inability to finance construction.

Special Funds and Priority Areas

Some K200 million was allocated to cover the purchase of new licenses in 1988, with an additional K400 million to be applied toward maintaining the 400 existing license agreements, according to officials. The amounts represent an increase of about 10% over what was spent in

Guide for Western Negotiators

Given the above-mentioned attitudes, problems and reforms, Western companies recommend the following tips when negotiating licensing deals in Czechoslovakia:

Emphasize the purchase of associated equipment as a way of shortening commissioning time. The long delay between acquiring a license and putting it into production has been a perennial target of criticism by Czechoslovak authorities. The Czech partner can speed up the commissioning time by demonstrating that it has assembled the necessary Western equipment to produce the licensed product once the license is approved. Western negotiators will find this a useful way to sell associated equipment in advance of the license.

Limit in the contract your liability for sub-supplies. Western firms have complained that products made under license do not meet specified standards. Such failures are often not due to any negligence on the part of the Western partner but to faulty materials delivered by Czechoslovak sub-suppliers. Experienced Western firms draw up contracts that protect themselves—and their reputations—against inferior products put out by the licensee.

Bear in mind the long time span between the opening of license negotiations and the start-up of licensed production when negotiating market restrictions. Companies with products that will enjoy strong sales in Western markets over the long term have good reason not to allow competition from licensed producers in Eastern Europe. But firms with no reason to fear competition four or five years in the future can often strengthen their position by selling a license without restricted market requirements.

Set fixed guarantee periods. As noted, the delay in starting licensed production after a license has been purchased can drag on for years. The Western seller should anticipate requests for longer guarantee periods, but he should also be wary. Purchased machinery may be stored in exposed areas, and thus be subject to water and other damage.

Get a local attorney. Firms recommend that an experienced Czechoslovak attorney or consultant be retained for assistance in drafting the contract and negotiating its provisions on technical matters. Such matters include the type of technical property rights to be licensed, protection of trade secrets, training of technicians, marketing territory, compensation, arbitration, termination and cancellation. Further details on patent and trademark applications should also be secured in consultation with legal counsel.

1987 and a full 20% above 1986 outlays. The high level of outlays for license purchases in 1988 reflects the Czechoslovak government's intention to keep the acquisition of Western technology central to its development strategy.

The electronics and engineering industries have supplanted chemicals as the priority areas for license imports in recent years. Currently, no fewer than 40% of all licenses acquired have gone to the electronics sector, while the metallurgical, heavy-engineering and chemicals sectors have each taken about 20%. Some industries have not been buying licenses at all.

Electronics took 10% of all industrial-investment funds during the 1986–90 plan period, with the Ministry of Electrical Engineering Industry reporting a budget of about K350 million for license purchases alone. This represents a significant shift from traditional investment patterns. Despite the over 1,000 R&D projects carried out annually in the electronics industry, only seven license contracts covering electronics-related projects have been signed on average each year. Moreover, the electronics sector in Czechoslovakia has accounted for fewer than 5% of all license fees paid, compared with 43% in Germany and about 30% in France and the UK.

A long-range program for the electronics industry foresees improvements in the production of control systems, computer hardware, semiconductor and optics components, micro-electronic integrated circuits and interactive graphic systems. Electronic medical equipment will also be a high investment priority—the major beneficiary of which will be the particle-accelerator plant planned at the Chirana facilities in Brno. License purchases in the consumer electronics sector, particularly video equipment, should also increase.

The metallurgy and heavy-engineering industry was budgeted to spend almost K400 million on purchases of foreign licenses over the 1986-90 period. The licenses are to assist in the restructuring of the industry, modernization of capacities and reduction of material and energy use. Licenses to manufacture equipment for nuclear power plants will continue to be sought in view of the fact that Czechoslovakia has become a major supplier of nuclear-engineering equipment to the Comecon countries.

Particular attention will be paid to introducing electronics and automation processes into the industry's products and production lines. The metallurgy and heavy-engineering sector accounts for nearly 30% of Czechoslovak industrial output and about a quarter of total industrial exports.

Growing industrial integration with the Soviet Union and other Comecon countries is affecting Czechoslovak investment in the chemicals industry. Czechoslovakia will restructure this sector to specialize in non-bulk and labor-intensive chemical production. The following sectors are to be modernized and expanded with the help of Western licenses: rubber and plastics; photographic chemicals; printing and paint; pure chemicals for electronics; glass-industry chemicals; detergents; pharmaceuticals; consumer-goods chemicals; pesticides; lubricant additives; textile and fiber industry chemicals; polyester; polyamide and cellulose fiber.

In the general-engineering industry licenses will be sought in technologies conducive to the efficient use of fuel and energy, raw materials and labor. Industrial robots and manipulators, transmission gear, hydraulic units and advanced transport systems will also require the purchase of Western technology.

Czechoslovakia's plans to modernize its automobile industry will require additional purchases of Western licenses. The automotive sector has been largely responsible for the general increase in license purchases since 1985. Skoda's new passenger automobile, "Favorit," has required about $100 million worth of licenses so far. Some major agreements associated with the project include licenses for disc brakes from Lucas-Girling, electrical equipment from Lucas (both UK), a carburetor from Pierburg and a clutch from Sachs (both Germany).

There is a continuing interest in updating the technology and raising the standard of consumer products, particularly export goods. Licenses may be sought covering production of food-processing equipment, household chemicals, consumer electronics and toiletries. Further sales are also possible for licenses covering brand-name beverages, clothing and cigarettes.

For Western firms, the surprise opportunity may lie in the field of environmental protection. According to officials at Polytechna, license purchases for "all aspects of environmental protection" will increase greatly in the next few years. Indeed, some 20–25% of all outlays for Western licenses in 1988 covered environmental-protection equipment and technologies. Highest priority within the sector will go to reducing harmful effluents in the iron and steel industry, treating sewage and water, and disposing of toxic waste.

Basic Licensing Procedures

Contact Organizations and Responsibilities

Polytechna (Panska 9, P.O.B. 834, CS-11245 Prague 1; Tel: 24-69-41, 24-89-41; Telex: 121-585) is the foreign trade organization (FTO) charged with handling the transfer of licenses, technical plans and blueprints, know-how and engineering and consulting services. The department responsible for importing Western technology is located at Politickych veznu 7, CS-11245 Prague 1; Tel: 26-88-51. The branch office for the Slovak Republic is located at Zelena 1, CS-89810 Bratislava; Tel: 384-89, 530-60; Telex: 092-278.

Polytechna is the principal contact for Western firms in cases of straight license sales, i.e. without the sale of associated machinery and equipment. The organization is also responsible for gathering information on outstanding technical achievements in foreign countries, with a view to what could be applied profitably within the Czechoslovak economy. Thus, keeping Polytechna regularly informed on license offers is one of the most effective ways a Western company can market its technology.

The State Commission for Scientific, Technical and Investment Development (SKVTIR), formed in 1984, also plays a key role in the transfer of technology in that it has jurisdiction over the country's technological development and investment programs. It strongly influences the shaping of industrial policy and becomes involved in questions relating to the acquisition of major equipment, technology and know-how from Western firms. Within the organization, the Department of International Cooperation is the major contact for Western firms.

SKVTIR's overriding function is to provide the State Planning Commission with long-range proposals covering both the import of technology and the direction of local R&D efforts. In general, the organization will approve a license acquisition where needed technology cannot be obtained through indigenous research, or where such research would prove too time-consuming or expensive. In considering a proposal, SKVTIR also weighs the estimated costs of purchasing the machinery and materials associated with the license. Successful proposals are passed on to the State Bank for funding.

SKVTIR approval is required on all purchases of pure technology, giving the organization not only the power to initiate the purchase of a given type of technology, but also ultimate veto authority over all technology imports. In cases where SKVTIR deems acquisition of a given license contrary to Czechoslovakia's own R&D program, it can (and does) withhold approval. Where large imports for priority projects are involved, i.e. with turnkey plants, SKVTIR and the appropriate federal or republic ministry will usually study the tenders and may even participate directly in the negotiations.

The VHJ, or industrial association, is a key partner for Western licensors trying to sell technology. Although all commercial contracts for imports of Western technology must be concluded with either Polytechna or another FTO, the VHJ can—and is encouraged to—initiate requests for technology imports for modernizing and rationalizing production capacities. Such recommendations can have an important influence on the final choice of the license.

Large end-user enterprises will occasionally maintain R&D institutes independent of the VHJ, or will have direct relations with their ministries without going through VHJ channels. Such enterprises should also be considered a key component of Western marketing efforts since they are nominally responsible for initiating technology innovation and new products.

The Decision-Making Process

SKVTIR is usually the organization responsible for making the initial decision on whether to purchase outside technology or develop it "in house." Once a decision to buy technology has been made, the Ministry of Foreign Trade is informed immediately. Ministry approval is required for all license imports, although its role in license purchases appears to be chiefly consultative.

After making a decision on a given technology, SKVTIR does not concern itself with the details of the eventual purchase agreement but must ensure that the purchase fits within the existing import plan. If necessary, the organization can make alterations to the plan. The purchase decision is then transmitted to both the relevant FTO (to begin the negotiations) and the VHJ or production enterprise.

Polytechna is selected to negotiate a contract when the deal involves only the purchase of technology (including patent and trademark rights, but without equipment, components, or other elements). For deals involving the purchase of technology in conjunction with plant and equipment, however, two possibilities exist: (1) the project is divided into two contracts, with Polytechna signing only the contract involving technology and an FTO representing the end-user signing the other contract; or (2) a single contract may be signed with the FTO representing the end-user. This second option requires Polytechna's approval. In nearly all cases, Polytechna will be asked to consult on the commercial aspects of a sale.

Licensing fees are paid from the concerned ministry's reserve funds on approval from the Ministry of Finance. Purchases specifically provided for in the import plan are financed by the Czechoslovak State Bank, which countersigns such a contract and provides payment guarantees. The State Bank is usually expected to fund the total package of the license, including associated imports.

Unplanned Imports

Occasionally, the initiative to purchase a license comes not from SKVTIR, but from the VHJ. Such unplanned imports of technology are usually made to cover immediate production problems. In all cases, unplanned imports must have the approval of the concerned industrial ministry, the Ministry of Foreign Trade and SKVTIR.

Under such an arrangement, the VHJ usually secures three competing license offers before approaching the relevant FTO to make the purchase. Where the VHJ has a particular preference for one of the three offers due to technical advantages, the FTO is obliged to take this preference into consideration. A preferred offer can only be rejected on the grounds of unacceptable price or payment conditions, and only after consultation with the competent ministry.

Taxes on Royalties and Fees

A 30–40% withholding tax is normally levied on all royalties and fees paid to foreign firms for licenses, patents, know-how and technical aid, although the effective rate can often be lowered to 5–10% within the context of a agreement for the avoidance of double taxation (see below). The tax on payments to foreign authors under copyright law is 25%. The tax on interest and rent due to foreign firms and nationals is 25%.

To avoid disputes over taxes or other unexpected deductions from license payments, contracts should stipulate that the Western licensor will receive net lump sums and net royalties.

Treaties with Austria, Belgium, Cyprus, Denmark, Finland, France, Germany, Japan, the Netherlands, Norway, Spain, and Sweden cover income and capital; those with India and Italy cover income only.

The contents of these treaties generally follow the provisions of the OECD Draft Convention for the Avoidance of Double Taxation, with the following special regulation:

Taxes on royalties arising in one state to a resident of another treaty state are limited to 5% except in the case of Japan (10%). In the event of royalties being transferred to a resident of a foreign treaty state, the resident will be taxed in that foreign state.

It is possible to have the purchasing FTO undertake all the Czechoslovak tax obligations, although a compromise rate of 5% paid by the Western seller is frequently demanded. Indeed, Western negotiators can argue that it is advantageous for the Czechoslovak FTO to undertake payment of such tax obligations, since the tax can then be paid with local currency instead of with the scarce hard currency that would have to be paid by the Western party—which would then have to bury the increased cost in higher prices.

Patents

Companies are generally satisfied with the quality of patent protection available in Czechoslovakia. The patent office in Prague lists thousands of Western patents and trademarks. Czechoslovak legal support is generally very capable, and fees remain reasonable.

Patents are granted either to an author or to his or her legal successor; the name of the author is always quoted in the Patent Letter. The patent owner is entitled to give consent for Czechoslovak or foreign exploitation of the invention (by license) or to assign the patent to another owner. Both the license to exploit a patent and a patent assignment must be in writing and must be registered in accordance with the law.

Patent rights are valid for 15 years from the filing date of the invention application, after which time they can be renewed. A six-month grace period is provided for patent renewal following the expiration date, but this is accompanied by a 100% fine.

Patents are not issued in Czechoslovakia for certain inventions, namely medications, chemical substances, foodstuffs, substances produced by nuclear reaction, processes pertaining exclusively to nuclear energy, and industrial microorganisms. Pesticides can be patented, but crop-protection techniques cannot be protected by either a patent or an author's certificate. This applies also to human and animal disease prevention, and to diagnosis and therapy techniques. These inventions are covered only by a special certificate.

Legislative Basis

The legal basis for the protection of inventions and industrial designs is provided for by Law 527/1990 in the series of laws on inventions, industrial designs and rationalization suggestions. Effective Jan. 1, 1991, the new law introduced an exclusive protection of inventions and industrial designs. Protection was extended to the industrial production of microorganisms, but not to foodstuffs or medications. The law also specified the ownership of a patent in terms of the individual or collective, rather than the state.

Patent protection is based on Czechoslovakia's participation in the 1883 Paris Convention on the Protection of Industrial Property, in its July 14, 1967, Stockholm version. The patent law also respects obligations connected to the harmonization of patent rights by the World

Intellectual Property Organization (WIPO). In principle, foreign citizens enjoy the same rights and are bound by the same duties, on the basis of reciprocity, as Czechoslovak nationals.

Domestic legal provisions of interest to foreigners include the statute on discoveries, inventions, improvements and industrial designs, which entered into force on Jan. 1, 1973.

An invention, in the meaning of this act, includes any solution of a technical problem that constitutes progress manifested by a new or higher effect. Moreover, the invention must be capable of industrial production or be applicable in the course of production or operation. Applications for protection of inventions must be submitted the Office for Inventions and Discoveries, whereupon the applicant is vested with the right of priority.

Author's Certificates

Czechoslovak law provides for a dual system of invention protection. Inventors have a choice between holding a traditional patent or getting what is called an "author's certificate." Most Western inventors opt for a patent, and thus maintain property rights to their invention, although a few author's certificates have been issued to Westerners. Czechoslovak or other Comecon inventors, on the other hand, are almost exclusively steered to the author's-certificate option. Under terms of an author's certificate, the ownership of an invention is transferred entirely to the state. The inventor receives compensation according to a statutory fee schedule up to K500,000. In cases where an invention has no immediately determinable market value, the amount of the award is decided by a commission, and depends on the usefulness of the invention to the Czechoslovak economy.

The term of an author's-certificate award is unlimited and payment is made on issuance of the certificate, regardless of when use begins. Westerners are paid in hard currency. Czechoslovak nationals can receive hard-currency Tuzex vouchers in cases where their invention is to be used abroad.

Applications for author's certificates are subject to the same examination rules as patents. Unlike patents, however, no filing fees for application or annual upkeep are required. Patents may be converted into author's certificates within the first seven years of issuance, provided no license has been previously granted.

Protection of Industrial Designs

An industrial design is any innovation in the external condition of a product, both planar and three dimensional, that is new and usable in industrial production. External condition in this respect consists of a particular external appearance, shape, contour, design or color, or in an arrangement of colors, or in a combination of these features. The industrial design is deemed usable in industrial production if goods can be repeatedly produced.

The subject matter of an application for industrial design is deemed new unless it has been known in Czechoslovakia or anywhere abroad prior to the date from which the right of priority has been vested in the applicant, from publicly accessible sources.

The legal provisions for the protection of inventions are generally applicable mutatis mutandis to protection of industrial designs. The industrial design for which a patent has been granted is protected for five years from the filing date of the application; the term may be extended upon request for an additional five-year period.

The Office for Inventions and Discoveries

The Office for Inventions and Discoveries (Urad pro vynalezy a objevy) is Czechoslovakia's patent office, located at Vaclavske namesti 19, PO Box 866, 11346 Prague 1.

The patent office is subordinated to the State Commission for Technical, Scientific and Investment Development (SKTVIR) and is responsible for administering the country's laws on discoveries, inventions, improvement designs, industrial designs and trademarks.

The office handles applications and examination procedures for patents, author's certificates, industrial designs and trademarks; rules in infringement on same; and maintains the Register of Trademarks.

The patent office is also charged with monitoring the inventions in its registers and promoting the use of significant inventions in the economy. Western firms holding valid claims have thus found it sometimes advantageous to enlist the services of the patent office in promoting their own license sales. Such actions have been successful when the company can prove that the license can solve specific economic problems or help fulfill requirements spelled out by the economic plan. The office publishes new patents in its official bulletin, the *Vestnik Urada pro patenty a vynalezy*. Patents are classified according to the Strasbourg agreement, to which Czechoslovakia is a signatory.

Application procedure

The Office for Inventions and Discoveries does not handle applications from foreigners for patents, author's certificates, industrial designs and trademarks. A patent application can be made only through one of three authorized Czechoslovak offices: UTRIN, Ustav technickeho rozvoje a informaci (Institute for Technical Development and Information) (U Sovovych mlynu 9, POB 1023, 11356 Prague); Advokatni poradna No. 1 (Czechoslovak Legal Offices 1) (Narodni trida 32, 11666 Prague); Advokatni poradna No. 10 (Czechoslovak Legal Offices 10) (Zitna 25, 11000 Prague).

In addition to the name and address of the applicant, all applications must have the following:

- name and address of the inventor (if different from applicant);
- power of attorney signed by the applicant;
- declaration from the applicant regarding authorship or assignment of right to apply for protection in Czechoslovakia;
- invention specifications and claims, in English, German or French (duplicate);
- invention drawings (one original and four copies); and
- documents proving priority, to be submitted within three months of filing the original application or proof of assignment of right of priority, to be submitted within three months of the original Czechoslovak filing date (in such cases, the signature of the original applicant must be certified by a notary public).

Compulsory Licenses

As in most other East European countries, Czechoslovak law provides in principle for compulsory licensing after four years of nonuse of a patented invention, if economic need can be shown. In practice, however, no case of compulsory licensing has been recorded since 1945.

The concept of dependent licenses is expressly recognized in Czechoslovakia. These are patents that cannot be worked without infringing on another dominant patent. In such cases, the owners of interrelated patents can agree to cross-license voluntarily or the patent office may order a compulsory license, with the royalties to be determined by the courts.

Infringement

There have been very few incidents of patent infringement involving foreign citizens or firms. And most of these issues have been settled between the parties without resort to the courts. There is no precedent of a foreign patentee recovering a judgement for infringement before the courts in Czechoslovakia. This does not mean that a foreign patentee would not get a fair hearing in Czechoslovakia, but rather that state-owned enterprises would not knowingly engage in infringement.

In case of alleged patent infringement, the patentee has the option of requesting the Czechoslovak patent office to determine the facts (under Section 43 of the Czechoslovak Patent Law) or to sue in court directly (under Section 124, part G of the law). If the patent office finds infringement, the parties have an opportunity to negotiate a settlement or bring the controversy before the court. If the patent office rules in favor of infringement on a given set of facts, this ruling is binding on the courts as well as on all other state organs and organizations for the same set of facts.

An alleged infringer can counter a patent-infringement claim in the courts by bringing a nullity action in the patent office. If a nullity action is started after an infringement suit has been brought to court, the court will suspend its proceedings until the patent office completes its nullity action. This procedure can take one or two years. In patent-office decisions, each side is responsible for its own costs and fees. If an infringement action is started directly in court, the issue is decided by experts, either within the patent office or with another appropriate office. Only the court can award damages; in a court action the loser must bear all costs and fees. The lawyers' fees are dependent on the value of the controversy.

While infringement litigation between Czechoslovak enterprises and foreign patentees is very rare, a considerable amount of litigation exists between Czechoslovak enterprises and their employees seeking compensation for unauthorized use of their inventions covered by author's certificates. The amount of such reward is set by Decree No. 106 of Dec. 12, 1972, and can be substantial.

Validity and Revocations

Questions of validity can be decided only by way of a nullity action in the patent office. If validity is brought to issue in an infringement suit, hearing of the lawsuit will be postponed until the validity issue is adjudicated by the patent office.

Total or partial revocations and oppositions are adjudicated by the patent office. No oral arguments are available in these proceedings. Oral interviews with examiners are available, and rejections are decided by an appellate forum within the patent office, referred to as the "second instance."

The decision of the second instance is final, and further appeal is not possible. However, errors in law can be contested by the attorney gen-

Licensing Experience in Czechoslovakia

Most Western firms report good experiences in licensing production in Czechoslovakia. On balance, local licensees exhibit a high degree of technical skill and are normally very sensitive to key Western concerns, including quality control. Moreover, issues such as trademark and patent protection are treated very seriously. According to one Western manager active on the Czechoslovak market for seven years, "Our (licensing) agreement was an unqualified success by any measurement one chooses to use. We encountered no major headaches uncommon to licensing in other parts of the world."

The following is a list of Western licenses purchased by Czechoslovak organizations during the years 1986 and 1987. (The entries are in approximately chronological order.)

Equipment or technology covered	Western seller	Czech licensee
Reconstruction of aluminum mill	Ardal (Norway)	Kovohute (Prague)
Modernization of garment-making line	Veit (Germany)	Odevni prumsyl (Prostejov)
PMA oil additive	Albright & Wilson (UK)	Lucebni zavody (Kolin)
Float-glass processes	Pilkington (UK)	Sklo Union (Teplice)
Carburetor 2E3 for Skoda 781	Pierburg (Germany)	Motor (Ceske Budejovice)
Selenium drums	Apeco (Germany)	Zavody vseobecneho strojirenstvi (Brno)
Compact disks	ICM (Switzerland)	Gramofonove zavody (Lodenice)
Mixing organic materials	Gustav Eirich (Germany)	Moravske samotove a lupkove zavody
Desulfurizing coke-oven gas	Carl Still (Germany)	Zavody Vitezneho unora (Hradec Kralove)
Spin-casting cylinders	Gontermann Peipers (Germany)	Vitkovice (Ostrava)
Surface threading products	Egelhaaf (Germany)	Elitex (Liberec)
Loading equipment for the Skoda 781	Carl Schenck Germany	AZNP (Mlada Boleslav)
Cylinder-head gaskets	Elring (Germany)	CZGP (Gottwaldov)
Corn hybrids	Pioneer Hi-Bred (US)	Slovosivo (Bratislava)
Pressure-boiling iron	Lurgi (Germany)	Rudne doly (Jesenik)
Geared belts for automobiles	Maschinenbau Scholz (Germany)	CZGP (Gottwaldov)
Push-button switches	Gnad (Austria)	Tesla (Roznov)
Jeans, T-shirts and accessories	Lee Cooper (UK)	OZKN (Presov)
Steam turbines and turbine technology	MAN (Germany) and Alsthom Atlantique (France)	Skoda (Plzen)
VCR technology	Philips (Netherlands)	Tesla (Bratislava)

eral, who can compel the case to be reheard by the second instance. Patent-office personnel participating in the proceedings of the second instance are identical for patent, author's certificate, industrial design, trademark and marking-of-origin matters.

Patents of Czechoslovaks Abroad

Western firms employing Czechoslovak citizens should be aware that all inventions of such nationals become the property of the Czechoslovak state. Under the patent law of Jan. 1, 1973, every Czechoslovak citizen is required to register a new invention in Czechoslovakia no matter where he lives. This law also applies to the many Czechoslovaks who, having left the country without official permission, have been denied release from citizenship. Furthermore, under the same law the invention of a Czechoslovak citizen can be made available to other Comecon countries at the discretion of the relevant ministry or industrial association.

Trademarks

Czechoslovakia grants protection to trademarks in accordance with the Madrid Convention of 1891, in the 1957 Nice version, and the 1957 Nice Convention.

Local legal support for trademark protection is found in Act 174/1988 on Trademarks and Protected Designs. The law came into effect on Jan. 1, 1989, and supercedes the outdated 1952 provisions governing trademark protection in the country.

Registration

To register a trademark, companies must first submit an application to one of three organizations: UTRIN, Advokatni poradna No. 1 or No. 10 (see above for addresses).

Following approval, trademarks are registered with the patent office, the Office for Inventions and Discoveries (Urad pro vynalezy a objevy) (Vaclavske namesti 19, P.O. Box 866, CS-11346 Prague 1).

Before registration, trademark applications are subjected to a thorough patent search by the Office of Patents and Inventions. The patent office has the power to reject applications for trademarks that are similar or identical to those already registered. Firms desiring to use another company's trademark will have to secure prior permission.

The entity or organization for which the trademark is registered has the exclusive right to use the mark from the date of application. This right is not effective for former users of the same or a similar unregistered mark for the same products.

Trademarks are published in a special section of *Vestnik,* the same publication that publishes new patents. Interested parties can contest a registered mark within three years of registration on grounds that it does not meet registration criteria or that they are prior users. The following trademarks cannot be registered:

- those of generic character (with pharmaceuticals, those indicating the illness treated or raw materials used in its preparation);
- those that include false or deceptive indications (including dates or years if untrue, i.e. "the finest since 1854");
- those that conflict with the general public interest or international usage; and
- those that incorporate geographic names in any way.

The last point is unusual and was adopted as part of the new 1989 law. Legal experts note that only new trademark applications will be screened for geographic names. Currently registered marks employing a geographic reference will continue to enjoy full trademark protection and can be renewed.

Companies with such marks, however, are advised not to let them lapse before renewing. The patent office will not renew a trademark with a geographic name after protection on the mark has expired.

Duration of Protection

Trademarks are protected for 10 years from the date of application, with a further 10-year extension possible. The application for renewal may be filed in the course of the final year of the term of protection, at the earliest, but not later than three months following its expiration.

Rights to trademarks may be transferred only together with transfer of ownership to the organization on whose behalf they have been registered. In case of a corporate reorganization, consent of the Office for Inventions and Discoveries may be requested.

"Use" Provisions

Under the 1989 law, companies with a registered trademark are obliged to "use" that mark or risk losing protection for it. This is a burden on trademark holders that has never existed in Czechoslovakia before. In the past, it was possible to maintain a trademark with the registry without ever putting it into active use—convenient for firms wanting trademark protection without the obligation of selling to the country.

According to Section 19 of the law, trademarks can be cancelled on the grounds that the mark has not been used in some way for at least five years before cancellation proceedings have been filed. Cancellation proceedings can be initiated by a competing firm or by the patent office itself.

Firms will probably not have their trademarks cancelled outright due to nonuse but may be forced to prove that the mark is indeed "in use" if challenged by a new claim.

The law is still unclear as to what constitutes "use," but Czechoslovak legal authorities suggest that firms with inactive trademarks do the following to protect themselves:

- publish the mark periodically within the country (advertise in a general or branch-specific publication);
- send descriptive material or price lists with the trademark to potential customers; or
- send company letterhead to various individuals in the country (keep copies).

12
Hungary

A major component in the current restructuring of the Hungarian economy is the acquisition and implementation of new technology. Official plans for raising the technological standards of Hungarian exports led to increased imports of technology during the 1986–90 plan period. This trend to import technology from the West has continued in the 1990s. The chemicals, pharmaceuticals and electronics industries, as well as the agricultural and agro-biotechnology sectors, are the main areas in which Hungarian enterprises will seek Western technology.

In keeping with ongoing efforts by the Hungarian government to ease foreign and domestic trade, the bureaucratic procedures for importing licenses were eased in January 1989. In practice, however, imports of Western technology will continue to be evaluated against the government's goal of boosting hard-currency export goods competitive on OECD markets.

Purchases of Western licenses and know-how have increased. Levels in 1987 were higher than those in the preceding year (see the table on p. 186). Another area showing high growth is investment in organizational know-how, i.e. management.

In the past, many Hungarian factory managers were reluctant to introduce new technology, since the time required for retooling and other measures could endanger the fulfillment of their production plan. Managers have also argued that the import of licenses means the immediate expenditure of considerable funds, while outlays for the company's own R&D work can be spread over longer periods. The virtual elimination of quantitative targets from the last five-year plan was intended to encourage greater innovation on the part of enterprise managers.

Funds for license purchases can now come from a number of sources:

Enterprise development and technical development funds. The amount retained in the Enterprise Development Fund is calculated on the basis of value added and not of gross sales, so that the most profitable rather than the largest enterprises should get the most money to spend on innovation. In 1989 the government set up a Technical Development Fund to which all enterprises, including joint ventures with Western participation, have to contribute 4.5% of tax due.

OMFB (National Technical Development Office) and the Ministry of Industry. Both have special funds for promoting technology imports.

Bank credits. The National Bank of Hungary and the various commercial banks grant credits to supplement enterprise funds. The State Development Bank specializes in long-term credits for large-scale investments.

Direct state subsidies and interest-free loans are given to support investments to which the government has assigned high priority.

Approval Requirements

As of 1989, imports of licenses and know-how for products or services included on the new "liberalized import list" do not require special approval from the various ministries. These transactions are, however, registered with the Ministry of Trade for statistical purposes. The list covers some 40% of the country's import requirements.

Although this simplifies licensing procedures, it also increases the risk for a Western company since the transactions are not covered by state guarantees. In light of shortages of hard currency in Hungary as well as the increased risk of enterprises going bankrupt, Western businesses are advised to check up on the cash-flow situation of prospective Hungarian business partners.

For large purchases the National Bank of Hungary reserves the right to play a "consulting" role, usually for contracts larger than $1–1.5 million. This should help companies avoid costly pitfalls. For goods not on

Expenditures on License Imports in 1987
(million forints)

	Ruble	Other	Total	% change over 1986
Licenses and know-how	86	2,175	2,261	137
Designs	241	344	585	77
Expert services	20	71	92	80
Organization	3	57	60	214

the "liberalized import list," a proposal for the purchase of a license by a Hungarian enterprise must be approved by the Ministry of Trade.

In addition, all license deals, with or without purchase of related equipment, must be approved by the National Bank. The Foreign Trade Bank and (starting in 1990) all commercial banks are responsible only for the approval of license deals concluded within the framework of a cooperation agreement with a Western partner.

A proposed license purchase will be evaluated primarily on how well the licensed product will fit into the industrial restructuring program, whether production will be profitable and whether the product can be exported to the West. Factory experts and Western sellers may be called in to discuss jointly the planned acquisition of technology. Normally, the final contract will be approved without delay as long as the Hungarian enterprise stays within the terms of the negotiating permit.

The Licensing Agencies

In keeping with the current decentralization of Hungary's foreign trade system, any enterprise with foreign trade rights can buy licenses. By May 1989, more than 2,000 Hungarian enterprises had these rights. In addition, private individuals can also obtain foreign trading rights and undertake licensing transactions.

Three Foreign Trade Organizations (FTOs), however, have traditionally specialized in license sales and technology transfer: Licencia, Novex and Intercooperation. An enterprise considering the purchase of a license has the option of calling one of these "licensing" FTOs, but may also negotiate and conclude the deal directly with the licensor.

According to an official with Licencia, most Hungarian enterprises do not have the resources or expertise on hand to engage in licensing transactions. Even though in 1987 and 1988 many enterprises tried to conclude such deals without Licencia, Novex or Intercooperation, the contracts were reportedly often disadvantageous to the Hungarian companies involved.

It must be emphasized that none of the above-mentioned specialized FTOs has any exclusive right to promote or negotiate license contracts. About 90% of imported licenses and technologies are purchased either by the appropriate FTOs or by other enterprises with foreign trading rights; these are also responsible for the import of related products, machinery and equipment.

All the larger Hungarian FTOs—such as Transelektro, Chemolimpex, Chemokomplex, Medimpex and Technoimpex—have in-house licensing expertise. Joint ventures with Western participation have also purchased licenses without resorting to the specialized FTOs. Smaller

Hungarian enterprises, however, will probably need—at least in the short run—to continue relying on organizations such as Licencia.

Licencia and Novex

Both Licencia and Novex deal primarily with "pure" licenses—those without machinery and equipment purchases—and have highly qualified specialists, well versed in every aspect of technology-transfer negotiations. Enterprises may request them to undertake a search for a specific type of technology. The licensing FTOs carry out market research and are equipped to evaluate licensing options commercially as well as technically. Western companies can approach Hungarian enterprises with licensing proposals as well.

Specialized licensing FTOs work on a commission basis. Commissions are calculated on the license royalties paid by the Hungarian enterprise to the Western company, at times amounting to as much as 20% of the licensing fee. Services in recent years have also improved. Licencia, for instance, now also handles leasing deals involving license transfers.

Licencia reports that it is willing to pay a lump sum and royalties in licensing transactions. Buy-back is also an important form of payment for licenses, especially for less important technology.

Intercooperation

Intercooperation has a nonexclusive mandate to organize, promote and coordinate cooperation agreements based on product and production sharing and on the transfer of licenses and know-how. It also acts as a consultant to Hungarian enterprises working on cooperation agreements, particularly on commercial, financial and legal matters.

Intercooperation is mainly called in to manage cooperation deals (which may or may not involve license and technology transfers) if several foreign and Hungarian firms are involved in the same deal and if, due to its special features, the given field cannot be classified comfortably within the sphere of activity of any single FTO.

License Payments and Taxes

A 25% value-added tax is withheld on royalties resulting from patent licenses. There is no tax on royalties from know-how licenses. If equipment or machinery is included in the licensing deal, customs duties must also be paid.

Hungary has treaties for avoidance of double taxation with numerous countries. Additional treaties are presently being negotiated with Spain, Greece, Portugal and Turkey. The treaties are based on the OECD Draft Convention for the avoidance of double taxation with respect to

Licensing Experience in Hungary

In recent years, a growing proportion of Hungarian pharmaceuticals products has been produced in accordance with Western licenses. In 1975 only 32 licenses were purchased to manufacture drugs; by 1980 this figure had increased to 67, and by 1987 it had reached 110. Western licenses are also purchased in the electronics, food-processing, packaging and machinery sectors.

In keeping with its overall policy of encouraging Western companies to have an ongoing interest in the Hungarian economy, the Hungarian government encourages the import of licenses in the context of cooperation or joint venture deals. It is hoped that this device will give the Western company an incentive to pass improvements in the license on to the Hungarian producer.

Henkel's Persil

Henkel Budapest, a joint venture set up in 1988, has started production of Persil washing powder and Picobello shoe varnish in Hungary under licenses provided by the West German firm Henkel. The Tiszamenti chemical works handles the production of Persil.

Persil is packaged in 3-kg cardboard boxes and costs less than when imported. Ninety-five percent of the ingredients used in Persil are sourced from local raw materials producers.

Videoton

Videoton, Hungary's largest manufacturer in the electronics field, remains a major user of Western licenses. The company employs 20,000 people, some 4,000 in computing alone. It first specialized in radio and TV receivers, but moved into the manufacture of data-processing equipment in 1971 with computers and software production accounting for one third of the company's production volume. In the mid-1980s Videoton began manufacturing video-recording equipment, further expanding its range of activities.

The first licenses that Videoton bought in the computer field were from France's CII in 1969 for minicomputers. Videoton subsequently bought licenses from US Data Products for line printers and from West Germany's Siemens for memories and other computer components.

Videoton has also purchased licenses from and engaged in joint development with Sweden's Data-Saab, especially in the field of

(Continued)

computers for banking operations. SEMS (France) sold the Hungarian enterprise a license for more than $300,000 in 1980 to keep its minicomputer line up to date. Data Products sold a $700,000 license to produce printers.

More recently, Videoton purchased a license for a head-printer assembly from a US company through a joint venture that it established in 1984 with Walters Microsystems (UK). Thomson Electronics provided the license to manufacture color television sets in 1988.

In addition to computers and software, Videoton has moved into the manufacture of video equipment, purchasing a license and know-how from Japan's Akai Electric in 1984 for the Akai V3 videotape recorder. Videoton planned to produce some 3,000 units in 1985, mostly for use in Hungarian schools. Akai signed its production cooperation agreement with Videoton shortly after a similar deal was signed by Matsushita Electric with Orion. In 1988, Videoton embarked on a program to produce CD players based on a Philips license. Production and marketing of the CD players started in 1989.

taxes on income and capital. Treaties with Austria, Belgium, Brazil, Cyprus, Denmark, Finland, France, Germany, Greece, India, Italy, Spain and Switzerland cover income and taxes; those with Japan, the UK and the US cover income only; and the treaties with the Netherlands and Sweden cover direct taxes generally.

Patents

By registering a patent in Hungary, a foreign patentee can stop Hungarian enterprises from producing the patented item illegally and prevent foreign competitors from putting it on the market in Hungary. The National Office of Inventions (NOI), the successor to the Patent Office created in 1895, has the final responsibility in patent matters and acts as an authority with nationwide powers.

The NOI can be contacted at the following address:

Országos Találmányi Hivatal (National Office of Inventions)
Budapest, V., Garibaldi u.2
H-1370 Budapest, POB 552
Tel: 112-4400
Telex: 22-47-00

Foreign applicants must be represented by a Hungarian patent attorney when they file with the NOI. In 1989, some 6,000 patents were filed with the NOI, half of which were by foreign firms. New patents are announced in the official journal of the NOI, the *Official Gazette of Patents and Trademarks (Szabadalmi Közlöny és Védjegyértesít)*. The Patent Collection Office stores some 16 million patent specifications.

Patent Agents

Among the organizations in Hungary that are available to represent foreign patent applicants are the following:

Danubia Patent Bureau
Budapest, V., Bajcsy-Zsilinszky út 16
H-1368 Budapest, POB 198
Tel: 118-1111; 117-1055
Telex: 22-5872

Lawyers' Association No. 2
Budapest, V., Szalay u. 13
H-1363 Budapest, POB 23
Tel: 132-4790; 111-2096

Lawyers' Association No. 14, Patent Bureau
Budapest, VII., Rákóczi út 8/a
H-1072 Budapest, Rákóczi u. 8/a
Tel.: 122-7875

Lawyers' Association No. 16, Patent Bureau
Budapest, VI., Dalszínház utca 10
H-1061 Budapest
Tel: 153-3733; 111-2786

Lawyers' Association No. 23
Budapest, VI., Andrássy út 53
H-1062 Budapest
Tel: 153-4733; 122-1705

Lawyers' Association No. 26, Patent Bureau
Budapest, VII., Klauzál tér 3
H-1364 Budapest, POB 64
Tel.: 122-4411; 142-1781; 142-4309

Lawyers' Association No. 29, Alvopatent Patent Bureau
Budapest, I., Fö utca 19
H-1251 Budapest, POB 11
Telex: 22-5692
Fax: 135-0535

Danubia is responsible for the protection of intellectual property and the administration of patents. Its duties include the acquisition and maintenance of Hungarian inventions abroad; protection of trademark and industrial property rights; maintenance of a research file on the protection of industrial property abroad; and the acquisition of related documentation. Danubia accepts commissions from both private individuals and enterprises.

The patent bureau maintains relations with some 80 countries. It files patent applications abroad for about 350-400 Hungarian inventions every year. Since Hungary joined the Patent Cooperation Treaty in 1980, it can acquire simultaneous patent protection in 35 contracting states by means of a single application for international protection. The accession to PCT ensures advantageous financial conditions as well. Danubia provides regular information to its foreign clients on current issues of the Hungarian law on patents and keeps domestic enterprises informed on changes effected abroad in the legislation of industrial property law.

Danubia has about 50 patent and trademark agents and lawyers and presently is still the only office entitled to represent Hungarian investors abroad. This is expected to be changed in the near future. Danubia is also affiliated with the Licencia organization.

The patentee may grant a license for exploitation of his invention in exchange for royalties. A contract of exploitation may be invoked against third parties only if the patent is recorded in the Patent Register. Right of exploitation under a licensing contract is granted on an exclusive basis only if it is expressly stipulated. Sublicenses may be granted only with the express consent of the patentee.

The Patent Information Center

The Patent Information Center operates the Industrial Property Library within the National Office of Inventions. The center provides information through its collection of data on patent issues and its own publishing activity. It publishes the monthly *Gazette of Patents and Trademarks,* the official journal of the NOI, as well as the official Hungarian patent specifications. In addition, it provides an information guide for inventors and a guide to trademark and industrial design matters.

The Industrial Property Library houses a collection of national and foreign patent specifications, consisting of about 16 million pieces. The library also maintains a database containing bibliographic data of Hungarian patent documents from 1970, which is accessible to the public. The full address for the library is as follows:

National Office of Inventions
Szabadalmi Tára/Industrial Property Library
Budapest, V., Perczel Mór u. 2-4.
H-1374 Budapest, POB 552.
Tel.: 153-2255, 153-2589

Patent Regulation in Hungary

Conventions. Hungary is a signatory to the World Intellectual Property Organization Convention of 1967; the Paris Convention of 1883; the Stockholm Act of 1967 and the Patent Cooperation Treaty of 1970.

Basic laws. Novel processes may be patented under the following Hungarian laws: Law No. 2 of 1969 on patent protection of inventions, as amended by Decree Law No. 5 of 1983; the decree implementing Law No. 2 of 1969, as amended by Decree No. 4 of 1983; Decree No. 9 of 1969 concerning court proceedings in patent matters; Announcement No. 3 of 1983 of the NOI President on procedural rules governing patent applications; and Announcement No. 4 of 1983 ordering the complete examination of certain patent applications.

Types and duration. Patents of inventions are granted, but not patents of addition. Any solution that is new, progressive, technical and capable of practical application can be patented. A Hungarian patent is valid for 20 years from the date of filing.

Unpatentable. Inventions relating to foods, medications, and chemically produced products are not patentable; the processes for manufacturing these items are patentable. Plant varieties and animal breeds, and the processes for obtaining them, are patentable, as are processes involving the use of microorganisms.

Application and examination procedure. The inventor or his assignee may apply for a patent. Foreigners must appoint a patent attorney domiciled in Hungary to represent the applicant before the NOI.

A complete examination—which covers novelty and progress—is compulsory for certain patent applications. In other cases the NOI undertakes a deferred examination before publishing the essential features of the application in the Official Gazette. Subsequent examinations can be requested within four years of publication of the application.

The results of the NOI's examination may be reviewed by submission to the Metropolitan Court of Budapest. Further appeals may be made with the Supreme Court.

"Prior use" claims may be made by anyone who had been manufacturing or using the invention in the country or had made preparation to do so before the registration date.

(Continued)

Infringement. Anyone who unlawfully exploits a patented invention may be prosecuted. A patentee may request an injunction from the Court, claim damages from the infringer and request seizure of infringing instruments and products.
Compulsory licensing takes effect if the patentee has not worked the invention in Hungary or if he has not undertaken preparations to grant a license to someone else within four years of the filing date or within three years of the grant of a patent. Exceptions may be made if the patentee can justify his inaction. The Ministry of National Defense can request that any patent or application be worked for reasons of national defense. Compensation to the patentee is fixed by the Court.
Fees. The fee for patent application is F2,000 for a complete examination, and F1,000 for a deferred examination or any subsequent examination. For maintenance of the patent, the annual fees start at F3,000 and increase by F3,000 after every five-year increment.

Trademarks

The legal protection of trademarks in Hungary is considered up-to-date by Western businessmen. The National Office of Inventions is the competent authority for the registration of trademarks, which are protected under the Hungarian Law on Trademarks (Law No. 9 of 1969). Hungary is a signatory of the Madrid Agreement on Trademarks. It is advisable to have trademarks registered in Hungary even if the product is not to be immediately exported to Hungary, as registration can be used to protect future business.

The principal requirement for registration is that the trademark be "distinctive." The Hungarian Office of Inventions, for example, refused to renew the American trademark Bakelite and the German trademark Perlon because they had no distinctive character and were used as generic denominations. Trademarks such as Cellophane, Chartreuse, Chiffon, Cord and Saccharine were declared generic denominations. On the other hand, the trademarks Dictaphone and Plexiglas were classified by the Hungarian Office as maintaining a distinctive character. By "generic" the office understands that the name in question is used in a general way for indicating the goods.

These decisions are subject to revision every 10 years when the mark comes up for renewal. Nonuse for five years may cause trademark removal from the register, but the occasional mention in an advertisement is sufficient to establish use. Trademarks liable to create confusion will not be registered. Through licensing agreements, trademarks often become the subject of commercial transfer. Thus Coca-Cola, Pepsi-Cola, Fiat and other trademarks appear in Hungary on Eastern Europe products.

As with trademarks in the West, the question of priority is all-important. Generally the date on which the application arrives at the National Office of Inventions establishes priority. In cases defined by special legislation, the filing date of the foreign application may take priority.

All proceedings of trademark infringement fall under the exclusive territorial and material jurisdiction of the Metropolitan Court of Budapest, which consists of three judges with professional knowledge in trademark cases. The Hungarian Trademark Act inflicts similar sanctions as the Patent Act (see above). An example is the misuse of the trademark Tungsram, for which the infringing party was fined a high sum by the Hungarian Court.

The Hungarian Trademark Law of 1969 focused primarily on safeguarding the consumer's interest rather than protecting the owner against competition. Protection is granted only to registered trademarks. In cases of infringement of unregistered trademarks, the owner can only claim redress on the basis of the Hungarian Civil Code and the Law Against Unfair Competition.

The Patent Bureau Danubia provides assistance to Western firms in formulating trademark applications, as well as monitoring services of trademarks, handling renewals, trademark searches and so forth. New trademarks are published in the *Official Gazette* of the National Inventions Office.

13
Poland

Over the course of the 1980s, Poland bought only 18 Western licenses, compared with about 30 annually in the late 1970s. The fall-off has been caused by acute cash shortages and misgivings that stem from bad experiences with license purchases in the 1970s. Also contributing to the low level of license purchase is Poland's failure to renew a number of licenses that expired in the early 1980s.

Recentralization of R&D over the last few years has put license purchases under far closer central supervision than was the case previously. Despite official rhetoric about modernization and the pressing need to accelerate technological progress, Poland is continuing its very selective license policy. This is due to both lack of funds and the continuing difficulty in obtaining credits.

Poland would like to direct its own license sales to the West European countries, particularly Austria, Finland, Germany, Italy and Spain. From 1981 to 1987, Poland exported 40 licenses to Western countries out of a total of 53. Trade with the developing countries has fallen during the 1980s, resulting in a disappointing level of exchange. Exports to developing countries comprises only 11% of Poland's total, with no license imports at all.

The Program of Development of Science and Technology for 1986-90 stated explicitly that of total planned spending of Z1 trillion ($5.9 billion equivalent in 1986) on R&D, only $375 million will involve hard currency. The plan allocated some $90 million for license purchase in 1990.

The relatively small amount of money allocated in the five-year scientific and technical development program, however, does not mean that Western companies will not receive license-related inquiries from Polish enterprises or that very large deals involving credits, such as recent licensing agreements with Fiat (Italy), are impossible. Although central allocations for license purchases will be difficult for Polish enterprises to obtain, enterprises may still draw upon their hard-currency retention accounts for this purpose.

Policy Background

Officials realize that Poland cannot isolate itself from technological trends in the West. The bitter licensing experiences of the 1970s, however, have led officials to regard the purchase of technology with extreme caution. To a certain extent, licensing deals have even been discouraged in favor of other forms of business. The licensing requirements that Poles especially object to are

- market restrictions that limit or prohibit the sale of licensed products to specific countries or areas;
- contractual obligations that commit the Polish partner to ongoing purchases of components and materials;
- contracts without adequate guarantees from the Western partner that a given technology can be made to work in practice to specified quality parameters; and
- contracts involving untried technology or technology that will need modification during implementation.

According to Polish officials, these factors were frequently found in license deals of the 1970s and have continued to the present. This has created an atmosphere of distrust between Polish industry and their potential Western partners.

During the period 1971–80, Poland purchased 459 licenses (see the table on p. 198). Of that total, according to a government study done in 1981, 10% were wholly unnecessary. Some 75 of the licenses never found their way into production, and the $500 million spent on the licenses and $5.5 billion spent on associated capital goods yielded only $3 billion in additional exports. The real cost, the study notes, adding fuel and raw-material imports, was much higher. Although 90% of the license outlay was spent in the West, only 40% of the licensed products exported went to countries with hard currency.

The engineering and chemical sectors experienced the greatest problems in getting technology into production. A review of 250 license projects in the sectors showed that 100 had not been fully utilized. Polish sources blame both unrealistic contract conditions and poor performance by Polish contractors for the failure.

The greatest obstacle restricting license purchase is the lack of hard currency. At present, the only way for the Poles to increase license im-

License Imports From the West (1971–88)

Years	Number of licenses
1971–75	316
1976–79	143
1980–88	18

ports would be to step up license exports (and exports in general). To escape this vicious circle, which hurts all aspects of foreign trade, trade officials have recommended the selective development through license purchases of certain industrial branches with export potential. All license imports must exhibit this "export multiplier effect"; that is, they must produce exports that outstrip the cost of their imports.

Licensing Procedures

Polish officials see the failure of extensive license purchase in the 1970s to yield appreciable return as being partly due to the lack of a central policy. This led, they reason, to frequent duplication, acquisition of unnecessary technology and the acceptance of unfavorable purchasing conditions.

As a result, a new State Committee for Scientific and Technical Progress (Komitet dla Spraw Nauki i Postepu Technicznego, Swietojarska 5/7, Pl-00950 Warsaw, Tel: 31-22-21) was set up in 1984 to oversee the entire technology sector and to supervise license purchases.

The main task of the Committee is to organize, coordinate and supervise the incorporation of new technology and scientific research into Polish industry. The body is assigned the task of preparing guidelines for the government's scientific and technological policy and supervising cooperation in this field with other countries.

The Committee is the coordinator of the Program for Development of Science and Technology for 1986–90.

The Central Fund for License Purchases

The government has also set up a special hard-currency fund to finance imports of Western technology. The new Foreign Exchange Fund, which forms part of a larger Central Fund for the Development of Science and Technology, is administered by the Committee for Scientific and Technical Progress.

With new financing now at its disposal, the committee is likely to become increasingly influential in economic planning and should constitute a potential target for future Western sales promotion and marketing.

Four factors appear to have influenced the decision to set up the fund: a shortage of cash for distribution among importers; the failure of reform mechanisms to stimulate technological change; the urgent need to narrow the technological gap between Poland and the West; and the increasing demand imposed on Polish science and technology by the Comecon integration programs.

New license-purchase regulations

In another move to increase central control over license imports, the government introduced stricter license purchase regulations as of Jan. 1, 1986. State Council Decree number 184 of Nov. 15, 1985, replaced the 1978 law on license imports and exports. The regulations multiply the number of institutions that must be consulted prior to purchase and, at the same time, tighten the commercial and organizational criteria for imports of new Western technology. These measures are likely to prolong negotiation periods for Western companies as well as increase the headaches associated with the talks.

All potential license purchasers must submit the following information concerning the proposal to the organization that oversees its activities (such as its industrial association or related ministry):

- technical characteristics of the proposed license import;
- planned costs and benefits of the license during its validity;
- sources of financing, implementing and developing the license; and
- the opinion of a Polish R&D institute on whether the technology could be developed domestically during the period when the license would be valid.

Proposals are then submitted through the enterprise's parent bodies to the Office of Scientific and Technical Progress and on to its committee for approval. Final approval rests on the full consent of the ministries relevant to the license, the Polish bank that is to finance the purchase, the State Energy Inspectorate and the State Committee for Norms, Standards and Quality.

Selling Licenses to Poland

All prospective Polish buyers must submit an application to its parent body containing the points listed below. Companies may find knowing these points helpful in preparing their negotiating and sales efforts. Applications must include

- a detailed description of the license, the technical and functional parameters of the machinery, equipment and product, as well as an evaluation of the modernity of the technological processes involved;
- a comparison of expected expenses with economic benefits accruing from the prospective application of the license;
- a source of financing for the purchase;
- an evaluation of the possibilities of tying the licenses to a buy-back agreement with the seller;
- a statement from the responsible R&D institute that no possibility exists for using local organizations to solve the problem covered by the license;
- a description of the type and volume of imports accompanying the main license and any sublicenses; and
- documented proof, unless an exemption is granted, that the value of license-related imports do not exceed 25% of the cost of the materials and elements necessary for licensed production.

The potential Polish buyer must also show that the license

- saves energy and raw materials (and preferably consumes inputs available domestically or obtainable in other socialist countries); and
- offers high-quality and profitable production, increases productivity and exports, and can mesh with existing Polish technology.

The Role of Polservice

The foreign trade organization (FTO), Polservice (Szpitalna 5, POB 335, 00-959 Warsaw, tel: 27-80-61, telex: 813-539) is used as a negotiating partner when licenses span several industries or are required by nonindustrial institutions, particularly in the scientific fields.

Polservice also exports technical and consulting services including construction of plants and assembly of equipment abroad.

The role of Polservice in license purchases has diminished somewhat, with the decentralization of foreign trade under the recent economic reforms. Indeed, Polservice has not bought a license from the West for several years.

Taxes on Royalties and Fees

In principle, Poland withholds taxes on license fees and royalties at a graduated rate rising to 30%. The tax obligation can be contractually assigned to the purchasing FTO. The Ministry of Finance, however, is reluctant to approve such provisions for net license payments, and on a number of occasions the tax obligation on a contract has been reduced, but not waived. The taxes a licensor must pay ultimately depend on his negotiating position.

Double-Taxation Treaties

Tax reductions on license fees and royalties exist where Poland has concluded bilateral tax treaties with other countries. Poland has 16 treaties on double taxation currently in force with Western countries (see below). The terms of these treaties, though based on the OECD Draft Convention for the avoidance of double taxation, vary from country to country.

Under the treaties, royalties arising in one state and paid to a resident of another state may be taxed in that other state. If license fees and royalties are taxed in the country in which they arise, the standard Polish tax rate of 30% is reduced to 10% in the cases of France, Denmark, Belgium, Sweden, the UK and the US and eliminated altogether in the cases of Germany and Austria.

The US example

Under Article XIII(3)(a) of the 1977 double-taxation treaty with the US, the term "royalties" is broadly defined to include "payments of any kind received as consideration for the use of, or the right to use...any patent, trademark...plan, secret formula or process, or for information concerning industrial, commercial, or scientific experience or skill (know-how)."

The reduced royalty rate applies only to royalties paid for "the right to use property or rights...within (Poland)"—Article XIII(5). To the extent that a license includes rights under non-Polish patents—for example, with respect to export into other countries—the reduced rate of withholding on royalties would be inapplicable. Under Article V(1), however, since such royalty income would be from non-Polish sources, Poland would have no jurisdiction to tax such royalties at all.

If technical services are rendered for training personnel, payments for such services do not qualify as royalties within the meaning of the treaty. Such fees for personal services should ordinarily be free of Polish tax unless they too are deemed effectively connected to a permanent establishment of the US enterprise within Poland.

Article XV exempts from Polish tax income received for professional services, including the services rendered by "engineers, architects...and others" who are within Poland for a period of less than 183 days during the taxable year. However, this article appears to refer only to self-employed persons rendering such services. Thus, professional service income of companies for services rendered by their employees is not covered by this exemption. It is covered, however, by another exemption—that for business profits of US companies not having a permanent establishment in Poland—Article III.

If the US licensor has a permanent establishment in Poland (for example, at its building site or a commercial office) then royalty income effectively connected to that permanent establishment—such as for know-how in erection of the plant—would no longer qualify for the reduced withholding-tax rate but would be deemed a profit of the permanent establishment taxable by Poland as such. Once the licensor's permanent establishment is dismantled after completion of erection, the royalties would no longer be effectively connected to an existing permanent establishment and would then qualify again for the reduced treaty-established withholding rate.

Under Article VI(2)(f) of the treaty, the term "permanent establishment" is defined to include "a building site or construction or assembly project that exists for more than 18 months." The 18-month period begins "when work physically commences" at the site. If a US company is found to have a permanent establishment within the meaning of the treaty within Poland, then the enterprise is fully taxable by Poland to the extent that profits are attributable to that permanent establishment—Article VIII(1).

Patents

Poland is a party to the Paris Convention on protection of intellectual property, including the provisions of the 1967 Stockholm revisions, and is a member of the World Intellectual Property Organization. In keeping with the convention, an applicant from a member country enjoys in Poland the same protection of intellectual property rights as a national of Poland, and can also base a claim or priority of up to 12 months on an earlier application filed in a convention country.

The basic Polish legislation providing for the protection of patents and inventions is the Law on Inventive Activity of Oct. 19, 1972 (published in *Dziennik Ustaw*, 43/72), and the Order of the President of the Polish Patent Office of Dec. 12, 1984. The 1984 Order is of little importance for Western applicants except for a change in regulations relating to unity of inventions, which, contrary to previous practice, does not allow claims on a composition or process of production of an active substance to be subsumed under one application.

Industrial designs are protected on the basis of a 1962 law on inventions, modified by the Council of Ministers decree of Jan. 29, 1963, on the protection of industrial designs.

Types of Patents

The law provides for the granting of four kinds of patents: a provisional patent with a validity of five years, an exclusive patent with a validity of 15 years from the date of the application, and patents of addition and subsequent patents, whose duration is the same as that of the main and dependent patents. Polish law does not provide any possibility of prolonging the legal force of a patent or provisional patent beyond the period for which it has been granted.

A provisional patent is granted after a limited examination, which consists of checking whether the invention has been disclosed in previously submitted applications. However, by filing a request for full examination within four years from the application date, a provisional patent may be converted into a full patent valid for 15 years. Examination is carried out after filing a request and payment of the examination fee, which is to be paid before expiration of a six-month period after publication of the application.

An exclusive patent is issued after full examination as to worldwide novelty. The Patent Office announces the submission of the application 18 months after the date of priority. The protection afforded by a process patent also covers the immediate product of the process. Anyone who, on the priority date, is exploiting the invention in good faith or is preparing to do so may continue to exploit it on the same scale after the patent is granted.

A patent of addition, or subsequent patent, may be obtained by the owner of a patent for improvements or supplements to his invention if these constitute an invention but cannot be applied on their own. More than one patent of addition may be granted to the principal patent. Validity of the patent of addition expires with the validity of the principal patent. When the principal patent lapses for reasons not affecting the invention covered by patent of addition, however, the first patent of addition matures into an independent patent and remains in force for the period for which the principal patent was granted.

Dependent patents are granted for exploitation of inventions that would encroach on a patent granted with earlier priority (earlier patent) to another party. This kind of patent becomes independent when the earlier patent expires.

An inventor's certificate is used in Poland only as a means of recognizing the inventor. It identifies the inventor as the creator or author of the invention and may be a basis for remuneration. It does not provide exclusive rights or any other form of protection. It is generally issued to Polish inventors, and although of no benefit it will be awarded to foreign inventors if requested. The certificate is awarded simultaneously with the patent to which the certificate relates. The utility model is defined as "a new and useful solution having a technical character that concerns the shape, construction or composition of an object having a stable form." Publication follows after the statutory conditions have been examined, within nine months from the day the application is filed or after 18 months from the priority date, whichever expires earlier. Protection is granted after a limited examination. If a patented invention has the features of a utility model, a request may be filed to convert the patent into a utility model. If justified, the utility model can be converted into a patent after payment of the fee for a full examination. If a patent has been refused, an applicant may request utility-model protection for the same invention within two months of the date of such a decision.

Patents are not granted for foodstuffs, pharmaceuticals and substances produced by chemical and radioactive processes, though the processes for producing them may be patented. Exploitation of patents is compulsory. The patent holder must work his invention within three years of the granting of the patent. Exploitation must be within the framework of the national economy and continued for the duration of the validity of the patent.

Industrial Designs and Models

The procedure for protecting industrial designs and models is similar to that for patents. Since Poland is not a party to the Hague Convention of November 1925 on the international deposition of industrial designs and models nor to the Locarno Convention of October 1968 on the international classification of industrial designs, all applications are subject to regulations set down in the Council of Ministers decree of Jan. 29, 1963, on the protection of industrial designs and the patent law of May 31, 1962.

A design eligible for protection is any new embodiment of an object affecting the shape, the properties of the surface, arrangement of lines, drawing, or color rendering the object a special and original appearance, destined for reproduction in industry or handicraft and having aesthetic value.

Industrial designs are protected for a period of five years, and the protection may be extended for a further period of up to five years.

Co-ownership

If an invention has been conceived by more than one party, the ownership of the invention belongs jointly to all the inventors so that the right to obtain a patent belongs also to the co-inventors. If they have not contractually defined their respective shares in the invention, it is understood that each holds an equal share in the invention. Unless a contract signed by the joint owners of the patent stipulates otherwise, each joint owner may work the invention himself without the consent of the other co-owners. A co-owner, however, cannot transfer his rights to the patent nor allow any person to work the invention without the consent of all the co-owners of the patent.

Application Procedures

Although the national authority on intellectual property rights is the Polish Patent Office (Urzad Patentowy), all applications and dealings by foreign individuals or companies concerning patents, trademarks and industrial designs must be made through one of two authorized agencies established for this purpose. They are at the following locations:

Patpol
(Patent Attorney Office of the Polish Chamber of Foreign Trade)
ul. Stawki 2, P.O.B. 168
Pl-00950 Warsaw
Tel: 395-845/21/38
Telex: 814-361
Telegram: Patpol Warszawa

Polservice
Foreign Trade Enterprise
ul. Chalubinskiego 8, P.O.B. 335
Pl-00950 Warsaw
Tel: 27-80-61
Telex: 814-906
Telegram: Polservice Warszawa

Polservice handles the bulk of foreign patent applications at present, but the services and fees of both agents are identical. The main activities of the two groups include:

- submitting patent, industrial models, designs and trademarks;
- giving legal and technical guidance in patent matters;
- preparing patent applications and documentation (drafts, translations, etc.) according to the regulations of the Patent Office;

- researching literature concerning the patents and technological matters that may be involved;
- representing foreign persons at the Patent Office and at its Board of Appeal;
- providing consultations concerning industrial property protection; and
- advertising license sales possibilities in the Polish press.

Documents required

For patent and utility-model applications, the following documents must be provided to the agent:

- an order requesting representation service, with the name and address of the applicant;
- the name and address of the applicant;
- the names and addresses of inventors and their citizenship;
- an instruction as to the kind of protection;
- the date on which the application is to be filed;
- a power of attorney, which need not be notarized;
- a specification on an invention, and claims, triplicate signed by the applicant or his agent on A-4 size paper;
- drawing, if indispensable to the understanding of the invention;
- an abstract of the specification including the most important particulars contained in the specification, claims and drawings up to 120 words;
- a document confirming the right to the patent if the applicant is not the inventor; and
- an inventor's declaration if he wants to obtain an inventor's certificate and to be mentioned in the specification and other documents issued by the Polish Patent Office.

When filing an application claiming any convention priorities, it is necessary to point out the dates, country and if possible the numbers of the original applications. Within four months of filing the application in Poland, it is necessary to file the following:

- the priority documents;
- a document confirming the applicant's right to priority (only if the original applications were not filed in the name of the applicant in Poland); and

- the allocation of the priority dates (for each Polish claim only one priority date can be claimed).

All the documents filed must be translated into Polish. Both offices accept the documents prepared in convention languages and provide the necessary translation.

Infringement and Legal Recourse

Legal recourse in cases involving infringement of patent or utility models requires that the patent holder send written notice to the infringer demanding cessation of infringement. If the infringement is not terminated by a stipulated date, suit may be filed in the district court where the alleged infringer is domiciled. The period of the statute of limitations in infringement matters is three years from the date when legal action is filed. It runs separately for each infringement.

Claims supporting infringement of patents may be filed before the common courts, preferably in the district where the infringement occurred. The Western partner can be represented in these proceedings by an attorney from Zespol Adwokacki No. 40 (Lawyers' Office No. 40), the only institution authorized to provide legal service to foreigners. Neither the Lawyers' Office No. 40 (Ul. Hiberna 13, 00-012 Warsaw; Tel: 27-48-75) nor the patent representatives from Patpol and Polservice can be hired to monitor the market for possible patent infringements. This much the patent holder must attempt himself.

Production and import of a product produced under patent are in practice considered to be covered by product patents, and Art. 54 of the law states that "in the case of a patent for a process to manufacture a new product, any product that can be obtained by means of the patented process shall be presumed to have in fact been produced by that process."

If the patented process is worked outside Poland, and the product so produced is introduced into Poland, the Polish process patent has been infringed. A person accused of infringement may defend himself by showing that the product was produced in a different way than the process covered by the patent. This would appear to give the Polish process patent a degree of extraterritorial effect under normal Western concepts of infringement.

The successful plaintiff may obtain an injunction against further infringement, and also "the surrender of any profits realized or the payment of damages." Additionally, the plaintiff may require the infringer to publish an explanatory statement in the press. If the infringement was intentional, the infringer may be required to pay a "suitable sum of money" to the Central Technical Organization for the purpose of encouraging inventive activity. The court may also issue orders regarding the disposition of infringing articles, "articles manufactured unlawfully," and elements used in their manufacture.

Compulsory Licensing and Annulment Proceedings

Poland, like all Comecon countries, makes legal provisions for compulsory licensing which are in fact more detailed and all-embracing than most other East European laws. However, no known use of these provisions has been made against Western firms.

Art. 46 of the law on inventions stipulates that if it can be shown that "the invention is necessary for the implementation of the tasks forming part of the economic plan," and the patent holder is not willing to reach a voluntary agreement on licensing or, according to Art. 40, if an invention has not been worked within four years of the date of filing or three years from the date the patent was granted, whichever is later, a compulsory license can be obtained. Compulsory licensing is also provided for in the case of patents of addition.

According to Art. 65, before instituting such a proceeding, the interested economic unit in Poland must approach the patentee for "voluntary surrender" of the patent, and try to conclude a contract for assignment of the patent. The compensation to be paid the patent holder may be paid over a period of time or in a lump sum. Although there are ceilings prescribed on the amount that can be paid, these ceilings may be exceeded if the patent is of "special significance for the national economy."

Annulment proceedings may be brought by individuals or by the Public Prosecutor in the public interest. Patents may be expropriated for national defense reasons and "for the implementation of tasks forming part of economic planning."

The law does not define the differences between compulsory licensing, annulment and expropriation, and since there are no precedents, the subject remains academic.

Trademarks

Poland is a member of the Madrid Agreement, which provides trademark protection in all member countries through registration with the World Intellectual Property Organization in Geneva. Poland is also a party to the Nice Accord regulating the international classification of products and services, and is a signatory of the Paris Convention on the Protection of Industrial Property and the Stockholm Act of 1974.

In 1985, a new trademark law was ratified to fine-tune existing Polish legislation and bring it into line with international conventions. As a

Licensing Experience in Poland

Western firms that have been in Poland for any length of time have undoubtedly noticed the more restricted licensing opportunities of the 1980s. The Poles are negotiating much harder these days than in the boom years of the 1970s, and sales possibilities, in general, have been reduced by to the hard-currency shortage. Lengthy and difficult negotiations, the constant problem of financing, and the mutability of the Polish economic environment are all part of the tough conditions that companies face in selling licenses to the Poles.

The Fiat saga

The "licensing deal of the decade," without a doubt, would be Fiat's agreement with the FTO Pol-Mot to modernize the compact and mid-sized automobiles produced in Poland since the late 1960s. The deal illustrates a number of difficulties facing a Western license seller in the Polish market. While not all agreements are as difficult as this one, the deal was typical in many ways.

The negotiations lasted several difficult years. There was some competition for both deals, but Fiat had been expected to win the contract for the compact-car license (which it did finally in September 1987). Before achieving this, though, Fiat had to promise loans of $500 million for the modernization of the FSM car plant. The funds would also be distributed among some 40 metallurgical, engineering and chemical factories supplying the project. The new model is scheduled to go into production in 1991. Repayment of Fiat's loan is supposed to come from hard-currency export sales of the auto.

For the mid-sized deal, Fiat negotiated long and hard in a much publicized duel with the Japanese car manufacturer Daihatsu. In July 1987, Fiat President Giovanni Agnelli stated that Fiat had "apparently" lost the deal to Daihatsu due to the Japanese's superior technology and better financial terms. The negotiating continued, however, and finally in September 1988 Fiat came out the winner. Among the main factors behind the firm's triumph was Fiat's flexibility with respect to financing.

Only three months later, though, the Polish government announced that it had changed its concept of how the Polish automotive industry should develop and suspended the final signing of the mid-sized deal. According to the new view, the government would like to abandon the mid-sized car altogether in favor of an even greater production of smaller cars. Thus, not only had the second licensing deal with Fiat been put in doubt, but the first agreement for the compact car was changed as a result.

side benefit, the new law helps to establish more secure market conditions for foreign companies operating in the country. The number of trademark registrations has grown in Poland over the last few years and now totals around 20,000.

To protect their trademarks in Poland, applicants must take the additional step of filing an application with the Polish Patent Office.

According to the 1985 Polish law, the first applicant is entitled to registration. A person who can later prove prior use of a registered trademark can apply for its cancellation and re-register the mark himself. A registered trademark vests exclusive rights to the owner and is enforceable by him against its unauthorized use by others. Trademarks are registered for a period of 10 years from application filing date and are renewable for like periods.

The 1985 Trademark Law also introduced the following new features:

- producers with registered marks are obligated to put the trademark to use;
- products must bear their registered trademarks (if this and above requirement are not met, the trademark will be invalidated);
- services are now eligible for trademark protection; and
- protected marks and their symbols must be precisely defined not only in terms of word, form and figurative design but also ornamentation and color composition.

Application Procedures

With the exception of documents concerning the original granting of trade protection outside Poland, all applications must be submitted in Polish. They must contain the name of the firm, its location and field of activity, the product connected with the trademark, a list of the product and types of products that will fall under the particular trademark, the kind of trademark, and, if possible, the way in which the trademark is attached to the product. The firm should also include the power of attorney if one is used, the original registration in a foreign country and its date of issue. One month after the date of application in Poland, the applicant can make a statement that he claims a priority of issue.

Infringement and Legal Recourse

Recourse in the case of trademark violation is provided for in the 1985 Trademark Law as well as in the Law Against Unfair Competition of 1926. Applicability of the latter is questionable in view of the lack of precedents. However, on Jan. 23, 1991, the Constitution Tribunal confirmed that this law is applicable in Poland.

Trademark infringement is defined as occurring when the marks are deceptively similar when placed on similar goods, creating confusion as to the source of the goods. The use of surveys and testimony of witnesses can be used in proving one's case. Infringements can be ascertained by surveillance of the marketplace, a service provided by both Polservice and Patpol.

In the case of trademark infringement, the owner of the trademark or his licensee may take action to halt the infringing activities. The first step is to notify the infringing party in writing in an effort to settle the matter amicably. If this fails and if the alleged infringer has a registered trademark of his own, the plaintiff may petition under the Trademark Law for cancellation in whole or in part of the infringer's registration. The petition is filed with the Patent Office.

The Trademark Law further provides that an adjudged infringer must give to the trademark owner "the benefits obtained, make restitution for the damages, and remove the effects of the infringement of rights." Also, the infringer must publish the verdict or decision in the press, and if the infringement was deliberate, further compensation must be paid for the "moral wrong." Lastly, the decision may require removal of forged marks from goods, wrappings, price lists and other papers, and removal of supplies of marks and the implements for forging the mark.

The statute of limitations is three years. The statute does not state when the period commences, but it is indicated by "the filing of the claim, separately as to each infringement." The running of the period is also "suspended in the period between the filing date of the trademark for registration at the Patent Office and the registration date of this (plaintiff's) mark."

The rights enumerated above would be enforceable by filing an action in one of the district courts in Poland, either where the infringement occurs or where the defendant is domiciled.

In addition to the civil remedies enumerated above, the Trademark Law provides for heavy fines and even imprisonment (or both) for trademark infringement. The head of the enterprise or person responsible for making or marketing the goods is liable for such punishment. In certain instances the prosecution may be instituted by the injured party.

Procedures are also available whereby the owner of an unregistered mark who has become well known in Poland can request the Patent Office to reject the application of another party for the same or similar mark, or to invalidate the registration of the other party, if already granted. The period within which a person may apply for revocation of a trademark by another party is five years.

Trademark Infringement in Poland

Everyone familiar with the Polish market for consumer goods knows that it is overrun with goods labeled with pirated brand names. Adidas and Puma sneakers, Smurfs cartoon figures, and Wrangler and Levi's jeans—to name but a few—are all pirated by small-scale producers for sale on the local markets.

An interesting twist to the situation is that Polish consumers usually prefer the original and will not always purchase the pirated good. Because of this, some pirated goods are exported to other Eastern European countries by individual Poles to conduct illegal sales of these goods where customers are not so in the know (or at least not so choosy).

Most companies are aware that their goods are pirated on the Polish market. But because the country is such a small market and the company's commercial interests are usually not threatened, firms close their eyes to goods produced illegally under their name. During 1988 and 1989, at least two Western companies decided that the pirating of their goods was intolerable and took legal action against the illegal producers.

In a case still pending in a Warsaw court, Christian Dior of France has charged a Polish company with illegally reproducing its perfume "Poison" on the local market. Christian Dior demands that the Polish company immediately withdraw its version of Poison from the market, publicly account for its infringement in the Polish press, and pay damages to Dior in a certain but undisclosed proportion of profits made on the pirated perfume.

In a less extreme case, Salomon, a manufacturer of sporting equipment, threatened a small-scale manufacturer with legal action if he did not cease production of shoulder bags marked with the firm's logo. The Polish manufacturer stopped producing the bags with the company's name before suit was filed.

The recent Western interest in protecting trademarks in Poland is causing some Polish foreign trade officials to believe that there might be a Western "crackdown" on illegal producers. Certainly the next year or two will prove or disprove these fears. At least companies now have the precedent that it is possible to pursue a trademark violator, and that effective action can be taken against product pirates.

14
Russia

For decades, two organizations, Litsensintorg and Vneshtekhnika, held the state monopoly over foreign trade in technology and licenses in the Soviet Union. Technology purchases emphasized the needs of the military sector and were often unaffordable for the civilian sector. With the formal, legal breakup of the USSR in 1992, the former Soviet laws applying to technology and licensing agreements have been in a state of flux. As of this writing (in the first quarter of 1992), none of the individual republics except Lithuania had passed its own intellectual property laws as yet (and the Lithuanian legislation that does exist is very short and pertains essentially only to company names and trademarks). The Russian republic has made the most headway, however, as it has put forward a number of draft proposals that, while not yet official policy, are on their way to superseding the older Soviet legislation.

Since the Russian republic is the most advanced, then, this chapter will concentrate mainly on licensing conditions in that republic.

A Market in Transition

Today the Russian market is suffering the problems of transition. The old USSR laws have either lost their force or have become hopelessly outdated, while the new Russian norms regulating intellectual property relations are still in the phase of confirmation.

Nevertheless, in the framework of existing law all enterprises now have the right to conclude licensing agreements directly with foreign companies or through Litsensintorg (which has been transformed into a state-owned commercial firm, but at the same address and with the same subdivisions). All limitations on import of foreign technology have been lifted. Foreign firms have even received the right to sell a single license to various Russian enterprises, forming a separate licensing agreement with each. In the past, state technology-import policy emphasized avoidance of repeat purchases of the same technology. The guiding principle was that the state acquired the new technology and then distributed it to domestic producers as needed.

Russian enterprises in the military sector are also slowly obtaining the right to exchange technologies with foreign partners. Thus the producer enterprises now have the right to export not only the finished T-80 tank and MIG-29 airplane but also the production technologies for their manufacture. Proposals for technological cooperation are being made ever more frequently to Russian producers in the field of rocket science and space technology.

Certain limitations on the export of military technology have been retained, but a number of Russian companies seeking foreign funds for conversion projects are reportedly bypassing such administrative barriers by establishing limited commercial structures for such operations. Reportedly the administrative authorities in the military industrial sector approve of such steps and are cooperating with establishment of such structures.

The only state organ still performing a supervisory role in the field of technology transfer is Rospatent (Ilinka 5/2; SU-103012 Moscow; Tel: 925-16-61; Fax: 230-27-67, 230-23-48; Telex: 411-431a; Chief of Protocol Department Mikhail V. Kuperev). However, Rospatent's role is purely one of state registration of technological ownership, rather than policy implementation.

There is no state organ currently supervising the financial or commercial conditions of technology trade, and there is currently no legal approval process for such agreements. Such approval was required under all-Union foreign trade regulations in effect until Jan. 1, 1992, however, and analysts believe that the approval requirement may be introduced anew under Russian regulations currently still being debated in parliamentary subcommittee. If so, the approval would be required from the Department of Licensing of the Russian Ministry of Science, Higher Schooling and Technology (SU-103905 Moscow, Tverskaya ul. dom 11; tel: 229-95-93).

It is recommended that interested parties ask this body for a review of licensing contracts in the meantime, despite the absence of a formal requirement. Their written finding could help preclude problems with the Customs Administration, which is still operating under all-Union procedures.

The institutes of the Russian Academy of Sciences are reorganizing their activities along commercial lines and have accumulated experience in technology barter deals. Such deals are currently free of all regulatory restrictions and customs duties.

There is a Russian profit-tax law, however, which foresees the imposition of a 15% tax on royalty transfers—again, though, this law is not currently in force and exists only in draft form. When and if it is finally passed, it will be retroactive, however, covering all of 1992.

The Russian parliament has also adopted a package of laws on intellectual property in the first reading, which means that the laws may still be revised and will go into effect only after presidential signature. Under these laws, patents will for the first time be classified as a tradeable commodity, including ownership for up to 20 years. Foreign legal entities obtain the same ownership rights as local organizations under the draft laws, although they will be required to register their patents or trademarks locally.

Western companies whose products are currently traded or will be traded in Russia are strongly advised to protect their trademarks as early as possible under the new regulations. Under USSR trademark laws, Western lawyers warn, there were a few cases in which a local organization tried to register a foreign company's trademark as its own property before the foreign firm took notice of the action. The foreign firms affected then apparently had a great deal of trouble untangling their intellectual property rights.

The Russian draft law foresees the possibility of a local firm or person applying for an international patent.

The draft trademark law has been submitted for review by the Paris Union for Protection of Industrial Property. One improvement foreseen by the Russian draft law—compared with the USSR law passed in 1991—is that locally based joint ventures and wholly owned foreign subsidiaries will be permitted to file for local patent protection for innovations developed locally.

The 1991 USSR Code

Until the draft legislation is approved, however, the 1991 USSR law will continue to be enforced. It is a strong piece of legislation, in fact, and many Western companies will benefit from the regulations, which created new incentives for their exports to and imports from the USSR, including know-how. In the past they were confronted with an atmosphere characterized by a lack of legal protection of their intellectual property.

The law "On Inventions in the USSR," which came into effect on July 1, 1991, belongs to a limited number of the all-union legislative acts that are not likely to lose their importance in the light of the increased independence of the former constituent republics. The law broadens the range of objects protected by patent; extends the patent validity period from 15 to 20 years; eases the procedures involved in obtaining a patent; and establishes tax concessions connected with the development and use of inventions.

The implementation of the law was made the responsibility of a newly formed State Committee for Patenting, or Gospatent. This act broke the patent monopoly of the USSR Chamber of Trade and Industry (Soyuzpatent), giving inventors a chance to choose between the two main patenting agencies. A special Patent Court has been assigned to settle all disputes arising from the practical implementation of the law.

The items that can be regarded as inventions and, consequently, protected by patent, are listed in Article 1 of the legislation. They include a device; a means; a substance; a staple of a microorganism; a culture of plant or animal cells; as well as an entirely new employment of an old device, a means, a substance or a staple of a microorganism.

The word "substance" in this case specifically implies medical and chemical products. The word "means" includes both methodology and products received by this methodology. It also covers objects that are usually unprotected by patent laws in many countries, such as preventive care, diagnostics and the treatment of diseases.

Western investors will no longer find many of the problems that have hindered their operations in the Soviet market for decades. One important obstacle was the impossibility of obtaining patents for inventions in particular industries. This was especially true in such export-oriented sectors as chemicals and pharmaceuticals, where patents for substances, obtained by certain chemical processes, were not issued at all. No patents were given for medical substances, methods of preventive care, diagnostics, health care and veterinary treatment either. Another obstacle was the state's monopoly covering usage of all inventions made in Soviet territory.

Protecting JV Inventions

The law is aimed first of all at protecting inventions made in the Soviet Union. However, Soviet citizens and persons without citizenship permanently residing abroad, as well as foreign juridical persons—including joint ventures—based in the USSR, can also apply for Soviet patent protection either directly or through their agents in the former Soviet Union registered with Gospatent.

Unlike patent legislation in most Western countries, the author (authors, co-authors) of an invention, i.e. a physical person, is guaranteed primary rights for his invention (Art. 4). He may, at his own discretion, grant those rights to other physical and legal entities such as the company that employs him, and so forth. This provision, however, is not applied to companies with foreign capital share that has foundation documents extending the right of the company over all inventions made by the staff (Art.49).

Joint ventures and subsidiaries may also get patents for their inventions abroad. The only condition attached to this is that they should first apply for a patent in the USSR (Art.49).

Five-Year Tax Exemption

A five-year tax exemption is one of the biggest advantages offered by the July 1991 law. It is applied to profits, including foreign currency profits, received from the implementation or sale of inventions. The same provision is applied to companies that use bought or licensed inventions, and to those producing equipment necessary to put an invention to use. Tax-exempt status may be extended by decision of the USSR Cabinet of Ministers, or the governments of the respective republics, for inventions that are of particular importance for the economy, especially in the fields of health care and environmental protection (Art. 28).

However, one important drawback to the law is that a number of subjects are not clearly recognized as inventions (Art. 1). First of all, Western and local companies involved in the development and production of computer systems are virtually unprotected by the patent legislation. Furthermore, it will be rather difficult to patent some scientific discoveries such as genetic engineering.

Not an Invention

The areas not recognized as inventions include the following:

- scientific theories;
- methods for the organization of economic management;
- conventional signs, schedules and rules;
- means of fulfillment of thinking operations;
- algorithms and software;
- projects and schemes for site, building and facility planning; and
- improvement of aesthetic design.

Despite these limitations, the law is still a considerable step forward for licensing in the ex-Soviet Republics, and the Russian legislation that is under debate and development in that republic's parliament is likely

Licensing Opportunities in the Former USSR

Western firms are increasingly accepting Eastern European licenses and technology as payment for goods or services. This approach to financing deals is becoming popular especially with firms looking for lower-cost R&D alternatives. As one trading-company executive noted, "High-tech products are now being offered in countertrade deals as well."

"R&D in East European countries represents new and profitable opportunities for Western firms," commented another trade consultant. The trend includes swapping manufactured goods for patents, licenses or the "rental" of scientists and technologies. In one interesting deal, Philips (Netherlands) bartered low-end electronic products for the full-time use over several years of a group of talented Soviet software programmers. The classic example of East-to-West technology transfer was the purchase of the Czechoslovak polymer license some years ago that is used to manufacture soft contact lenses.

Historically, most EE licenses in use in the West come from the former Soviet Republics (mainly Russia), which have sold well over 300 separate processes, inventions and innovations to Western companies. In many cases, the technologies were developed by the USSR's military industry and often meet international standards. While military-sponsored research or production organizations used to be off-limits for Western firms seeking new technology, this has changed significantly in recent years. Reductions in military spending have encouraged some scientific organizations to find Western partners who can help develop and commercialize their untapped technology base.

In one recent example, a firm acquired the technology of special filters for air-raid shelters. Such contracts may become more difficult to negotiate, however, owing to the ongoing shifts in decision-making from central ministries and authorities to the republics. Numerous German, Belgian, Swedish, Italian, British, Spanish, Austrian und US firms have concluded license deals in sectors such as ferrous and nonferrous metallurgy, process engineering, machine building, chemicals, the food industry, agriculture, industrial construction, microbiology and the production of medical equipment.

Foreign buyers have included Nippon Kokan (Japan), Italimpianti (Italy), Newton Chambers (UK) and Altos Hornos (Spain), the latter producing equipment for dry coke quenching under a Soviet license. The Japanese use USSR-developed purification plants for treatment of industrial wastes. McDermott (US) purchased a technology for welding of large-diameter pipes.

Since basic research is becoming increasingly expensive in the West, many companies are actively looking for opportunities to tap technology bases outside their own R&D departments. As the Russian republic is the most developed in this area, Western experts suggest several options to Western companies interested in structuring a license in the republic. Options include the following:

- acquiring a process (e.g. a chemical process) that carries no patent in the respective Western country. In these cases, the Russians prefer to follow the Soviet practice of setting up a lump-sum agreement rather than a running royalty payment before patent disclosures have been made. Under this setup, the Russian licensor gets his money much faster that under a royalty deal. Many Western companies also request worldwide exclusivity in order to incorporate the technology into several products;
- purchasing information and technical data in the current state of development and securing worldwide exclusivity. Also in this case lump-sum payments are preferred;
- negotiating an agreement to pay the sum in "phases" linked with the performance guarantees set forth in the licensing contract; and
- agreeing on a combination of down payment and royalty fees where good patent protection exists. (See above for a discussion of the July 1991 Soviet patent law.)

But the most interesting developments may very well open up in connection with the acquisition of former Soviet enterprises. If an enterprise is assigned to a buyer, in general its patent rights are also transferred to the acquiring company unless the government issues restrictions with respect to a certain product or technology.

to build upon the principles it established rather than go back on them. For its part, the Supreme Soviet regarded it as a pilot project. According to its resolution of May 31, the Supreme Soviet is to evaluate the practical effects of the law by Aug. 1, 1992, and then, should the need arise, amend or further add to it. While historical events have since forestalled such an evaluation in the Soviet context, the Russian legislative body, for one, has clearly taken up the same mandate.

Appendix **A**

What to Include in a Foreign Licensing Agreement

I. Definitions
  A. Product
  B. Territory
    1. manufacturing
    2. sales (optional)
  C. Parties (subsidiary)
  D. Fees and down payments
    1. conversion rate
    2. convertibility guaranties
    3. royalty base—percentage of:
      a. licensee's total production, including products other than licensor's;
      b. licensee's production of licensor's models and comparable models;
      c. licensee's production of licensor's models only; or
      d. savings generated
    4. equity interest or right to acquire stock (optional)
    5. right to buy percentage of production
    6. requirement of volume in given time period, or yearly minimum payment
  E. Confidential disclosures
  F. Export rights
  G. Transfer of title; foreign-based company

- H. Foreign taxes: who pays
- I. Arbitration
- J. Place of jurisdiction
- K. Right of termination, plus reopening clause
- L. Term of agreement
  1. corresponding to years of production, regardless of time lapse between signing of agreement and licensee's picking up model
  2. when patent licensee signs agreement, tied to life of patent
  3. automatic renewal clause, with minimum advance notice
- M. Accounting provisions
- N. Option to buy
- O. Management participation
- P. Licensor's capital investment (if any)
- Q. Schedule of payments and form of invoice penalty clause for late payment
- R. Weights and measures system to be used

II. Grant
- A. Patents (plus "identifiable information")
  1. acknowledgment of validity
  2. reversion of rights or title in case of expropriation, bankruptcy, etc.
  3. protection, including cost of infringement, prosecution
  4. cross-licensing, including improvements
  5. exclusivity
  6. immunities outside country of manufacture
  7. acquired patents (right to them by acquisition)
- B. Trademarks
  1. acknowledgment of validity, especially where they cannot be registered
  2. reversion in case of expropriation, bankruptcy, etc.
  3. protection, including cost of infringement, prosecution
  4. quality and advertising control
  5. trademark registration, user agreement
- C. Right to services (and charges for them)
  1. training
  2. access to plant
  3. know-how
  4. term of services
  5. technical material
  6. exchange of commercial information on price of components, equipment

7. purchase of equipment, sale of components
8. start-up supervision

III. Other
  A. Host government approval of agreement and remittances; non-validity of agreements until received
  B. Noncompetitive clause
  C. Retention of sales rights
  D. Recognition of preexisting exclusive licensees
  E. Right to license components
  F. Interchangeability of parts among licensees
  G. Right to audit
  H. Exact reproduction of trademark (no adulteration)
  I. Caveat regarding laws of country of licensor: "total agreement subject to any laws, regulations or restrictions of...[country]"

Appendix B
Typical Licensing Agreements

The following documents represent "typical" licensing agreements for trademark and know-how transfers in Argentina and Brazil. They are included here because their comparison demonstrates how the operating environments in different countries determine the issues to be addressed in the contracts.

The editor would like to thank Edwin C. Bullock and Diana Muller of the law firm Kuhn and Muller for making these texts available; the comments included with the contracts are theirs.

I. Trademark and Know-How License Agreement for Argentina

License Agreement

AGREEMENT made this first day of November, 1991 between ________________, a corporation organized and existing under the laws of ____________ and having its principal place of business at ________________________________ (hereinafter referred to as "Licensor") and ________________, a corporation organized and existing under the laws of ________________ and having its principal place of business at ____________________ (hereinafter referred to as "Licensee").

WHEREAS, Licensor is the exclusive owner in the Territory (as hereinafter defined) of the entire right, title and interest in the Trademarks (as hereinafter defined);

WHEREAS, Licensor is in possession of valuable know-how relating to certain techniques and methods of manufacture and packing relating to the Licensed Products (as hereinafter defined);

WHEREAS, Licensee desires to utilize such know-how to enable it to manufacture and sell the Licensed Products in the Territory under the Trademarks; and

WHEREAS, Licensor has agreed to make available to Licensee such know-how and to permit Licensee to manufacture the Licensed Products and give to Licensee the right to use the Trademarks in relation thereto on the terms and conditions hereinafter set forth.

NOW, THEREFORE, in consideration of the foregoing and the mutual covenants herein contained, the parties hereto agree as follows:

1. Definitions

As used in this Agreement, the following terms shall have the following meaning:

(a) "Licensed Products" shall mean

(b) The "Trademarks" shall mean the trademarks set forth in Schedule A and any additional trademarks as may be agreed to in writing between the parties hereto from time to time.

(c) "Technical Information" shall mean all know-how, designs, materials, production methods and techniques, formulae, specifications, directions and standards for manufacturing and packaging the Licensed Products which are furnished from time to time by Licensor to Licensee and all subsequent modifications, improvements and additions thereto.

(d) "Territory" shall mean Argentina.

(e) "Net Sales" shall mean Licensee's invoice price of the Licensed Products sold hereunder less cash, quantity and freight discounts actually taken and actual returns for defective Licensed Products, value added taxes, sales taxes, and customs duties, if any.

(f) "Contract Year" shall mean each twelve (12) month period commencing on the first day of November and ending on the thirty-first day of October.

2. Grant of License

(a) Upon the terms and conditions hereinafter set forth, Licensor grants to Licensee and Licensee hereby accepts, for the term of this Agreement, the exclusive right and license to use the Technical Information and the Trademarks for the manufacture, packaging, distribution and sale of the Licensed Products in the Territory.

(b) The license granted hereby specifically excludes any right to use or apply the Technical Information or the Trademarks to manufacture and assemble any Licensed Product or other items in any country outside of the Territory or to assist or procure the manufacture or use of the Licensed Products outside of the Territory.

3. Term of License

The initial term of this Agreement shall be a period of four years commencing on the Effective Date and terminating on the thirty-first day of October, 1995, unless sooner terminated as provided herein. The Licensee shall have the option to renew this Agreement for one renewal term of four years commencing November 1, 1995, provided that Licensee gives written notice to Licensor of its intention to renew no later than April 30, 1995, and provided further that as of that date Licensee is not in default of any of the terms of this Agreement.

4. Royalties

Licensee agrees to pay to Licensor on all Licensed Products sold hereunder a royalty of five percent (5%) of Net Sales.

In the event any sale is made a special price to any of Licensee's affiliates or subsidiaries or to any other person, firm or corporation related in any manner to Licensee's officers, directors or major shareholders, there shall be a royalty paid on such sale based upon the price generally charged the trade.

5. Minimum Royalty

The following constitute minimum royalties for each Contract Year:

First Contract Year	$150,000.00
Second Contract Year	$175,000.00
Third Contract Year and each Contract Year thereafter	$200,000.00

Licensee's failure to pay to Licensor in any Contract Year the applicable minimum royalty shall be grounds for termination of this Agreement by Licensor but shall not result in other liability of Licensee nor provide a basis for monetary recovery by Licensor.

6. Payments

(a) During the term of this Agreement, Licensee shall pay to Licensor no later than thirty (30) days after the end of each quarter of each Contract Year the royalty due to Licensor pursuant to Paragraph 4 for said quarter.

(b) All royalty payments and other amounts due Licensor pursuant to this Agreement shall be payable in United States currency, unless another means of payment is required by the Government of Argentina, in which case such other means of payment shall be employed. The rate of exchange shall be the one authorized by the Central Bank of Argentina as of the date of invoice with respect to royalty payments, and as of the date the payment became due with respect to other amounts due to Licensor.

(c) Licensee shall in no event, without Licensor's prior written authorization, be entitled to set off any amounts which Licensee may claim to be owed to it by Licensor for any reason whatsoever, against any royalties owed to the Licensor pursuant to this Agreement.

7. Advertising and Promotion

(a) Licensee shall include in all advertising and promotion of the Licensed Products a prominent statement or notice identifying the Licensed Products as having been manufactured, packaged and sold under license from Licensor.

(b) Licensee agrees to consider the advice and suggestions of Licensor with respect to Licensed Product advertising and promotion. Licensee further agrees upon request of Licensor to promptly discontinue any advertising or practice reasonably deemed by Licensor to have a detrimental effect. Licensee shall not advertise the Licensed Products outside of the Territory.

8. Maintenance of Records

(a) Licensee shall keep separate true and accurate books and records in which there shall be reflected all manufacture and sales of Licensed Products, all refunds, returns and discounts in connection therewith, and the amount of royalty payable to Licensor pursuant to this Agreement. Licensee shall maintain such books and records for a period of five (5) years following the years to which they pertain. In the event that a controversy or litigation develops between the parties, Licensee agrees to maintain such books and records until such time as the controversy or litigation is resolved.

(b) Licensee agrees to furnish to Licensor, within thirty (30) days after the end of each quarter of each Contract Year, a statement, verified by a duly authorized officer of Licensee, showing the total of all sales of Licensed Products and all returns and trade discounts during the quarter of such Contract Year then ended and a computation of the royalty payable to Licensor pursuant to Paragraph 4 of this Agreement. Within forty-five (45) days after the end of each Contract Year, Licensee shall furnish to Licensor a statement for the Contract Year then completed, certified by the chief financial officer of Licensee, containing the same information required to be contained in the quarterly certified statements on an annual basis. Receipt or acceptance by Licensor of any of the statements furnished, or of any sums paid, pursuant to this Agreement, will not preclude Licensor from questioning their correctness at any time.

(c) For the purpose of verifying the figures reported in any statement or report furnished by Licensee hereunder, a representative or representatives of Licensor may, during the term of this Agreement and for a period of three (3) years thereafter, upon reasonable notice to Licensee, examine any or all of the books and records which Licensee is required to maintain pursuant to Subparagraph (a) of this Paragraph 8, and all other records, documents and material in the possession of or under the control of Licensee (including, but not limited to, production records) relevant to calculating royalties with respect to the subject matter of this Agreement. Such books of account and records shall be made available to Licensor's representatives for examination at the premises of Licensee during normal business hours.

9. Quality of merchandise

Licensee agrees that the articles covered by this Agreement at all times shall be of high standard and of such style, appearance and quality as to protect and enhance the Trademark and the goodwill pertaining thereto, shall meet Licensor's quality standards and specifications, and shall be manufactured, sold, distributed and promoted in accordance with all applicable laws and regulations.

Licensee agrees to submit to Licensor, without cost to Licensor, for its approval five (5) samples of each of the Licensed Products to be made by it under this Agreement, together with all cartons, labels, containers and packing and wrapping materials, and shall not sell any Licensed Products which do not have Licensor's written approval prior to sale. If any significant change is made in the quality, workmanship or design of any previously approved Licensed Product, Licensee shall submit five (5) samples of such changed Licensed Products to Licensor for approval pursuant to this Paragraph, and shall not sell such changed Licensed Products prior to receipt of written approval by Licensor of all changes. Licensee agrees that all Licensed Products made and sold under this Agreement shall be of the standards of material, workmanship, design and performance equal to the samples and specifications approved by Licensor.

Licensor shall have the right to inspect the Licensed Products and methods of manufacture on the premises of Licensee during regular business hours upon reasonable prior notice.

10. Trademark use and marking

(a) All Licensed Products sold or distributed by Licensee under this Agreement shall be marked with the appropriate trademark notice, which shall be of proper form and content and properly displayed, in a manner that is in compliance with the applicable provisions of the trademark laws of the Territory. All packing, containers and material illustrating, utilizing or featuring the Trademarks shall also be appropriately marked with any trademark notices required by applicable law.

(b) Licensee agrees to use the Trademarks only in the form approved by Licensor. All use of the Trademarks on the Licensed Products and on labels, packaging and in advertising must faithfully reproduce the form approved by Licensor. Approval of form of use of the Trademarks, once given, shall be continuing.

(c) Licensee is prohibited from using any trademark other than the Trademarks on any Licensed Products and other products which are confusingly similar in design configuration to any of the Licensed Products.

11. Ownership of trademarks

Licensee acknowledges Licensor's exclusive right, title and interest in and to the Trademarks in the Territory and elsewhere and will not at any time do or cause to be done any act or thing contesting or in any way impairing, or tending to impair, in any respect such right, title and interest. In connection with the use of the Trademarks, Licensee shall not in any manner represent that it has any ownership in the Trademarks or registrations thereof, and Licensee acknowledges that use of the Trademarks shall not create in Licensee's favor any right, title or interest in or to the Trademarks, but all strengthening through use of the Trademarks by Licensee shall inure to the benefit of Licensor. Licensee agrees to do all reasonable acts requested by Licensor to confirm ownership by Licensor of the Trademarks, permit maintenance of the Trademarks, and, upon termination of this License Agreement, to convey all rights in and to the Trademarks to Licensor and to terminate the rights granted to Licensee hereunder to the use of the Trademarks.

12. Default and termination

(a) This Agreement may be terminated forthwith in the event of bankruptcy or judicial or administrative declaration of insolvency of either party, or in the event of government expropriation of any of the assets of either party which relate to their activities as contemplated by this Agreement.

(b) In the event that either party shall fail to perform or observe any term, condition, agreement or covenant in this Agreement to be performed or observed by it, and said party (A) shall have received written notice of such default and (B) shall have failed, within thirty (30) calendar days after its receipt of such notice, to cure such default then and in such event the other party may, at its option, terminate this Agreement and all rights, licenses and privileges granted hereunder, immediately.

13. Effect of termination

13.01 In the event of termination of this Agreement (A) Licensee will cease to be an authorized licensee of Licensor and all rights, licenses and privileges of Licensee hereunder shall forthwith terminate and revert automatically to Licensor, and (B) without limiting the foregoing:

(a) Licensee shall immediately pay all sums due and owing to Licensor;

(b) Licensee shall furnish to Licensor within thirty (30) days after termination of this Agreement a statement showing the number and description of all Licensed Products it has on hand, which statement shall be verified by a duly authorized officer of Licensee;

(c) Upon termination of this Agreement, Licensee shall have the right to sell its remaining inventory of Licensed Products, under the Trademarks, through its normal trade channels and in accordance with the terms of this Agreement for a period of not more than ninety (90) days. Licensee shall, within thirty (30) days after the end of such ninety (90) day period: (i) furnish to Licensor a statement of all sales of Licensed Products after the termination date and a computation of the royalty payable hereunder in respect to such sales, and (ii) pay to Licensor the royalty provided for in Paragraph 4 on all sales of Licensed Products by Licensee after the termination of this Agreement, and Licensee shall be bound by all of the other terms and provisions of this Agreement so long as it shall continue to sell any Licensed Products. All Licensed Products remaining after the aforesaid time period must be destroyed or delivered to Licensor at no cost to Licensor;

(d) Upon termination of this Agreement Licensee shall not thereafter manufacture any Licensed Products, and upon expiration of the ninety (90) day period described in Paragraph 13.01(c), Licensee shall not thereafter distribute, sell, or advertise any Licensed Products or other products under the Trademarks, or variations or simulations thereof, nor shall it use the Trademarks in any way in connection with its business operations.

13.02 The termination of this Agreement shall be without prejudice to the rights of Licensor and Licensee, and such termination shall not relieve either party of any of its obligations to the other party existing at the time of termination.

14. Notices of infringement

Licensee shall give notice in writing to Licensor of any infringement of the Trademarks which shall come to its knowledge and, when requested, shall cooperate with Licensor in stopping such infringements. Licensor shall determine in its sole discretion whether to institute legal action with respect to any infringement which may occur, and the cost of any such litigation or the policing of rights granted by Licensor hereunder shall be paid by Licensor and any proceeds shall be retained by Licensor.

15. Indemnification

(a) Licensee shall indemnify and hold harmless Licensor from any liability, loss, damage, cost or expense (including reasonable attorneys fees) arising out of any use, manufacture, distribution, sale or exploitation of any Licensed Products or any breach by Licensee of any term, covenant or condition of this Agreement.

(b) Licensor shall indemnify and hold harmless Licensee from any liability loss, damage, cost or expense (including reasonable attorneys fees) arising out of any claim that use of the Trademarks in the Territory infringes any trademark or other intellectual property right of any third party.

16. Confidentiality

(a) Licensee acknowledges that all Technical Information furnished by Licensor to Licensee during the term of this Agreement is the property of Licensor and is of a highly confidential and secret nature.

(b) All of such Technical Information is to be used by Licensee solely for the purpose of carrying out this Agreement. Licensee shall keep in strict confidence the aforesaid Technical Information and shall not, for any reason whatsoever, reveal, disclose, sell or transfer any part of such Technical Information, directly or indirectly, to its own employees or agents or to any third party except as permitted by the terms of this

Paragraph 16. Licensee shall at its own cost take all precautions and steps which may be reasonably requested in order to protect such Technical Information. Nothing herein shall be interpreted as prohibiting Licensor at its own expense from bringing such legal actions within or outside the Territory as Licensor shall deem to be in its best interest.

(c) Licensee shall have the right to disclose Technical Information only to those of Licensee's employees who will require the same in order for Licensee to carry out this Agreement.

(d) Licensee's obligations set forth in this Paragraph 16 shall survive and remain in force for a period of 5 (five) years after the expiration or the termination of this Agreement.

17. Assignment; sublicenses

Neither this Agreement nor the license granted by this Agreement may be assigned or otherwise transferred by Licensee without the prior written consent of Licensor. Licensee may not grant any sublicenses without the prior written consent of Licensor. Any purported assignment, transfer or sublicense in violation of this provision shall be null and void. Licensee shall not have Licensed Products manufactured for Licensee by a third party without the express prior written consent of Licensor.

18. Amendments, waivers, approvals and consents

(a) No amendment of, or waiver, approval or consent permitted or contemplated by this Agreement shall be valid or effective for any purpose as against any party unless stated in a written instrument executed by each party.

(b) No waiver by any party, whether express or implied, of any provision of this agreement or of any breach or default of any party shall constitute a continuing waiver of such provision or any other provisions of this Agreement, and no such waiver by any party shall prevent such party from enforcing any and all provisions of this Agreement or from acting upon the same or any subsequent breach or default of the other party of any provision of this Agreement.

19. Interest on late payments

If any party shall fail to make any payment due under this Agreement within thirty (30) days after the due date, interest shall accrue and be payable on such unpaid principal amount from and after the date on which the same became due at a rate equal to (i) fifteen percent (15%) per annum or (ii) the highest rate of interest legally permissible, whichever is lower.

20. Notices

All notices and other communications which are required or which may be given under the provisions of this Agreement shall be in writing and shall be mailed by registered mail, postage prepaid, return receipt requested.

If to Licensor, addressed to:

and

If to Licensee, addressed to:

All notices and communications shall be effective on the fifth business day after the date on which they are mailed. Either party hereto may change its address by written notice to that effect to the other party in accordance with this section.

21. Governing law

This Agreement is executed and made in contemplation of its interpretation and effect being construed in accordance with the laws of Argentina.

22. Jurisdiction

In the event of any litigation between the parties to this Agreement, based in whole or in part upon claims arising out of or relating to this Agreement, Licensor and Licensee hereby exclusively designate and consent to the exclusive jurisdiction in the courts of Argentina.

23. Entire agreement

This Agreement constitutes the entire agreement among the parties hereto with respect to the subject matter hereof and supersedes all prior agreements and understandings, oral or written, among the parties with respect to the subject matter hereof. No representation, warranty, promise, inducement or statement of intention has been made by any party which is not embodied in this Agreement, and no party shall be bound by, or liable for, any alleged representation, warranty, promise, inducement or statement of intention not embodied herein.

24. Filing of agreement

Immediately upon execution of this Agreement, Licensee shall file it at its own cost with the National Institute for Technology Transfer (INTI) for information purpose only, as provided for by Argentine Law. Licensee shall keep Licensor fully informed of all steps taken by it in connection with such filing and promptly provide Licensor with copies of any documents submitted in connection therewith, and copies of the filing certificate or any other paper issued by INTI.

IN WITNESS WHEREOF, the parties hereto have caused this Agreement to be executed by their duly authorized officers as of the date and year first above written.

LICENSOR

By: ______________________________

LICENSEE

By: ______________________________

II. Trademark and Know-How License Agreement for Brazil

If the Territory were to be Brazil rather than Argentina, the National Institute of Industrial Property (INPI) may well require two separate agreements—one for use of the trademark and one for the supply of technology. Historically, INPI has required recordal of agreements on a category-by-category basis, with the four categories being:

(a) exploitation of patent;
(b) use of trademark;
(c) supply of technology; and
(d) rendering of technical and scientific assistance services.

However, under new resolutions it may be possible to record agreements containing characteristics of more than one category. If a single agreement is allowed to be recorded containing both a trademark license and a license for know-how, the preceding License Agreement would be modified to include the following changes to the enumerated paragraphs:

Paragraph 1(b) The "Trademarks" shall mean the registered trademarks set forth in Schedule A and any additional registered trademarks as may be agreed to in writing between the parties hereto from time to time.

Comment: In Brazil, the payment of royalties under a trademark license agreement is authorized only with respect to registered trademarks originally applied for in Brazil under the Paris Convention priority term and only during the initial ten-year period following registration.

Paragraph 2(b) The license granted hereby specifically excludes any right to use or apply the Technical Information or the Trademarks to manufacture and assemble any Licensed Product or other items in any country outside of the Territory or to assist or procure the manufacture or use of the Licensed Products outside of the Territory, provided, however, that nothing herein shall be construed to limit Licensee's right to export from the Territory Licensed Products manufactured within the Territory.

Comment: Licenses may not impose any restrictions on the exportation from Brazil of the licensed products. If this may result in conflicts with the rights of exclusive licensees of the licensor in territories outside of Brazil, one solution which might be attempted is a provision allowing the Brazilian licensee to export to any country, but prohibiting sales to any party other than the exclusive licensee in each country where the licensor has or may in the future have an exclusive licensee.

Paragraph 3 The term of this Agreement shall be for a period of five years commencing on the Effective Date and terminating on the thirty-first day of October, 1996, unless sooner terminated as provided herein.

Comment: Agreements for the transfer of technology have traditionally been limited to a five-year term. Note that because this Agreement also includes a trademark license for which a royalty is paid, it presupposes that registration of the trademark has occurred within the five years preceding the date of the Agreement.

Paragraph 4 Licensee agrees to pay to Licensor on all Licensed Products sold hereunder a royalty of one percent (1%) of Net Sales.

In the event any sale is made at a special price to any of Licensee's affiliates or subsidiaries or to any other person, firm or corporation related in any manner to Licensee's officers, directors or major shareholders, there shall be a royalty paid on such sale based upon the price generally charged the trade.

Comment: The maximum royalty which has been permitted in trademark licensing agreements has been one percent.

Paragraph 5 It will be the mutual goal of the parties that sales of the Licensed Products in the Territory achieve levels which will generate royalties for each Contract Year consistent with the following guidelines:

First Contract Year	\$150,000.00
Second Contract Year	\$175,000.00
Third Contract Year and each Contract Year thereafter	\$200,000.00

Comments: No restrictions can be placed upon a licensee's ability to industrialize, market, commercialize or produce the licensed products. Therefore, minimum royalty levels may be accepted in a license agreement only if used as guidelines rather than as an obligation of the licensee.

Paragraph 6(b) All royalty payments and other amounts due Licensor pursuant to this Agreement shall be payable in United States currency, unless another means of payment is required by the Government of Brazil, in which case such other means of payment shall be employed. The rate of exchange shall be the one authorized by the Central Bank of Brazil as of the date of invoice with respect to royalty payments, and as of the date the payment became due with respect to other amounts due to Licensor.

Comment: The language of this provision is not significantly different from that of the contract for Argentina. It is important to note that in countries such as these which have seen high inflation rates, the date upon which the exchange rate is applied can greatly influence the amount of royalties received. Where as here the payment is to be in U.S. currency, establishing the exchange rate as of the date of invoice of the licensee's sale will protect the licensor from the effect of local currency inflation between the date of sale and the date of payment. Moreover, establishing a specific date for purposes of determining the exchange rate will protect the licensor from the possibility of the licensee selecting in each instance the rate most favorable to it in a period of fluctuating rates.

Paragraph 9 Licensor undertakes to exercise effective control over the specifications, nature and quality of the Licensed Products manufactured by Licensor and identified by any of the Trademarks. Licensee agrees that the articles covered by this Agreement at all times shall be of high standard and of such style, appearance and quality as to protect and enhance the Trademarks and the goodwill pertaining thereto, shall meet Licensor's quality standards and specifications, and shall be manufactured, sold, distributed and promoted in accordance with all applicable laws and regulations.

Licensee agrees to submit to Licensor, without cost to Licensor, for its approval five (5) samples of each of the Licensed Products to be made by it under this Agreement, together with all cartons, labels, containers and packing and wrapping materials, and shall not sell any Licensed Products which do not have Licensor's written approval prior to sale. If any significant change is made in the quality, workmanship or design of any previously approved Licensed Product, Licensee shall submit five (5) samples of such changed Licensed Products to Licensor for approval pursuant to this Paragraph, and shall not sell such changed Licensed Products prior to receipt of written approval by Licensor of all changes. Licensee agrees that all Licensed Products made and sold under this Agreement shall be of the standards of material, workmanship, design and performance equal to the samples and specifications approved by Licensor.

Licensor shall have the right to inspect the Licensed Products and methods of manufacture on the premises of Licensee during regular business hours upon reasonable prior notice.

Comment: The first sentence has been added because the Trademark Law in Brazil specifically requires that a license agreement must contain the obligation of the licensor to keep effective control over the specifications, nature and quality of the licensed articles or services.

Paragraph 10(c) Except as otherwise provided in this Paragraph 10(c), Licensee is prohibited from using any trademark other than the Trademarks on any Licensed Products. The Licensed Products may bear in addition to the Trademarks a trademark which is the property of Licensee, provided that (i) said trademark is registered in Brazil, (ii) the said trademark is not displayed or used on the Licensed

Products in a more prominent manner than the Trademarks and (iii) the said trademark is not displayed or used in a manner which gives the impression that it forms a single unit with any of the Trademarks.

Comment: It has been required that trademark license agreements include a clause giving the licensee the option of using its own trademark together with the licensor's trademark on products covered by the license agreement, and of using its own trademark when it manufactures or commercializes other products in addition to those which are specifically identified by the trademark to which the license refers. The rationale for this is that when the licensee uses the licensor's trademark, it is not developing a market for itself but for the licensor who owns the trademark, and upon termination of the license agreement the licensee will lose the market to the licensor.

Paragraph 16(a) Licensee acknowledges that all Technical Information furnished by Licensor to Licensee during the Term of this Agreement is the property of Licensor and is of a highly confidential and secret nature.

(b) All of such Technical Information is to be used by Licensee during the Term hereof solely for the purpose of carrying out this Agreement. Licensee shall during the Term hereof keep in strict confidence the aforesaid Technical Information and shall not during the Term hereof, for any reason whatsoever, reveal, disclose, sell or transfer any part of such Technical Information, directly or indirectly, to its own employees or agents or to any third party except as permitted by the terms of this Paragraph 16. Licensee shall at its own cost take all precautions and steps which may be reasonably requested in order to protect such Technical Information. Nothing herein shall be interpreted as prohibiting Licensor at its own expense from bringing such legal actions within or outside the Territory as Licensor shall deem to be in its best interest.

(c) Licensee shall have the right to disclose Technical Information during the Term hereof only to those of Licensee's employees who will require the same in order for Licensee to carry out this Agreement.

Comment: A Brazilian firm is free to use technology as it pleases once the term of a technology-transfer contract has expired. For this reason a licensor may wish to negotiate a lump-sum payment or other payment plan acceptable in accordance with prevailing legislation and ordinances by monetary and exchange authorities, separate from royalties, for any technology rights granted in conjunction with a trademark license.

Paragraph 24 Immediately upon execution of this Agreement, Licensee shall file at its own cost with INPI a request for recordal of this Agreement together with all other required documents, as provided for by Brazilian Law. Licensee shall keep Licensor fully informed of all steps taken by it in connection with such filing and promptly provide Licensor with copies of any documents submitted in connection therewith, and copies of all certificates and documents issued by INPI.

Comment: Unlike Argentina, filing is not merely for informational purposes. Recording (i.e., approval) by INPI must be secured before payment by the licensee to the licensor will be permitted.

Appendix C
Questions to Ask When Fixing a Price on Patents Abroad

- Is the product patented in the licensor/parent country?
- Is it patented in the potential licensee's country?
- Is it patented in the potential licensee's export markets?
- Has the patent ever been actively protected in any of these markets?
- Does the patent truly "cover" the product or process? (Some patents may mean little if the product or process may be easily varied to avoid violating the patent.)
- How new and valuable is the product or design? How long will it remain valuable?
- Do other firms offer a comparable product or technology, and if so, what do they charge?
- Could local producers in the licensee's country develop the same or similar techniques or products?
- Do your licensee's competitors have comparable technology or products, and are they paying royalties?
- How much, and how quickly, do you expect the licensee to add to or alter the process or product?
- Are there cross-licensing possibilites?
- Does the licensee need help in getting started and securing a strong grip on the market?
- Is this agreement going to lead to other agreements?

- Do you want equity participation, or even eventual 100% ownership of the license? If so, do you want to acquire it gradually through royalty payments, or by a one-shot purchase at a later date?
- Is there an option to purchase equity at a given price?
- Is there a large initial (cash or equity) payment? Or is disclosure to be paid for in installments?
- Can you persuade the licensee to make a down payment representing its share of your own R&D?
- Will the licensee agree to a minimum annual royalty?
- Will there be continuing flat fees for technical assistance, etc? Are your out-of-pocket expenses covered?
- Is the royalty based on a volume factor that increases the royalty as sales mount?
- Do you want to provide an incentive by lowering the royalty rate as sales approach the marginal level and become more difficult and expensive?
- Will you cover or share your licensee's promotion and advertising expenses?
- How fast is the market growing? Is licensing the best method of maintaining or increasing your firm's share of the market?
- Will the licensee agree to short renewal dates? Will he agree not to produce for a fixed period after the agreement expires? Is the license readily cancelable?
- Will the licensee agree to limit use of your trademark to certain export markets? Will he agree to use your distributors in export markets?
- What have you charged in other countries?
- Is licensing your principal long-term aim in international operations?
- Is your prime purpose to crack the market and establish your brand name in preparation for later investment?
- Is local government approval for the licensing agreement and/or royalty rate required? What royalty rates does it normally approve?
- Would industry in the licensee's country benefit from your licensing of this patent?
- What marketing areas will you give the licensee?
- Will local manufacture lower the country's imports or increase exports?

- Will the licensee agree to sell to you at cost plus manufacturing profit in its home or export markets?
- Will you accept blocked royalty payments? For how long?
- What are the local tax rates on royalties?
- Should royalties be kept low and technical assistance fees high (for local tax reasons)?
- Do you wish to use low royalties and high flat fees to increase taxes payable at the parent/licensor level at the expense of taxes payable abroad?
- What charges made by you can the licensee claim as deductible expense in this country?
- What are you own cash needs, now and later on?

Index

Annulment in Poland, 208
Application fees for registration of intellectual property, in Mexico, 41
Arbitration in Taiwan, 95
Argentina, 1–14
legal context in, 2–8
copyright and, 7–8
industrial models and designs and, 6–7
patents and, 5–6
trade names and, 5
trademarks and, 2–5
licensing experience in, 9–10
taxation in, 14
technology transfer in, 8, 10–13
approval criteria for, 11–12
practical advice regarding, 12
trademark and know-how license agreement for, 223–233
Author's certificates in Czechoslovakia, 177

Brazil, 15–33
copyrights in, 21–24
royalty remittances and, 32
on software, 22–24
federal legislation in, 16–17
international treaties of, 15–16
licensing and technology transfer in, 24–26
remittance restrictions and, 25–26
requirements of, 27
licensing experience in, 28–30
piracy problems and, 28–29
trade-secret theft and, 29–30
patents in, 17–19
remittance restrictions and, 19
unpatentable products and, 18–19
practical matters regarding, 26–27, 31
Brazil (*Cont.*):
tax consequences in, 31–33
tax incentives and, 32–33
tax rates on royalty remittances and, 32
trademark and know-how license agreement for, 235–238
trademarks in, 19–21
remittance restrictions and, 20–21
royalty remittances and, 32

Cartels in Venezuela, 55
China (*see* People's Republic of China; Taiwan)
Compulsory licensing:
in Czechoslovakia, 179
in Hungary, 194
in Poland, 208
Confidentiality, technology transfer and, in Mexico, 38–39
Copyrights:
in Argentina, 7–8
in Brazil, 21–24
royalty remittances and, 32
on software, 22–24
in India, on intellectual property, 161
in Mexico, of intellectual property, 42
in People's Republic of China, 139–143, 151–152
in Taiwan, 102–103
on intellectual property, 106
in Thailand, 117–118
in Venezuela, 53
on software, 53
Countertrade clauses in People's Republic of China, 134
Cultural issues in Thailand, 124–125
Czechoslovakia, 167–184
contact organizations and responsibilities in, 172–174

Czechoslovakia (*Cont.*):
decision-making process in, 174
guide for Western negotiators in, 170
licensing experience in, 181
patents in, 176–180, 182
application procedure for, 178–179
author's certificates and, 177
compulsory licenses and, 179
Czechoslovak patents abroad and, 182
of industrial designs, 177–178
infringement and, 179–180
legislative basis for, 176–177
Office for Inventions and Discoveries and, 178–179
validity and revocations and, 180, 182
problems in, 168–169
reforms in, 169
special funds and priority areas in, 169, 171–172
taxes in, 175–176
trademarks in, 182–184
duration of protection by, 183
registration of, 182–183
"use" provisions and, 183–184
unplanned imports in, 175

Double-taxation treaties in Poland, 201–202

Equity links in Mexico, 42
Exports in People's Republic of China, 138

Foreign-investment requirements in India, 158–160
incentives and, 159–160
investment classifications and, 158–159
Franchise guidelines in Mexico, 36, 39
Funding:
in Hungary, 185–186
in People's Republic of China, lack of, 133, 135

Government attitudes toward business, in Thailand, 120

Hungary, 185–195
approval requirements in, 186–187
funding in, 185–186
licensing agencies in, 187–188
intercooperation among, 188
licensing experience in, 189–190

Hungary (*Cont.*):
patents in, 190–194
application and examination procedure for, 193
compulsory licensing and, 194
fees for, 194
infringement and, 194
patent agents and, 191–192
Patent Information Center and, 192
regulation of, 193–194
unpatentable products and, 193
payments and taxes in, 188, 190
trademarks in, 194–195

Imports, unplanned, in Czechoslovakia, 175
India, 153–166
foreign-investment requirements in, 158–160
incentives and, 159–160
investment classifications and, 158–159
industrial designs and models in, 161, 164
industrial policy in, 155
intellectual property in, 160–162
copyrights and industrial designs and, 161
patents and, 160–161
trademarks and trade names and, 161–162
patents in, 163
on intellectual property, 160–161
payment in, 162, 164
restrictions on royalties and fees and, 162, 164
tax consequences in, 166
technology transfer in, 156–158
approval requirements for, 157–158
trademarks in, 161–164
on intellectual property, 161–162
Industrial designs and models:
in Argentina, 6–7
in Czechoslovakia, trademarks and, 177–178
in India, 164
intellectual property and, 161
in Japan, 77
in Mexico, intellectual property and, 42
in People's Republic of China, 149
in Poland, 204

Industrial designs and models (*Cont.*):
in South Korea, 86
in Taiwan, 106
in Thailand, 122
in Venezuela, 60
Industrial policy in India, 155
Infringement:
in Czechoslovakia, 179–180
in Hungary, 194
in People's Republic of China, 150–151
in Poland, 207–210, 210–212
in Taiwan, 100
Intellectual property:
in India, 160–162
copyrights and industrial designs and, 161
patents and, 160–161
trademarks and trade names and, 161–162
in Mexico (*see* Mexico, intellectual property in)
in Taiwan (*see* Taiwan, intellectual property in)
International conventions, Taiwan's membership in, 107
International disputes of Japan, 75, 77–78
International legislation in Venezuela, 55
International treaties:
of Brazil, 15–16
of Poland, 201–202
of Venezuela, taxes and, 65
Inventors' certificates in Mexico, intellectual property and, 42

Japan, 66–78
industrial designs and models in, 77
international disputes and, 75, 76–78
legislative framework in, 68–72
Foreign Exchange and Foreign Trade Control Act and, 70–72
patents and, 69–70
royalty payments and, 72
trademarks and, 70
patents in, 69–70, 76
practical matters in, 73–75
pharmaceuticals and, 74–75
tax consequences in, 72–73
technology transfer in, 68
trademarks in, 70, 76–77
Joint ventures in Russia, protecting inventions of, 216–217

Know-how:
licensing and know-how agreements:
for Argentina, 223–233
for Brazil, 235–238
in Venezuela, 50

Licensing:
compulsory:
in Czechoslovakia, 179
in Hungary, 194
in Poland, 208
in Russia, opportunities for, 218–219
Licensing agreements:
for Argentina, 223–233
for Brazil, 24–26, 235–238
remittance restrictions and, 25–26
requirements of, 27
items to include in, 220–222
for Thailand, registration of, 119
Licensing experience:
in Argentina, 9–10
in Brazil, 28–30
piracy and, 28–29
trade-secret theft and, 29–30
in Czechoslovakia, 181
in Hungary, 189–190
in Poland, 209
in Thailand, 126
in Venezuela, 62–64
Batman movie and, 64
pirate production and, 64

Mexico, 34–44
benefits of licensing in, 35–36
disadvantages of licensing in, 36–37
intellectual property in, 36, 40–42
application fees and, 41
copyrights and, 42
industrial designs and models and, 42
inventors' certificates and, 42
patents and, 41
regulatory framework and, 40
trademarks and, 41–42
practical matters in, 40, 42–44
regulatory framework in, 37–40
intellectual property and, 40
technology transfer and, 38–39
tax and financial considerations in, 40
trade secrets in, 36
Monopolies in Venezuela, 55

Patents:
- in Argentina, 5–6
  - pharmaceuticals and, 6
- in Brazil, 17–19
  - remittance restrictions and, 19
  - unpatentable products and, 18–19
- in Czechoslovakia (*see* Czechoslovakia, patents in)
- fixing prices on, questions to ask and, 239–241
- in Hungary (*see* Hungary, patents in)
- in India, 163
  - on intellectual property, 160–161
- in Japan, 69–70, 76
- in Mexico, on intellectual property, 41
- in People's Republic of China (*see* People's Republic of China, patents in)
- in Poland (*see* Poland, patents in)
- in South Korea, 84–89
  - corporate response and, 86–89
- in Taiwan, on intellectual property, 97–101, 104–105
- in Thailand, 115–117, 121
- in Venezuela, 50, 57, 59

Payments:
- in Brazil, restrictions on
  - licensing and technology transfer and, 25–26
  - patents and, 19
  - trademarks and, 20–21
- in Brazil, tax rates on, 32
- in Hungary, 188, 190
- in India, 162, 164
  - restrictions on, 162, 164
  - restrictions on royalties and fees and, 162, 164
- in Japan, 72
- in Mexico:
  - regulation and, 39
  - tax considerations and, 40
- in People's Republic of China, 135–138
  - progressive-payments clauses and, 136
- in Taiwan, 95
- in Thailand, 122–123
- in Venezuela, 54–55
  - payment instruments and, 58
  - taxes and, 60–61

People's Republic of China, 127–152
- copyrights in, 139, 142–143, 151–152

People's Republic of China (*Cont.*):
- countertrade clauses in, 134
- finding partners in, 128–129
- industrial designs and models in, 149
- legal context in, 129–133
  - negotiating and approval requirements and, 131–133
  - technology transfer and, 129–131
- patents in, 139, 142–146, 148
  - Chinese language in patent applications and, 145
  - importing patented products and, 145
  - pharmaceuticals and, 145
  - product patenting and, 144–145
  - protection prior to grant of patent and, 145
  - software and, 145
- practical matters in, 133, 135–139
  - disagreements over 'appropriate' technology as, 138–139
  - disputes as, 139
  - exports as, 138
  - lack of funding as, 133, 135
  - overlapping jurisdictions as, 138
  - payment terms as, 135–138
  - secrecy as, 135
  - trademark licenses as, 138
  - training as, 138
  - updating as, 139
- tax consequences in, 152
- technology transfer in, 140–142
  - confidentiality and, 131
  - dispute-resolution and, 131
  - export provisions and, 131
  - performance tests and, 131
  - tie-in arrangements and, 131
- trademarks in, 138–143, 146–151
  - infringement and, 150–151

Pharmaceuticals:
- in Argentina, 6
- in Japan, 74–75

Piracy:
- in Brazil, 28–29
- in Mexico, 43
- in Venezuela, 64

Poland, 196–212
- licensing experience in, 209
- licensing procedures in, 198–199
  - Central Fund for License Purchases and, 198–199
  - new regulations and, 199

Poland (*Cont.*):
patents in, 202–208
application procedures for, 205–207
co-ownership of, 205
compulsory licensing and annulment proceedings and, 208
industrial designs and models and, 204
infringement and legal recourse and, 207–208
types of, 203–204
policy background in, 197–198
selling licenses to, 199–200
Polservice and, 200
taxes in, 201–202
double-taxation treaties and, 201–202
trademarks in, 208, 210–212
application procedures for, 210
infringement and legal recourse and, 210–212
Politics in Thailand, 124–125
Prices, fixing on patents abroad, questions to ask and, 239–241

Registration expenses in Venezuela, 54
Regulation:
in Hungary, 193–194
in Mexico, 35–40
technology transfer and, 38–39
in Poland, 199
in Venezuela, 46–48
Republic of China (*see* Taiwan)
Revocations in Czechoslovakia, 180, 182
Royalty remittances (*see* Payments)
Russia, 213–219
areas not recognized as inventions in, 217, 219
joint venture inventions in, 216–217
licensing opportunities in, 218–219
1991 USSR code and, 215–217, 219
taxes in, 217
transition of market in, 213–215

Secrecy in People's Republic of China, 135
Service fees in Venezuela, 54–55
Software:
in Brazil, copyrights on, 22–24
in Mexico, regulation and, 39
in People's Republic of China, patents on, 145
in Venezuela, copyrights on, 53
South Korea, 79–92
attracting foreign technology to, 80–83
foreign-investment preferences and, 82–83
future in, 92
industrial designs and models in, 86
legislation in, 89–91
patents in, 84–89
corporate response and, 86–89
tax consequences in, 91–92
trademarks in, 84–89
corporate response and, 86–89

Taiwan, 93–110
intellectual property in, 96–103, 106–107
copyrights on, 102–103, 106
enforcement of intellectual property rights and, 103, 106–107
industrial designs and models and, 106
international conventions and, 107
legal matters regarding, 107
patents and trademarks on, 97–101, 104–105
pressure for change regarding, 101–102
licensing outside system in, 107–108
patents and trademarks in, 97–106
application and issue of, 99
infringement and, 100
on intellectual property, 97–101, 104–105
local agents and, 98
patent licensing and, 101
subject matter and, 98–99
trademark licensing and, 100–101
working/use and, 100
practical matters in, 108–109
tax consequences in, 109–110
technical-cooperation agreements in, 95
Taxes:
in Brazil, 31–33
tax incentives and, 32–33
tax rates on royalty remittances and, 32
in Czechoslovakia, 175–176
in Hungary, 188, 190
in India, 166
in Japan, 72–73
in Mexico, 40
in People's Republic of China, 152

Taxes (*Cont.*):
  in Poland, 201–202
  in Russia, 217
  in South Korea, 91–92
  in Taiwan, 109–110
  in Thailand, 123–124
  in Venezuela, 58, 60–61, 65
    corporate income tax rates and, 61
    royalty remittances and, 60–61
    tax treaties and, 65
Technical-cooperation agreements in Taiwan, 95
Technology fees in Venezuela, 54–55
Technology transfer:
  in Argentina, 8, 10–13
    approval criteria for, 11–12
    practical advice regarding, 12
  in Brazil, 24–26
    remittance restrictions and, 25–26
    requirements of, 27
  in India, 156–158
    approval requirements for, 157–158
  in Japan, 68
  in Mexico, regulatory framework and, 38–39
  in People's Republic of China (*see* People's Republic of China, technology transfer in)
  in South Korea, 80–83
    foreign-investment preferences and, 82–83
  in Venezuela, 48
Thailand, 111–126
  industrial designs and models in, 122
  legal context in, 114–119
    copyrights and, 117–118
    patents and, 115–117
    registration of licensing agreements and, 119
    trademarks and, 118–119
  licensing experience in, 126
  patents in, 115–117, 121
  political and cultural considerations in, 124–125
  practical matters in, 119–120, 122–123
    government attitude toward business and, 120
    legal tradition and, 120, 122
    payment issues and, 122–123
  tax consequences in, 123–124
  trademarks in, 118–119, 121–122
Trade names:
  in Argentina, 5
  in India, intellectual property and, 161–162
Trade secrets:
  in Brazil, theft of, 29–30
  in Mexico, 36
Trademarks:
  in Argentina, 2–5
    trade names and, 5
  in Brazil, 19–21
    remittance restrictions and, 20–21
    royalty remittances and, 32
  in Czechoslovakia, 182–184
    duration of protection by, 183
    registration of, 182–183
    "use" provisions and, 183–184
  in Hungary, 194–195
  in India, 161–164
    on intellectual property, 161–162
  in Japan, 70, 76–77
  in Mexico, on intellectual property, 41–42
  in People's Republic of China, 138–143, 146–151
    infringement and, 150–151
  in Poland, 208, 210–212
    application procedures for, 210
    infringement and legal recourse and, 210–212
  in South Korea, 84–89
    corporate response and, 86–89
  in Taiwan, on intellectual property, 97–101, 105
  in Thailand, 118–119, 121–122
  in Venezuela, 50, 57, 59–60
Training in People's Republic of China, 138
Treaties, international:
  of Brazil, 15–16
  of Poland, 201–202
  of Venezuela, taxes and, 65

Validity in Czechoslovakia, 180
Venezuela, 45–65
  foreign-investment regulations in, 46–48
  industrial designs and models in, 60
  legal context in, 48–55
    Copyright Law and, 53
    Decree Law 727 and, 51–52
    Industrial Property Law and, 49

Venezuela (*Cont.*):
international legislation and, 55
know-how and, 50
licensing restrictions and, 50, 52–53
patents and, 50
proposed bill on monopolies and cartels and, 55
registration expenses and, 54
royalties and fees and, 54–55
software and, 53
trademarks and, 50
licensing experience in, 62–64
Batman movie and, 64
Venzeula, licensing experience in (*Cont.*):
pirate production and, 64
patents in, 50, 57, 59
practical matters in, 56–58
patent and trademark protection and, 57
payment instruments and, 58
tax consequences in, 58, 60–61, 65
corporate income tax rates and, 61
royalty remittances and, 60–61
tax treaties and, 65
technology transfer in, 48
trademarks in, 50, 57, 59–60

About the Author

BUSINESS INTERNATIONAL, a member of *The Economist Group*, has been providing the international business community with political, economic, and business information since 1954. Their operations span 75 countries, and include 300 consultants, analysts, and researchers. Through publications and seminars, BI provides vital information used by more than 1,000 of the world's leading companies to take advantage of emerging opportunities in global business markets.

About the Editor

THOMAS J. EHRBAR is Director of Reference Services and Global Online Publications at Business International Corporation. Formerly, he was editor of BI's global licensing publication, *Investing, Licensing, & Trading Conditions Abroad.*